CRAZY OLD LADIES

Crazy Old Ladies

The Story of Hag Horror

Caroline Young

BearManor Media
2022

Published in the United States of America by:

BearManor Media

4700 Millenia Blvd.
Suite 175 PMB 90497
Orlando, FL 32839

bearmanormedia.com

Printed in the United States.

Typesetting and layout by BearManor Media

ISBN—978-1-62933-997-9

Contents

Acknowledgments

Firstly I'd like to thank my agent Isabel Atherton of Creative Authors who was so enthusiastic about the concept of this book, and to Ben Ohmart of Bear Manor Media for taking it on. Stone Wallace, who edited the manuscript and provided such warm and enthusiastic feedback, gave encouragement to me that this book was an important project.

Thanks to Dennis Bartok of the American Cinematheque who took the time to speak to me about his friend Curtis Harrington. Foster Hirsch also allowed me to pick his brains on the subject, and invited me into a conversation with Piper Laurie at The Lamb's Club. I loved hearing Mark Lester's stories of his time working with Shelley Winters on *Whoever Slew Auntie Roo?* Shar Daws also shared with me fantastic insight into Diana Dors and her experience working with Joan Crawford.

Thanks also to Kristine Krueger at the Academy of Motion Pictures Arts and Sciences, who offered invaluable assistance in helping me research at the Margaret Herrick Library, and Steve Chibnall who granted me a wealth of material from the Hammer Horror archives at De Montfort University, Leicester.

This book is for all the women who have been told they are too old, or washed-up, or crazy, and for the women whose lives don't follow the expected trajectory, and are made to feel they are less, because of it. And finally, here's to all the wonderful actresses I featured in this book, who have brought joy and inspiration to so many different generations, in the past, and in the future.

Introduction

It all started with *Judy*. The spark of an idea for this book was ignited while watching the 2018 film, starring Renee Zellweger as Judy Garland. It told the story of the singer's fraught time in London in 1969, after signing up to a five-week run at the Talk of the Town nightclub, as she battled serious addiction problems, coupled with money and relationship worries. It was a heartbreaking account of the pressures of fame and the treatment of women as they get older; a parable of the fate of successful actresses who are eventually discarded by the movie studios they had worked so hard for and often bankrolled. Garland was a victim of the fickle nature of stardom, and would die just a few months later, at the age of forty-seven, from an accidental drug overdose.

Around the same time, a number of films and television series recounted similar tales. There was 2017's *Film Stars Don't Die in Liverpool*, with Annette Bening as Gloria Grahame, the bad girl of 1950s Hollywood whose last years were spent doing regional English theater and taking on roles in cheap horror movies. *Stan & Ollie* (2018) offered a male perspective, telling the story of 1920s comedy act Stan Laurel and Oliver Hardy when they embarked on a reunion tour of Britain's variety halls in 1953. They'd signed up for the gigs to earn some much needed income, as well as to raise their profile for an anticipated comeback. And there was Ryan Murphy's *Feud*, the 2017 FX TV series which told the story of the rivalry between Joan Crawford and Bette Davis, during the making of *What Ever Happened to Baby Jane?* and *Hush, Hush Sweet Charlotte*.

As a woman approaching forty, I resonated with this theme of society's perceptions of women, and particularly single women, as they get older. It was the old adage, played out in Hollywood, that as a woman hit that milestone, she could feel the chill, that awareness that she would soon be considered over the hill, cast out of the leading roles, and no longer viable as a romantic heroine. Instead, she'd have to make do with bit parts as elderly spinster aunts, the bitchy office boss who sacrificed love for her career, or the old crone in a creepy house who casts a spell on the younger protagonist, unleashing all sorts of horror.

There have been notable exceptions in recent years. Jennifer Lopez defied all of these conventions when she played a stripper in *Hustlers* (2019) at the age of fifty, as well as playing romantic lead in a series of aspirational rom-coms throughout her forties. Sixty-two year old Linda Hamilton reprised the role of tough-as-nails Sarah Connor in *Terminator: Dark Fate* (2019) and sixty-year-old Jamie Lee Curtis returned to the *Halloween* franchise as Laurie Strode forty years on from her first encounter with Michael Myers, and this time she was a more cynical, tougher version of the character. The film broke records as the biggest opening weekend for a horror film starring a woman.

While these opportunities seemed like massive progress for the depiction of older women on screen, the common thread for Hamilton and Curtis was that both of these characters, fearless, strong women in their sixties, had a single-mindedness that edged close to madness due to a sense of loss in their past. To be viable and to show their motivation, they had to be incomplete somehow, and it reminded me of all those horror movies of the 60s and 70s that depicted the flawed, lonely, embattled older woman who serves as a warning against feminism due to her rejection of a normal family life. They were depicted in wheelchairs, or with a walking stick, they kept cats around them, or boxes of mementos from their past. These included the glamor photos of their younger years, which only served to remind them of their lost looks, lost loves, and lost children. Women are defined by their status as wife and mother, and if they fail to achieve this, then typically they are considered unfulfilled, and therefore unstable.

At the heart of this book is the study of a subgenre of 1960s and 1970s horror films known as "Hag Horror," "Hagsploitation," "Psycho-biddy" and "Grande Dame Guignol." These films, well within the boundaries of camp, tended to cast an aging movie star as the monster, or victim, who lives in a creepy home with a creaking staircase that offers an easy metaphor for her descent into madness, with her basement or attic as the womb-like space that holds her darkest secrets.

What Ever Happened to Baby Jane? is considered the film that launched a subgenre of middle-aged horrors, and I started from there when it came to developing this book, *Crazy Old Ladies*. I looked at the gothic horror films that came after *Baby Jane*, and the films that came before it. *Sunset Boulevard* laid the groundwork with its faded Hollywood grandeur set within a crumbling gothic mansion, which holds the hopes and dreams of a once beautiful actress who is morphed into a grotesque caricature.

I also wanted to explore the later life stories of some of Hollywood's most iconic actresses, from Bette Davis and Joan Crawford, to Gloria Grahame, Gloria Swanson and Piper Laurie. Other stars who embraced the genre included Shelley Winters, Veronica Lake, Debbie Reynolds, Joan Fontaine and Olivia de Havilland.

The actresses who played these parts often lived beyond their gender expectations, despite the promotion of their beauty and glamor as an aspiration for regular women. To make it to the top in Hollywood required hard work and dedication, and often this was at the expense of following the traditional path of being a stay-at-home wife and mother. They earned reputations on set for being difficult and uncompromising, for exhibiting "unfeminine" characteristics, because they believed in perfecting all aspects of their performance. As Cary Grant once commented: "Women who want to be actresses have a disease. Wanting to be a star is all-enveloping. It's not a very feminine pursuit."

Both Crawford and Davis were in later life chastised for their mothering skills; they were punished with tell-all books for not being the soft mother they were expected to be; rather they were working women who had to be tough to survive. In the myths of Hollywood, it was more fun to tear these successful women down for their perceived lacking and their rejection of traditional female roles.

Judy Garland may have opted out of debasing herself in B-movie horrors, preferring to put on dazzling stage shows instead, but her life formed the basis of the central, monstrous character in the 1967 camp classic *Valley of the Dolls*, in which she very nearly starred. The scope of this book also took me to two of the most groundbreaking horror movies of the time, *Rosemary's Baby* and *The Exorcist*. While these films may not initially seem to fit the "Hag Horror" subgenre, they illustrate the fears of the time, playing up to the worries around feminism with depictions of older women, combined with a clash between tradition and youth, and statements on how the cult of celebrity had replaced the worshipping of God.

Recently, the genre seems to have been reignited with a stream of movies that have utilized similar themes. In 2019's *Ma*, Olivia

Spencer is the aging loner who befriends and then terrorizes a group of teenagers as a result of the painful memories from her past that she struggles to forget. In *Run* (2020) Sarah Paulson plays an abusive mother who deliberately drugs her paralyzed daughter, and traps her in an upstairs bedroom, to prevent her from leaving her. Edgar Wright's *Last Night in Soho* (2021) cast Diana Rigg, in her last film before her death, as a creepy landlady whose secrets from her past are hidden in her creaking boarding house. Just as the films of the 60s and 70s represented the cultural clash between the older generation and the countercultural youth who bitterly protested the Vietnam War and fought for Civil Rights and Women's Liberation, today's battle is between the Baby Boomers and Generation Z, who find each other's cultural and political stances perplexing.

The title I chose for this book is deliberately provocative – it's a twist on some of the unflattering terms women are called when they reach what's euphemistically known as "a certain age." Jack Warner referred to Bette Davis and Joan Crawford as "washed up old bitches" when he initially turned down the chance to produce *What Ever Happened to Baby Jane?* And the films are peppered with the insults of "Old Hag," "Old Bag," and "Old Witch" when referring to women. The aim of the book is not to insult or degrade. Rather, it examines the way older women are depicted in cinema, by delving behind the scenes of the making of some of the classics in the genre, exploring the societal context of the period, from political unrest, the women's liberation movement and the switch from the cosseted Studio System to the ever-increasing violence and salacious sex of New Hollywood. Above all it's a celebration of some of the most iconic stars of the Golden Age of Hollywood, telling their stories of the later years of their careers.

1 "She is a star..."

Joan Crawford made her entrance on stage wielding an axe.

In January 1964, at the age of fifty-eight, the Hollywood grande dame began an exhaustive tour across the United States, with personal appearances at big city and small town cinemas to publicize her new horror film, *Strait-Jacket*, directed by B-movie master William Castle. Attracting huge audiences of all ages, Joan was only too happy to meet the adoring public who clamored to see the star in full glamor; a movie legend of the 30s and 40s, which now seemed like the distant past.

Because she sat on the board for Pepsi-Cola, she was able to travel across the country on the luxury Pepsi jet, with Columbia Pictures distributing a list of her requirements for each stop. These included a bedroom each for her publicist, her maid Anna Brinke, known as "Mamacita," and the two pilots; and a rider including pens, pencils and paper, red and yellow roses, one bowl of peppermint lifesavers, several buckets of cracked ice, 100 proof Smirnoff vodka, Beefeater gin, Moët and Chandon champagne, and a case of Pepsi-Cola. As the list of instructions made clear, "Miss Crawford is a star in every sense of the word; and everyone knows she is a star."

The tour kicked off in New York, traveling to three theaters a night for seven days across Manhattan, Brooklyn, the Bronx, Queens and Staten Island. The first stop was Loews cinema in the Bronx, and William Castle remembered: "Two blocks away from the theater I could see the beams from the klieg lights traveling across the sky - and then I saw the people. Mob would be a better word. Hundreds of people surrounded the theater. Police were trying to hold them back. As the bus pulled up in front of the theater and Joan Crawford, magnificently dressed, stepped down, there was a roar. The crowd went wild…Joan threw kisses to the crowd, thanked them for coming, and then disappeared backstage. The theater was sold out for the six o'clock show."

To introduce the movie, Crawford appeared on stage with a cardboard axe, and this moment of pure camp thrilled the young audience, many of whom hadn't been born when she was starring in *The Women* in 1939, or even when she won her Academy Award for *Mildred Pierce* in 1946. When the screening began, they might not have understood the significance of her entrance in *Strait-Jacket*, doing the Joan Crawford walk, where her broad shoulders become their own character. They may have howled with laughter at the over-the-top moments of horror, with fake heads being lopped off and rolling on the ground, or when, as a woman in her sixties, she seduces her daughter's boyfriend by teasing her fingers into his mouth. Yet Crawford was utterly convincing in the over-the-top role and despite being widely panned by critics, audiences embraced the film.

"Joan Crawford has picked some lemons, some very sour lemons, in her day, but nigh the worst of the lot is *Strait-Jacket*, in which she showed up at neighborhood theaters yesterday," wrote *The New York Times*' Bosley Crowther in January 1964. But the film's success affirmed Crawford's reinvention as a horror queen.

Strait-Jacket was one of a new breed of horror movies that exposed a big name star to thrills and shocks, and which would later be referred to as "Hag Horror," "Hagsploitation," "Psycho-biddy" or "Grande Dame Guignol." It was a sub-genre launched on the back of 1962's *What Ever Happened to Baby Jane?*, the hugely-successful gothic horror starring Crawford and her long-standing rival Bette Davis, whose decades-long feud had become the stuff of legend. It was also the rare film that demonstrated that two older women could headline a successful movie, and triggered a trend for other older actresses to ham it up in horror, while cashing the often-generous check.

"Of course she rationalized what she did," said director George Cukor. "Joan even lied to herself. She would write to me about these pictures, actually believing that they were quality scripts. You could never tell her they were garbage. She was a star, and this was her next picture. She had to keep working, as did Bette."

As a way to boost their flagging careers, silver screen beauties like Gloria Grahame, Ann Sothern, Tallulah Bankhead, Miriam Hopkins, Veronica Lake, Barbara Stanwyck, Lana Turner, Yvonne De Carlo and Ruth Roman all took up the horror mantle to varying degrees of success. The characters they played were typically once-glamorous women preoccupied with their past and unable to move on. The films often showed old clips and real life glamor shots of the actresses from their glory days, which their character displays in their home; a knowing reference first used in *Sunset Boulevard* (1950), where Gloria Swanson's younger glamor shots and film clips stood in for her character Norma Desmond. Similarly, in *Die! Die! My Darling!* (1965) Tallulah Bankhead lent real life portraits of herself from her twenties to be used for a scrapbook belonging to her character, Mrs Trefoile.

It is a truth universally acknowledged that once actresses reached their mid-thirties, they would find the good roles were few and far between, and that if they didn't maintain their youthful vigor, the powerful studios could label them as "has-beens."

For women, youth has always been entwined with beauty, and as actresses got older, they were considered to now be lacking some of that original appeal. Leading men like Cary Grant, Gary Cooper and Clark Gable continued to romance much younger women on screen, even when they were in their sixties, yet a woman who was over forty was unlikely to be considered as a viable love interest. There were, of course, exceptions. Ingrid Bergman was 42 when she starred with Cary Grant in the romantic comedy *Indiscreet* (1958), and fifty-something Anna Magnani simmered with brooding sensuality opposite Marlon Brando in *The Fugitive Kind* (1960).

Even a bombshell like Marilyn Monroe began to worry she would become less relevant as she reached her mid-30s. For actresses, the fear of aging was not just for vanity; it was deep-rooted in their career. They would lose out on lead roles in quality scripts and would instead be relegated to the spinster, the matron or the tragic, desperate older woman. If she'd lived, Monroe would likely have been considered the past-it sex-pot, ridiculed and pitied as if she was desperately trying to cling to her looks.

Myrna Loy, star of MGM's hugely popular *The Thin Man* in 1934, found out for herself that older actresses were treated badly by Hollywood. "The studio no longer cared about us," she said. "They kept us locked into our old images while they concentrated on giving the good roles to newcomers. If we complained they had ways of forcing us out, of making us quit." But she also wondered if exploitative horror films were detrimental to these stars, particularly Bette Davis. "Is it worth playing all those demented old ladies to maintain that status?"

Rather than continuing to play romantic leads, older, unmarried women on screen were typically shown to be pathetic figures or mentally unstable, driven mad by their single status and their lost looks, and it was this trope that formed the basis of "Hag Horror." Peter Shelley, in his 2009 book *Grande Dame Guignol Cinema* noted that there were two roles for a woman in this genre. "She could be a mentally unstable antagonist, pining for former glory or her lost youth, or as a Woman in Peril." He adds that, "Even if she is not unstable at the start, her mental health deteriorates as the film progresses. As a Woman in Peril she is also more vulnerable due to the loss of youth and of her looks, which brought her power."

Melodrama, gothic horror, stylized death scenes and a faded star slipping into mental deterioration were the defining markers of these films. They were what critic Roger Ebert in 1971 referred to as "the macabre genre of the menopausal metaphysical mystery movie." He described how they "seem to involve a couple of middle-aged ladies with shameful pasts, who make lots of trips up and down dark stairs and into unlighted cellars, get the hell scared out of them when dust mops fall out of the shadows, and end up hideously, with blood and feathers all over the place. Well, it's a way to pass an evening."

The titles of these films were also a literal description of the troubled, reclusive woman at the center of the story – there was *What Ever Happened to Aunt Alice?* (1969), *What's the Matter with Helen?* (1971), and *Whoever Slew Auntie Roo?* (1971). Even *Hush, Hush Sweet Charlotte* (1964), director Robert Aldrich's follow up to *Baby Jane*, was originally to be called *What Ever Happened to Cousin Charlotte?*

John Baxter in *Hollywood in the Sixties* described "Hag Horror" as celebrating "sado-gerontophilia," which insultingly implied that a woman over fifty couldn't be considered a viable sex symbol. The women in "Hag Horror" are spinsters, recluses and alcoholics, and tend to have a limited, or non-existent, sex life, which perhaps leads to their frustration. In *What Ever Happened to Baby Jane?* two unmarried sisters are forced to live together despite their hatred for one another, due to their rejection of societal norms.

The mentally unstable spinster was just one type of female monster in horror movies. Stereotypes also include the psychopathic mother in *Psycho* (1960) and *Carrie* (1976), the beautiful but deadly killer in *Sisters* (1972), the dangerous adolescent of *The Exorcist* (1973), and the woman who transforms into a mythical creature in *Cat People* (1942).

The older woman often exhibits unstable behavior because of a trauma of the past, typically the result of the loss of a child, or because they missed their chance of having a family due to the abandonment, or death, of a lover. They've either rejected the proper gender roles of being a good wife and mother, in favor of their unnatural desires, as in *Strait-Jacket*, or perhaps their child has died, as experienced by Mrs Trefoile in *Die! Die! My Darling.*

Without being able to fulfill their function as a mother, they are incomplete and driven to madness. They carry a deep wound from grief or from their resentment at a past rejection, pushing them further into a demented state, particularly as they realize, when looking at their aged reflection in the mirror, that their beauty is now gone. Sometimes their domineering maternal instincts, or their neglect through being a single mother with different lovers, prevents their child from being able to function normally in society. The mothers in *Strait-Jacket* (1964), *Berserk!* (1967) and *The Killing Kind* (1973) are blamed for their children being murderers, due to their atypical behavior outside the realm of what a "normal" mother should be like.

The tropes of the bad mother or twisted spinster are so ingrained in culture that they can be traced back to the myths of ancient civilizations. As Jude Doyle, author of *Dead Blondes and Bad Mothers*, writes: "This is the primal threat in our earliest stories: a woman who lives on the outskirts of civilization, rejected by her community; a woman who is old, ugly, asexual; a woman who is, alternately, too beautiful, too sexual, too self-possessed; a woman who knows things others don't know, and can do things others can't do. When the loop of patriarchy closes, it can feel inescapable."

The Furies of Ancient Greek mythology were vengeful crones who tore men apart, and were described as having snakes for hair and blood dripping from their eyes. Medusa, one of the Gorgon sisters, is similarly so hideous in appearance, with boar's tusks, snakes for hair, a gaping mouth and a beard, that she can turn men to stone if they look at her.

In Jewish folklore, Lilith was Adam's first wife, before she fled the Garden of Eden, and her marriage, so that she could be free from his control. As punishment, she was transformed into an evil demon of the night who preyed on children and women in childbirth. While she is sometimes hailed as an independent woman who chooses to reject the patriarchy, her isolation after being banished from Eden drove her to madness, transforming her into a terrifying figure and threat to the sanctity of the family.

During the witch trials of the sixteenth-century, women were accused of everything from cannibalism to child murder, from destroying crops to bringing on natural disasters like storms, fires and the plagues. Reginald Scot wrote in *The Discoverie of Witchcraft* (1584) that witches were "old, lame, blearie-eied, pale, ffowle and full of wrinkles; poore, sullen superstitious, and papists..." The witch is frequently portrayed as an older woman who has never had children, or whose children have died. She is lacking because she isn't a mother, and doesn't share the natural maternal instincts that women are expected to possess.

Midwives in the Middle Ages were considered suspicious, and often declared to be witches, because of their knowledge of women's bodies, particularly around childbirth and menstruation, which was often outside of the realms of men's understanding. A woman's body has long been thought to be full of horrors, from the moment when she has her first period to the gore of giving birth, and then with the changes that come through menopause.

Pliny the Elder wrote in *Natural History* that contact with menstrual blood "turns new wine sour, crops touched by it become barren, grafts die, seeds in gardens are dried up, the fruits of trees falls off...to taste it drives dogs mad and infects their bites with an incurable poison..." He underscored how women's bodies were considered to be grotesque, and despite their exterior beauty, they were dangerous and rotten inside.

"When woman is monstrous, it is almost always in relation to her mothering and reproductive functions - the archaic mother; the monstrous womb; the witch; the vampire; and the possessed woman," writes Barbara Creed in *The Monstrous Feminine*.

Women in the horror genre are often in fear that they are slowly going mad. In reality, women who suffered anxiety and depression in the nineteenth-century, and well into the mid-twentieth century, faced the possibility they would be committed to an asylum or forced to undergo electric shock treatment. There was a real lack of understanding around the issues affecting women, such as post-partum depression, PTSD and the menopause. These themes would play into the depiction of misunderstood women. Charlotte Hollis in *Hush, Hush Sweet Charlotte* (1964) is traumatized by the violent death of her lover, and is trapped in her family home because of her grief, as well as the rumors and gossip around her mental state, and she becomes the eccentric who the local children are both curious and terrified of.

In Victorian gothic literature, women were frequently victims of gaslighting; slowly driven mad or labeled hysterical by men. The female gothic tale can be traced back to Charlotte Brontë's *Jane Eyre* and the tales of Ann Radcliffe, where a weak woman is overwhelmed by the house she is trapped in, and haunted by memories, and people, from the past.

From its first incarnations in gothic stories, beginning with Edgar Allan Poe's *The Fall of the House of Usher* (1839) and *Jane Eyre*, the gothic house is where danger lurks - on the staircase, in the creepy attic or basement and, later, in the bathroom. The house is always something frightening, and which is reflective of the insanity that is central to the story. Important scenes take place on staircases, because they are treacherous, unstable, and act as a gateway between sanity and madness. This is evident in *The Haunting* (1963), where Hill House's staircases are the site of mysterious deaths. In the prologue, Hill House is occupied by an elderly woman, Abigail, whose mother died after falling down the stairs. Abigail hires a female companion to live with her, but when this assistant is too busy with a sexual transgression to come to Abigail's aid as she dies, she is eventually driven mad by the spirit of the house. She climbs up the spiral staircase with a rope in her hand, and flings herself off it with the noose around her neck.

The bathroom is the most private room in the house, a space for cleansing rituals, and where one is at their most vulnerable – because of this, violence in this space is particularly shocking. The basement or attic has a habit of luring in the hapless victim, and which represents the darkness of the womb; where Norman Bates hides the body of his mother, and where he takes on her persona.

While the female characters of "Hag Horror" allude to well-established fears around older women, the sub-genre, also sometimes referred to as "Grande Dame Guignol," can be traced back to the Grand Guignol Theater in the Pigalle district of Paris. André de Lorde was the most significant writer at the theatre, and from 1901 to 1926 he often used the stories of Edgar Allan Poe to create shocking, naturalistic depictions of violence on an underclass of prostitutes, criminals and urchins. He transitioned into silent film, working with D.W. Griffith on a 1909 short film called *The Lonely Villa*, and he would inspire several French films, including *The System of Doctor Goudron* in 1913.

Grand Guignol made a striking impression on genre director Curtis Harrington when he visited the theater on a trip to Paris with fellow avant-garde filmmaker Kenneth Anger in the early fifties. He credited it as being one of the "most meaningful" experiences of his time in Europe, even above meeting Jean Cocteau.

Alongside Robert Aldrich and William Castle, Curtis Harrington was one of the most creative directors in the female-led B-movie horror genre. His work included *Games* with Simone Signoret, *What's the Matter with Helen?* with Shelley Winters and Debbie Reynolds, and *The Killing Kind* with Ann Sothern and Ruth Roman. His love of the golden age of cinema was evident in his desire to cast some of Hollywood's most famous stars in his independent movies. In his films, Harrington also brought sympathy to his own monster women. Dennis Bartok, director of the American Cinematheque, and a friend of Harrington's, said that: "He may have sympathy for Ann Sothern's tyrannical mom in *The Killing Kind* or for Shelley Winters's hopeless, pathetic Helen Hill [In *What's the Matter with Helen?*] but he understands that they're monsters, true monsters of a very human kind, and that's what makes them so haunting."

As the feminist movement gained ground in the sixties, and women were being given agency over their reproduction rights with the advent of the pill, the concept of the independent woman was becoming a threat to patriarchy. The fifties had pushed family values to the fore, supported by a conservative sway in Hollywood which used female tropes to demonstrate to women that marriage was the only way to have a fulfilling life. By depicting older women in horror films who were mentally disturbed and scarred by the lost opportunities in life, they served as a warning to others – that this is how you'll turn out if you don't perform your assigned gender roles.

The supposed lesson for women was that if they were too focused on their career, they were destined to be pitiful figures who were single and childless, or would have their child turn against them. In *Rosemary's Baby* (1966) and *The Witches* (1966), starring Joan Fontaine, older women were shown to take up witchcraft as a substitute for sex, as it was a "secret power when normal powers are failing."

While these "Hag Horror" films, of mixed quality, were seen to be a low career point, many of the actresses enjoyed showcasing their acting skills to play complex, twisted characters. After all, it could be fun to camp it up, wield an axe and drag a dead body. "Hag Horror" was successful on two points – it appealed to the nostalgia of older moviegoers who wished to relive their youth by seeing their favorite icons on screen, and for younger horror audiences who watched these aging stars with a degree of irony.

Camp horror films could not match the quality of classics like *Grand Hotel* (1932) and *Mildred Pierce (1945), Dark Victory* (1939) or *All About Eve* (1950), yet these films were, by the sixties, considered old-fashioned and over-the-top, and often ridiculed by the counterculture generation. Bette Davis recalled that "Warner Brothers sent me a letter saying they wanted to use a clip from *Now Voyager* in *The Summer of '42*. They implied that they wanted to use it as a laugh. My lawyer wrote back saying, if they wanted a clip to laugh at, why didn't they choose a scene from one of their current films."

Young people had rebelled with rock 'n roll in the fifties, and the beat generation was introspective and mimicked the poorest in society, but it was the sixties that was marked by huge cultural changes, as the baby boomers came of age. The hippie movement became a phenomenon that encouraged a generation of "dropouts" who chose the concept of "free love" and burnt their draft cards to protest against the Vietnam War. In this context of a newly switched-on, politically-active and promiscuous generation, classic movies seemed outdated, and they demonstrated a clash between modern youth culture and the traditions of the thirties and forties.

"Peace and love and all of that is just fine," said Joan Crawford, "but there are limits to be observed. When I was young, I also broke some of the stuffy conventional rules. But, damnit, we obeyed the laws, respected our elders, and we always earned our own way. Kids today say they don't trust anyone over thirty. Does this apply to their parents, who seem to be paying for their freedom and rebellion?"

Older movies also seemed tame and out-of-touch due to the Motion Picture Production Code which insisted Hollywood studios follow strict moral guidelines to ensure there was no nudity, sex or graphic violence on screen. From its introduction in 1934 the Production Code, also known as the Hays Code after its creator Will H Hays, held a grip on Hollywood, but by the late fifties films like *Suddenly Last Summer* (1959) and *Psycho* (1960) circumvented the strict conventions to deal with shocking subject matters.

Through the sixties the Production Code was increasingly ignored as more violence and sex was shown on screen, and by 1968 it was abandoned in favor of a new film rating system. The decline of the Production Code allowed for a rise in horror films throughout the sixties, and laid the groundwork for the success of *What Ever Happened to Baby Jane?* and the grittier and more exploitative female-led horror movies going into the seventies. What could be more appealing than seeing these former A-list stars, who had only appeared in heavily-censured films of the past, now being tortured on screen or wielding sharp objects?

Having watched *What Ever Happened to Baby Jane?* over fifteen times on its release to marvel at its huge success, director William Castle dreamed of creating his own version with a grande dame of cinema. When he fortuitously met Joan Crawford one night at a party in the Hollywood Hills he immediately courted her, telling her he had a script written especially for her by *Psycho* novelist Robert Bloch. The film was *Strait-Jacket*. "I'm listening, Mr. Castle," she replied. It was here, in front of an audience of teenagers, that Joan Crawford found a new lease of power, enjoying every moment where she was treated like the star she was.

2. "All about has-beens…"

1950 was a big year for Hollywood. The town was reeling from Ingrid Bergman's Roman scandal, having abandoned her family and fallen pregnant to Italian filmmaker Roberto Rossellini while making *Stromboli*. On top of this, there was also the fear of Senator Joseph McCarthy, and his witch-hunt for suspected communist sympathizers in Hollywood. His House Un-American Activities Committee was a dark cloud that hung over those in the movie industry who even had the loosest of connections to the party. It was also clear to film executives that the new medium of television was a major threat to cinema, when the lure of cozying up on the sofa at home was more appealing than waiting in line outside movie theaters.

While it felt like the country was holding the City of Dreams to account, it also proved to be a year of strong films, particularly for women, and more specifically for older women. As 1950 was the year when *Sunset Boulevard* and *All About Eve* were released – two films that exposed the entertainment industry, revitalized the careers of two of the biggest stars that had come out of Hollywood, and which depicted older actresses suffering from the trauma of the aging process.

When Gloria Swanson emerged from the shadows of her gothic prison in *Sunset Boulevard*, she was laying the foundations for a new type of horror film. "Hag Horror" took the gothic and the Grand Guignol, and combined it with a theme of Hollywood-lost. While *Baby Jane* is considered the trigger for the "Hag Horror" genre, it was also kick-started by Gloria Swanson, an outdated silent star playing up to her reputation as a demonic diva, who can't allow herself to be relegated to the past. The word "Comeback" angers Norma. "I hate that word, it's a return!" she declares. "A return to the millions of people who have never forgiven me for deserting the screen."

As William Holden's character, Joe Gillis, narrates from beyond the grave: "It was like that old woman in *Great Expectations*. That Miss Havasham and her rotting wedding dress, and her torn veil, taking it out on the world."

Prior to *Sunset Boulevard* there were only a handful of films that offered an introspective look at Hollywood. These included *What Price Hollywood?* (1932), *The Death Kiss* (1933), *Hollywood Boulevard* (1936), *Bombshell* (1933) and *A Star Is Born* (1937), where the name of the faded, alcoholic star, Norman Maine, was the namesake of Norma Desmond. Playing with the theme of the fickle nature of Hollywood, director Billy Wilder and producer Charles Brackett added an element of the gothic, perhaps inspired by *The Spiral Staircase* (1946) in which iconic stage star Ethel Barrymore plays the mysterious bed-ridden elderly woman who is concerned for the safety of her mute companion under the threat of a serial killer.

"Two years ago we decided we wanted to do a story about Hollywood," said Brackett in 1950. "Someone suggested a relationship between a silent-day queen and a young man. She lives in the past, refuses to believe her days as a star are gone, and has sealed herself in one of those rundown, immense old mansions on Sunset Boulevard, amid a clutter of mementoes like the Louis XV commode and the huge gondola-shaped bed in her bedroom…

"This taut, pathetically grotesque woman, this manic-depressive driven to murder when her dream of love, her dream of success, the whole fabric of her life are shattered. To him she is a temporary haven, a meal ticket. It's pity that keeps him around the place. Pity. That's his story – the disaster of a man who pitied a woman."

Sunset Boulevard dealt with shocking themes for the time – a young writer who becomes a gigolo, a dominant older woman who pays for him, a dead monkey buried in the back garden, with the hint that the monkey was her past lover. Gillis must pay for his sin of selling himself out to an aging spinster who has stepped into the traditional male role. *Sunset Boulevard* was filmed in black and white at a time when Hollywood was entering into its Technicolor period. The monochrome adds depth and an old-world gothic quality, playing with the shadows and dark recesses of Norma Desmond's mansion, which Gillis describes as "a great big white elephant of a place, the kind crazy movie people built in the crazy twenties."

When we first see Norma Desmond, there's something vampiric about her –she wears sunglasses indoors, her claw-like hands are crossed in front of her chest, and she holds her cigarette holder like a weapon. The underlying theme of the film is not just about making a return from oblivion, like Baby Jane Hudson in *What Ever Happened to Baby Jane?*, but in making a return from the dead. "Undead," is how critic Lucy Fischer describes Norma Desmond, "who is technically alive yet mired in a state of suspended animation."

Death is referenced throughout the film. Joe Gillis narrates the story as a dead man, we first see Norma holding a funeral for her deceased monkey, her butler, Max, has the appearance of Dracula's manservant, and Norma Desmond's mansion has a creeping paralysis.

"Sunset Boulevard was all about has-beens," Sam Stagg writes in his authoritative guide to the film. In particular, Gloria Swanson's return to cinema after a long period of absence was tied to the publicity and the legend of the film. Pictures of the real Swanson from her glory days in Hollywood were dotted throughout Norma's mansion, reinforcing the idea of Gloria Swanson and Norma Desmond crossing over like a Venn diagram. "How could she breathe in that house so crowded with Norma Desmonds?" Gillis muses. Just as Norma shows off her Charlie Chaplin impression to Joe Gillis, Gloria did her own impersonation of Chaplin on screen in *Manhandled* in 1924. A clip of Swanson in *Queen Kelly* (1932) is shown as Norma plays her old films for Gillis on her home projector. These moments of nostalgia for the past, of lamenting lost beauty, would be a recurring theme in "Hag Horror."

It was Swanson who was in the minds of Billy Wilder and Charles Brackett when they first conceived the faded film star of their story. As well as drawing on Swanson's life, Brackett and Wilder shaped Norma Desmond through the life of tragic silent stars like Norma Talmadge and Mabel Normand, and the scandal around the murder of director William Desmond Taylor in 1922.

"We needed a passé star who has gone down the tubes," Wilder recounted. "And the reason we needed a real passé star to play her was because it's very difficult to find a woman in her sixties, let us say, who is undiscovered - where was she until sixty? It would be hard to believe she was ever a big star. So we went after one who had been big."

In the event Swanson refused the part, there was a wish list of potential actresses, including Greta Garbo, who were also being considered. After having left Hollywood abruptly in 1941, the elusive star's return to the screen was much anticipated, with various rumors over the last decade of a potential comeback. Other names included Mary Pickford, who was at ease in her retirement and is said to have turned the role down, Mae West, who was far too assured of her sexiness to play desperate, and Pola Negri, the vampish star who had disappeared from screens following the advent of sound. It wasn't until 1964 that she made a short-lived return in *The Moon-Spinners*, starring Hayley Mills, before going back to her retirement in San Antonio.

Brackett insisted to the *Saturday Evening Post* in July 1950: "Nobody else was considered for the part. We knew no time would be wasted getting into the story as soon as Swanson appeared on the screen. Youngsters who never saw her would immediately accept her as an old-time movie queen. Older fans would identify with the characterization and get a bigger emotional wallop from the story."

In the silent cinema era of the 1920s, Gloria Swanson was one of the most photographed women in the world, having shaped her own glamorous image amongst the vamps, flappers and moths. Famous for her extravagant lifestyle, she was the first actor to make $1 million, and one of the first women to independently produce her own films, having set up her own production company.

Her Hollywood lifestyle was far removed from the cramped apartment in the meatpacking district of Chicago where she was born on March 27, 1899. Her father was an Army captain and she spent her early years living in military posts in Florida and Puerto Rico. After returning to Chicago when she was fourteen, she paid a fortuitous visit to Essanay Studios where she was discovered and cast as an extra on a number of films. When she moved to

Los Angeles in 1916 with her mother following her parents' separation, she initially had ambitions to become a singer, but in the meantime was hired at Keystone studios to appear in Mack Sennett films.

"To be a motion player picture was like being in burlesque or something. It wasn't something I wanted to be," she remembered of those early days. "I wanted to be an opera singer, but somehow I got waylaid and got on the merry-go-round of the picture business and couldn't get off."

After signing with Famous Players-Lasky, she was directed by Cecil B DeMille in six of his epic movies, where she dripped with jewels, pearls and feathers, and had her head pawed by a lion in *Male and Female* (1919). Two of her own productions, *Sadie Thompson* (1928) and *The Trespassers* (1929) were sensationally successful. It was while filming *Madame Sans-Gêne* in France that she met her third husband Henri de la Falaise, Marquis de La Coudraye, and swept back into Hollywood as a marquise. Following the financial disaster of her ambitious, and unfinished production, *Queen Kelly*, Swanson's career entered into a period of decline throughout the 1930s.

In 1938 she made a permanent move to New York City, where she was one of the first stars to switch to the new medium of television, in 1948. WPIX offered her a lifestyle show, *The Gloria Swanson Hour*, where she discussed fashion trends, glamor on a budget and the latest restaurants and events coming out of New York. "Everyone told me that television was the future, that the number of sets in New York alone had suddenly risen in a year from 17,000 to 300,000," she said.

The show proved to be a hit, and she was in the process of signing on for another three years, when she was hospitalized for a stomach problem. After turning on the television set in her hospital room, she was horrified to see the cheap aesthetic of television, and realized it was not something she wanted to be involved with. She wrote her resignation letter, and an hour and a half later, she said she received a phone call from the casting director of Paramount, asking her to go to Hollywood to screen test for Billy Wilder's latest film. "I've made two dozen pictures for Paramount. Why would they need to test me?" she thought.

By the time Wilder was casting for *Sunset Boulevard*, Gloria Swanson hadn't appeared in a film since 1941's *Father Takes a Wife*. Yet she didn't live an isolated life in her Hollywood mansion – she was fulfilled by television work, her fashion line, Forever Young, her beauty line Essence of Nature, groundbreaking in its use of natural ingredients, and in her role as a mother of two children. Even without the movie roles, she continued to spend lavishly and live in luxury.

"Miss Swanson represents better than any other person, perhaps, a lush Hollywood era of high salaries and low taxes which is gone forever," wrote *The New York Times* in a profile in 1964. "With her gold bathtub, black marble bathroom, gold sink, home elevator to save walking up one flight, four secretaries, and Atlantic City boardwalk chair in which a manservant wheeled her around the lot, she probably did more, singlehandedly, to spread Hollywood's fame and glamour to the corners of the earth than any other star before or since."

As much as Swanson hated the idea of doing a screen test, the offer of a $50,000 salary and a suite at the Beverly Hills Hotel was, she said, "music to the ears of someone who had been creating a whole TV show for $350 a week." She arrived in Hollywood in January 1949, having been assured it was just a formality to see the chemistry between actor Montgomery Clift, whose casting as Joe Gillis had been announced in the press in December 1948. Yet he seemed to find it a difficult concept to do the film's love scenes with a woman in her fifties. "They told me that Montgomery Clift had objected, through his agent, to playing scenes of romantic involvement with an older woman," wrote Gloria in her memoirs. "Therefore, they shyly asked, would I mind doing another screen test, since now their fear was that I looked too young for the man they had chosen to replace Montgomery Clift."

By March 1949, William Holden had stepped in to fill the role, but there were concerns that the thirty-one year old would look too old compared with the youthful-looking Swanson. "Women of fifty who take care of themselves today don't look old," she told Wilder. "That's the point. Can't you use makeup on Mr. Holden instead, to make him look more youthful?" Wally Westmore, head of Paramount's makeup department, painted wrinkles onto Swanson's face to make her appear more haggard.

Gloria credited her youthful looks to her devotion to following a healthy diet, only eating organic foods, avoiding refined sugar and meat, and even taking her own nutritious sandwiches to dinner parties. She was a health food fanatic way before it became a fashionable craze. "It is insanity for citizens of the richest nation in the world to be slowly poisoned to death in order to satisfy the greed of the big food and chemical cartels," she wrote in her memoirs. In 1947 she had been diagnosed with a tumor in her uterus and was advised to undergo a full hysterectomy. Instead, she chose to overhaul her diet and cut out animal protein, which she believed aided her complete recovery.

As well as a return to Hollywood, *Sunset Boulevard* also marked Swanson's return to Paramount studios for the first time in decades, and the long-time crew members, with whom she worked all those years before, came out to greet her and cheer for her. Speaking with John Kobal in 1964, she said, "When I walked on that film set, the whole crew … I've known them all their lives … they hadn't seen me … it was like the prodigal had returned. There was such an atmosphere of camaraderie, it made everything so easy. I had every bit of help you can imagine."

This moment inspired Wilder to add into the script Norma Desmond's warm reception from the crew, as she makes her return to Paramount while Cecil B DeMille is filming his real-life movie *Samson and Delilah*.

While Norma Desmond is stuck in the past, she is also aware of modern fashion and beauty trends, and when Paramount's head designer Edith Head designed the costumes, she combined 1920s style with the latest fifties silhouette. "She was to be a poignant, sad character, a woman who didn't realize that she had passed her prime by thirty years," Edith later recounted. "Although her greatest moments were in her silent movie days, Norma Desmond tried to be as contemporary as possible by wearing fashionable styles, clothes and makeup; yet there was something about her that connoted a sense of the past, a bit of déjà vu. What Billy was telling me was that he wanted me to find some way of combining Jazz Age clothes with the New Look."

Billy Wilder crossed fact with fiction when it came to casting the supporting roles. Erich von Stroheim was hired as Norma's butler and former director. In real life von Stroheim had directed Gloria Swanson in the disastrous *Queen Kelly* in 1928. As well as destroying both their careers, she also lost almost a million dollars of her own money. Swanson hadn't seen von Stroheim for almost ten years, but they caught up like old friends. "I'm a very forgiving person, I never hold anything against anyone," she later said.

Norma plays bridge with her old acquaintances, known as the Wax Works, who were real-life silent-era stars - Anna Q. Nilsson, Buster Keaton, and H. B. Warner. There was a joy for older audiences in seeing these faces from the past, at a time long before the internet when it wasn't easy to find out what happened to old stars, and it contributed to making the film the most talked about production of 1950. Swanson herself commented that this bridge scene "came closest to giving us all the creeps, but it reminded us too, once again, of exactly who we were...Anna had recently returned to the screen as a character actress and looked splendid, but HB (Warner) appeared brittle, almost transparent, when he showed up. Buster Keaton, the fourth member of the bridge party, looked ravaged, as indeed he had been, by alcohol."

Paramount contract player Nancy Olson was only twenty-years-old when she was cast as Betty Schaefer, and had little knowledge of who Gloria Swanson was. This separation between the old and the new stars was highlighted by the modern costumes worn by the younger actors, and the sense of dust and decrepit style on the older characters. In the November 1950 issue of *Sight and Sound* James Agee wrote that in *Sunset Boulevard* "the silent era, and art, are granted a kind of barbarous grandeur and intensity" and that "the lost people are given splendor, recklessness, an aura of awe; the contemporaries by comparison are small, smart, safe-playing, incapable of any kind of grandeur, good or bad."

Rather than being conscious of her age in comparison to the younger actors, Swanson admired how Brackett and Wilder "had cleverly kept this ghostly world of oldies separate from the young

Hollywood aspirants who form the other half of Joe Gillis' life; therefore I had no scenes with Nancy Olson or Jack Webb."

Once the film was completed, Louis B Mayer held a VIP dinner party and private screening, with guests including Mary Pickford and Barbara Stanwyck. The Hollywood audience had been completely enthralled as the film played out, and were left in stunned silence for a moment as the credits began to roll, before bursting out into enthusiastic applause. Edith Head recalled how Barbara Stanwyck "had tears streaming down her face as she pushed her way up to congratulate Gloria. I heard later that Barbara had knelt down and kissed Gloria's lamé skirt in reverence. I only saw them embrace."

Swanson, in her memoirs, believed she was giving her fellow older stars hope that they too had the chance to make a dramatic comeback. She described how she "could read in all their eyes a single message of elation: If she can do it, why should we be terrified? She's shown us that it can be done!" Mae Murray, who was 65 at the time the film was released, commented after watching Swanson's performance: "None of us floozies was that nuts."

Norma Desmond may have failed drastically in her "return" to the screen, but Swanson was hailed as the comeback queen on release of *Sunset Boulevard*, embarking on a successful nationwide publicity tour, where she played up to her character as she gave radio interviews and made in-person appearances. *Screenland* wrote in December 1949: "This 51-year-old grandmother has just finished starring in *Sunset Boulevard* for Paramount, and granny is as glamorous today as she was when she made her first film – 63 movies ago."

Film critic Bosley Crowther believed that the true-to-life moments in *Sunset Boulevard* lay at the heart of its appeal. "This story of an aging movie idol, now forgotten and completely passé, living in dank, unhealthy luxury in an old, baroque mansion in Beverly Hills, nurturing herself on mad delusions and the bought love of a hack writer of scripts – this would not seem the pregnant substance of an extensively popular film. Let's not be highbrow about it. A large part of this picture's mass appeal must lie in its amazing exposure of a sordid and scandalous affair. What's more it's a Hollywood scandal – one of those ripe, juicy, poisonous exposes, spewing madness and degeneration…"

1950 was also the year that another film about an aging actress received critical acclaim and record-breaking Oscar nominations. *All About Eve*, written and directed by Joseph L Mankiewicz, dealt with similar themes, but rather than centering on Hollywood, the story took place in the New York theater world. Margo Channing (Bette Davis) is a successful actress in her forties who only realizes the threatening nature of younger actresses once she has let one into her life. Bette Davis in 1973 said: "Margo Channing was not a bitch. She was an actress who was getting older and was not too happy about it. And why should she be? Anyone who says that life begins at forty is full of crap. As people get older their bodies begin to decay. They get sick. They forget things. What's good about that?"

Before Bette made the role her own, a number of stars were considered for the role of Margo. Susan Hayward was thought too young at 34, and Barbara Stanwyck turned it down as she was afraid of being typecast as a declining star in her forties. Claudette Colbert was eventually signed up, but she was forced to drop out at the last moment when she broke a vertebra in her back. "Claudette could have played it beautifully … bitchily, icily, with a great elegance – a piss elegance, if you like," Mankiewicz said.

A decade before, Bette Davis had been Queen of Warner Brothers, ruling the lot with a succession of hugely successful films including *Jezebel* (1938), *Now Voyager* (1939), *The Letter* (1940), and *The Little Foxes* (1941). But when she had her third flop in a row with *Beyond the Forest* (1949), a film most famous for her much-quoted line "what a dump!," she asked to be let out of her contract. After nineteen years of bringing in millions of dollars for the studio, she was tired of "fighting for the right scripts." She later reflected that "I look with pride at some of the roofs of those sound stages. I am responsible for a few of them being built."

It was while making her first independent film, *Payment on Demand*, at RKO in 1950, that she received a call from Darryl Zanuck asking her to step into the role of Margo, if she could be in San Francisco to start filming almost immediately. She met Joseph Mankiewicz for dinner to discuss the character, and he told her that Margo Channing was "the kind of dame who would treat her mink coat like a poncho." Despite her difficult reputation, Mankiewicz found Bette to be "intelligent, instinctive, vital, sensitive – and above all, a superbly equipped professional actress."

While the director later stated he based Margo on an Austrian actress, Elisabeth Bergner, comparisons were drawn to Tallulah Bankhead, whose stage career seemed to echo Bette's film career. Tallulah had first taken the role of Judith in *Dark Victory* to the stage, had initially been lined up to star in the stage production of *Jezebel*, and had received rapturous acclaim for playing Regina in the initial production of Lillian Hellman's play, *The Little Foxes.*

Charles LeMaire had already completed costumes on the female cast members, but Bette Davis requested Edith Head be loaned from Paramount to Fox to design her costumes. Edith Head noted that she asked her researchers to gather stills of Bankhead for her research. "Some of the costumes were very extravagant, sexy evening gowns. Some of them were rather simple sport or daytime clothes. I had steeped myself in Tallulah, and everything looked as if it was made for her, yet the clothes complemented Bette. What you must understand is that Bette was becoming Tallulah Bankhead or Margo Channing, or whoever the hell she was supposed to be. That is her marvelous talent. She becomes her character. She is such a good actress that she makes clothes belong to her."

It was on the set of *All About Eve* that Bette met Gary Merrill, cast as Margo's partner Bill Sampson. As Margo feels threatened in her career by the younger ingénue, Bill is the stable support who convinces her to settle down and marry him. Their love affair crossed over into real life, with the two marrying shortly after production wrapped. It was Bette's fourth marriage; the last decade had held personal tragedies for her, despite her thriving career. After divorcing high school sweetheart Harmon Nelson in 1938, she married Arthur Farnsworth in 1940. She was widowed only three years later when he collapsed and died on Hollywood Boulevard, due to a skull fracture. Third husband William Sherry, who she married in 1945, was abusive and violent, and by the time of *All About Eve*, when she was in her early forties, she had wondered if a happy marriage would remain elusive.

"Margo Channing was a woman I understood thoroughly. Though we were totally unalike, there were also areas we shared," said Bette. "The scene in which - stuck in the car - Margo confesses to Celeste Holm that the whole business of fame and fortune isn't worth a thing without a man to come home to, was the story of my life. And here I was again - no man to go home to. The unholy mess of my own life - another divorce, my permanent need for love, my aloneness. Hunched down in the front of that car in that luxurious mink, I had hard work to remember I was playing a part."

Sunset Boulevard and *All About Eve* dominated at the 1951 Academy Awards, with both films nominated in many of the same categories, including Best Picture and Best Actress. While Gloria Swanson and Bette Davis gave career-defining performances, they lost out to Judy Holliday for her comedic turn in *Born Yesterday*, a film which also starred William Holden.

Gloria later wrote of her Oscar loss that "I honestly didn't care," and that "Judy Holliday, when she dared to look at me at all, seemed to be pleading for forgiveness." She felt that everyone "expected scenes from me, wild sarcastic tantrums. They wanted Norma Desmond, as if I had hooked up sympathetically, disastrously, with the role by playing it."

By the time she completed the publicity tour for *Sunset Boulevard*, Swanson found she was receiving requests for personal appearances and scripts were piling up on her desk. But when she read through them, she dismissed them as "awful imitations of *Sunset Boulevard*, all featuring a deranged superstar crashing toward tragedy."

Despite the critical-acclaim of *All About Eve*, Bette Davis struggled to find quality work throughout the fifties. She accepted a small role in *Phone Call from a Stranger* (1952), starring husband Gary Merrill, and then the lead role in *The Star* (1952). Combining the plots of both *All About Eve* and *Sunset Boulevard*, Davis played Maggie Elliot, a washed-up, alcoholic actress in her mid-forties who is forced to work in a department store to make ends meet.

"They can't put me out to pasture. Not me, I was a star," Maggie tells her agent Harry Stone, as she pleads with him over lunch to help her revive her career.

"That's right, and you won an Academy Award," he replies. "But there's no denying that fresh, dewy quality, well something else takes its place…it's tough, but that's what the public wants."

Davis was again nominated for an Oscar for *The Star*, but lost out to Shirley Booth in *Come Back Little Sheba*, a part she had been offered first. In a moment that echoed *The Star*, the decent scripts were no longer arriving at her door, and Davis moved to Maine with Merrill, where she settled into life as a housewife. She called her Cape Elizabeth home "Witch-Way," because "a witch lives there, and we don't know which way we're going." It was the first time she had stayed home while her husband earned money, and while she tried to find contentment in this life, it never fully satisfied her, or Merrill. "My Maine neighbors had expected Theda Bara, at least, in sequin sheaths," she wrote in her memoirs *The Lonely Life*.

In 1955, she made the decision to return to Hollywood when 20th Century-Fox lured her back with the offer of playing Elizabeth I in *The Virgin Queen*. It was her second turn at playing the monarch, and she earned plaudits for her dedicated transformation by bravely shaving back her hair. At forty-seven years old, she also brought her age and experience as she delivers a performance that reflects the queen's fears of the loss of beauty and lack of fertility, and her jealousy of the younger rival, Bess, played by Joan Collins, for the affections of Sir Walter Raleigh. While it proved to be a success, she found the roles becoming few and farther between. "I did not know then that I had entered what

I would later call my ten black years. For three of those years I worked very little, the result of two major physical problems," she wrote.

During the making of *Phone Call from a Stranger* she had fallen down a set of stairs and broke her back. She also underwent surgery for a condition that was later diagnosed as osteomyelitis of the jaw. Her recuperation from both of these took years, and at the same time, her marriage began to crumble. "The more distant my career seemed, the harder I worked at being a wife and mother, and the shakier my marriage grew," she said. "I loved making a home for him, but he did not at all like that domestic side of me. He wanted me to be Margo Channing."

The couple tried working together once more when they signed up for a nationwide tour of the stage show *The World of Carl Sandburg* in 1958. It was a great success, but their marriage disintegrated as they toured together, and as soon as the contract ended in San Francisco, they divorced. It was 1960, and Bette Davis was fifty-four, single and struggling to recover her once stellar career.

Gloria Swanson didn't want her future to be playing *Sunset Boulevard* over and over again, and so for her follow-up she chose *Three for Bedroom C* (1952), a light farce which received scathing reviews, with audiences disappointed that she wasn't Norma Desmond. Like many others who have played iconic characters, Desmond was so big and dominating that it ultimately had a negative impact on Swanson's career. There were talks for Gloria to star in a small screen version of *Sunset Boulevard* in 1956 for Robert Montgomery's television show, but plans didn't materialize. *Sunset Boulevard* instead became a gift for other older actresses, including a television version in January 1955, starring Miriam

Hopkins, and fifty-four years later, as an Andrew Lloyd Webber musical starring Glenn Close.

The reclusive, faded star roles would instead go to stars like Joan Crawford, Bette Davis, Olivia de Havilland and Tallulah Bankhead, in a series of similarly-themed horror movies with characters that seemed to hark back to the madness of Norma Desmond, and the fears of aging, as felt deeply by Margo Channing.

3. "Beautiful woman, talented, frustrated..."

Joan Crawford had a survivor's skill for adjusting her career to suit the times, and even as she turned forty in 1945, an age which tended to be a kiss of death for actresses, she stayed relevant by embracing cinematic trends.

Crawford's MGM contemporaries from the 1930s, Norma Shearer and Greta Garbo, had both retired from the screen before they could be dismissed as too old, and Bette Davis lamented that the 1950s were her "black" decade, but Joan refused to be cast aside by the business. Instead of bowing out, Crawford pushed her career by following societal trends reflected in cinema. Just as she had been the flapper in the twenties and the glamor girl of the Depression-era, in the 1940s she captured the post-war mood for darker stories of obsession and trauma. By the mid-fifties she fully embraced the fashion for melodrama, playing the lonely older woman struggling to find love.

"I'd been a flapper in an age of flappers, a sophisticated lady in an era of sophistication," she said. "When you're part of an era, you're not aware of trends at the time. I only knew that I wanted good parts, valid and varied parts, and that I battled constantly to try to get them. To no avail. From *Dancing Lady* on, every picture I made was formula."

By the outbreak of the Second World War the depression-era hoofers and Park Avenue princesses seemed old news, and there was a new generation of young stars at MGM studios, such as Lana Turner and Judy Garland, who appealed to the new breed of teenage bobby-soxers. Now placed in the "mature" category, Joan's appeals to MGM to give her more interesting roles went unheard, and in 1943 she was effectively pushed by Louis B Mayer into leaving the studio that had been her home for eighteen years. Instead, she chose to sign a contract with Warner Brothers, the studio where Bette Davis was making hit after hit. It was here that Joan found a new career as the tough, troubled woman of film noir, beginning with her Oscar-winning role in *Mildred Pierce* (1945).

During the Second World War, women from all backgrounds entered into the workforce to support the war effort in place of the men who were fighting overseas. While there was an expectation that they would return to their traditional roles once the war was over, many women were reluctant to give up their jobs and the newfound freedom that went with it. As men returned from war and transitioned back into society, they felt displaced and suspicious of these newly independent women. Hollywood reflected their fears in films that explored the dark side of humanity with tales of obsession, alcoholism and dangerous love. In *Humoresque*, released by Warners in December 1946, Joan plays a wealthy married woman with an alcohol problem, who flirts with younger men and falls dangerously in love with a talented young violinist (John Garfield).

"Of course, I fell in love with Helen, the woman who drinks too much, has too much time on her hands, too much love in her heart," Joan said. "Initially, there may have been scant sympathy for this dipsomaniac married woman, but when she walks at last into the sea with her lover's violin playing Liebestod, backed by full orchestra, it was uncompromisingly dramatic."

She followed it with *Possessed* (1947), where she played a schizophrenic, and like her other characters in this period, there was a sense of yearning and tragedy around a loss of youth. As she lies in a catatonic state in a psychiatric ward, the doctor who is treating her comments on the state of civilization and its effects on mental health. "Beautiful woman, talented, frustrated. Frustrated, just like all the others we've seen. It's always the same."

Post-war Hollywood was influenced by Italy's "neo-realist" filmmakers when making their own credible, socially-conscious films. Billy Wilder's *The Lost Weekend* (1945) was Hollywood's first realistic depiction of alcoholism, and *Crossfire* (1947) explored anti-Semitism and earned Gloria Grahame an Oscar nomination for Best Supporting Actress. As Senator Joseph McCarthy's communist witch-hunts gripped Hollywood in the late 1940s, the number of films that dealt with social problems declined. The "red scare" resulted in a drain of left-leaning creative talent, and Hollywood's output in the 1950s became more conservative, with a focus on the sanctity of the family and the promotion of Capitalism.

As well as the hysterical fear of Communism, the 1950s was also marked by other perils, including the possibility of nuclear holocaust, a moral panic around juvenile delinquency and its link to rock n' roll and the Beat Generation, and the threat to male supremacy, and society as a whole, as more women sought emancipation by entering the workplace.

The 1950 US census revealed that women now made up one third of the total workforce, and as they became more visible, there was a suspicion that they were not only taking jobs from men, but jeopardizing the traditions of the family. Anti-feminists Dr Marynia Farnham and Ferdinand Lundberg wrote the best-seller *Modern Woman: The Lost Sex* (1947). They claimed that the independent woman "is a contradiction in terms," and that women who chose not to have children or be married were abnormal. They proclaimed that "spinsters" shouldn't be allowed to be teachers, as they made bad role models for children. To counteract this threat, women were bombarded with messages from politicians, trade unions, and in the media, that their proper place was at home. The working woman haunted the melodramas of the 1950s, and her decision to pursue a career and remain unmarried revealed her own inadequacies.

For decades, it was known that women were the leading demographic at the cinema, making the decision as to what to see, a fact that Alfred Hitchcock knew only too well. In a 1931 article, he was quoted as saying: "The chief point I keep in mind when selecting my heroine is that she must be fashioned to please women rather than men, for the reason that women form three-quarters of the average cinema audience." During the Great Depression women flocked to theaters on rainy afternoons so they could gaze up at the silver screen, watching their favorite heroine dressed in recession-defying gowns. Joan Crawford's long eyelashes, framing large, earnest eyes, fluttered down at the audience, enraptured by her strong-willed characters looking for love – shopgirls, factory girls and burlesque dancers.

In the early 1950s producer Ross Hunter, in a bid to reverse the downward spiral of Universal, wanted to recapture the female matinee audience of the 1930s by providing a series of domestic dramas that dealt with issues that concerned them. Hunter was credited with boosting the finances of the studio with his extravagant and instantly recognizable Technicolor melodramas, particularly those directed by Douglas Sirk, including *Magnificent Obsession* (1954) and *Imitation of Life* (1959). Not only did Hunter cast glamorous actresses like Jane Wyman and Lana

Turner, whose careers were fading, but they also offered up an answer to concerns around gender roles. They allowed a space for female audiences to make sense of the changes in society through the overwrought emotional scenes and high-camp drama.

Marjorie Rosen in *Popcorn Venus* (1973), her feminist study of Hollywood films, coined the expression "The Woman Alone" to describe the stereotypical characterization of an unmarried, childless woman on screen. Rosen noted the shifting changes in how "The Woman Alone" was depicted. She was a dignified, sacrificing figure in the 1930s and 1940s, such as Claudette Colbert as the hardworking single mother in *Imitation of Life* (1934), Olivia de Havilland in *To Each His Own* (1946) and Bette Davis as the hand-wringing spinster-turned-beauty in *Now, Voyager* (1942). But by the 1950s, "The Woman Alone" became "a love-starved pariah" and "a creature so negative and pitiful that one can interpret the vogue as little other than a reinforcement of the decade's belief in marriage as salvation." The Wife, the Mother, and the Daughter became the only truly viable female alternatives in the film melodramas of the 1950s.

In the 1970s, feminist writers re-examined the depictions of women in melodrama, and concluded that women who resisted the conventions of society were punished in films, to serve as a lesson for women. Marjorie Rosen suggested that in the 1950s women's films became "'how tos'' on catching and keeping a man." Melodrama stirred emotions in its mostly female audience, such as heartbreak, despair and triumph, and the ending tended to provide a solution to the conflict. What the lesson seemed to be was that women were at their happiest when they followed traditional roles. If they delayed marriage, then they would be tormented by the thought that they could miss their chance and end up an old spinster, and would always wonder what could have been.

Molly Haskell in her seminal text on women in film, *From Reverence to Rape* (1974), argues that the film industry supported "the big lie…the idea of women's inferiority, a lie so deeply ingrained in our social behavior that merely to recognize it is to risk unraveling the entire fabric of civilization." She added that women are not "real women" unless they "marry and bear children, and even those without the inclination are often pressured into motherhood and just as often make a mess of it. The inequity is perpetuated as women transmit their sense of incompleteness to their daughters."

In *Belles on Their Toes*, the 1952 sequel to *Cheaper by the Dozen* (1950), Mrs. Gilbreth (Myrna Loy) is now a widow, balancing work with raising her twelve children. When her daughter Ann turns down the marriage proposal of an attractive doctor so she can help her mother, Mrs. Gilbreth tells her: "Is that why you think I've kept this family together? So I can have spinster daughters around the house?" Being a self-sacrificing widow was acceptable, but a spinster was not.

Olivia de Havilland in *Not as a Stranger* (1955) plays Kristina Hedvigson, an attractive but unsophisticated Minnesota Swede, who works as a nurse while hoping one day to have a family. Her spinster status is taken advantage of by Robert Mitchum's ambitious but poor student doctor, Luke, who marries her for her money. His friend Al (Frank Sinatra) tells Luke, "I think it's a dirty, stinkin' thing to do. You're takin' advantage of a poor squarehead who's afraid of being an old maid. You're lettin' yourself be kept."

By the time she starred in *The Damned Don't Cry* (1950), forty-five-year-old Joan Crawford found she was being scrutinized for any signs of aging. Director Vincent Sherman, concerned at the "lines in her face, around her eyes, and her neck," talked to Jerry Wald about the most flattering way to film her. They decided "we had better take Joan's appearance into consideration and write a different opening for our film. He thought she was very attractive, too, but she couldn't play a girl. It was all very delicate."

Similarly in *Goodbye, My Fancy* (1951) Sherman was instructed by Jack Warner to avoid doing any close-ups of Joan because her face gave away the clues that she was a woman in her forties. After completing the badly-received *This Woman is Dangerous* (1952) and no decent roles forthcoming, Joan asked for her contract at Warner Brothers to be terminated.

To leave a major studio at the age when leading female roles were hard to come by was a gamble, but it was worth it when she came across the novel *Sudden Fear* by Edna Sherry. She was immediately struck by its possibilities of reversing the concept that an actress in her late forties couldn't play a love interest with sexual desires. The story may have seemed progressive, but the plot still followed "The Woman Alone" trope. Myra Hudson is a successful playwright who longs for love, but she is duped by a younger man (Jack Palance) who marries her for her money, and, with his conniving girlfriend (Gloria Grahame), plots to murder her. The stereotypical sexpot younger rival is in direct opposition to "The Woman Alone," and her threatening presence would be a marker of Joan Crawford's later movies, and of 1950s melodrama, as a whole.

Made at RKO Pictures, it was Crawford's first experience as executive producer and she oversaw all aspects of the production, including hiring screenwriter Lenore Coffee, director

David Miller and cinematographer Charles Lang. She made the perceptive decision to take 40 percent of the profits in lieu of a salary, which ultimately netted her more than a million dollars, reversing her fortunes and placing her firmly back on the A-list. She was also nominated for an Academy Award, which put her in direct competition with Bette Davis in *The Star*. Walter Winchell reported: "While many female stars in Tinseltown are scrambling to find work in movies or television, Joan Crawford, with the smell of a new hit movie, *Sudden Fear*, on her hands, is lining up jobs for the next three years. She's putting all offers right next to the requests for dates, from every eligible male on both coasts."

After the criticism she'd experienced at Warners over her looks, it was no wonder she decided to get a facelift and cleavage-enhancement for her return to MGM for *Torch Song*. She told costume designer Helen Rose, "The face and the breasts are new, but my ass is the same." As an aging and neurotic Broadway star, *Torch Song* (1953) was hailed as the Technicolor version of *All About Eve*, but instead she was described by one critic as "a drag Queen let loose on film," with her orange page-boy hairstyle and garish makeup.

She followed *Torch Song* with another Technicolor movie, the western *Johnny Guitar* (1954), directed by Nicholas Ray, in which she played opposite whisky-voiced Mercedes McCambridge as her archrival. It was another flop, and Joan made a return to a formula that worked so well with *Sudden Fear* - that of the Older Woman in Peril. In the thriller *Female on the Beach* (1955), filmed at Universal, she played a wealthy widow who is preyed on by a handsome beach bum (Jeff Chandler) and where her younger rival is played by B-list blonde bombshell Mamie Van Doren.

Joan Crawford felt incensed at some of the new Hollywood stars who flaunted their bodies in what she considered to be cheap, too-tight gowns. According to photographer Eve Arnold, she took particular exception to Marilyn Monroe. "She doesn't even wear a girdle. Her ass was hanging out. She's a disgrace to the industry!" Crawford was the representation of the corseted older society, clashing with the new type of woman who her characters in her later movies would often be threatened by.

She signed up to a three-picture deal with Columbia Pictures, and the first of these films was *Queen Bee* (1955), where she played ruthless southern belle Eva Phillips, a character she described as a "total bitch." Eva is so terrified of getting older that she wears gloves and an eye-mask to sleep, and prefers to hide her wrinkles under her satin sheets as "nasty light" filters through the window. "Don't stand there staring at me and looking ridiculously young," she cries to her young houseguest, Jennifer.

"*Queen Bee* owed so much to Tennessee Williams. I felt like a Carte Blanche DuBois," Crawford said. While it had become increasingly difficult for women past forty to find quality roles, Tennessee Williams' plays and novellas offered rich characterization for their film adaptations; the type of lonely older woman who would be amped up in the horror films of the 1960s. Williams dealt with the themes of a yearning for lost youth, old-world glamor, and the plight of spinsters, who felt incomplete without a husband and children.

In *The Glass Menagerie* (1950), stage star Gertrude Lawrence played Amanda, a faded Southern Belle who clings to the memories of her past to escape the present. In *Suddenly Last Summer* (1959) Katharine Hepburn is Violet Venable, a widow who is ashamed of the homosexuality of her deceased son, and in 1961,

The Roman Spring of Mrs. Stone, Vivien Leigh took on the tragic title role of a widowed American actress who is taken advantage of by a younger lover in Rome.

Williams' plays also dealt with controversial topics that pushed the boundaries of the Production Code. In *Cat on a Hot Tin Roof* (1958) Big Mama (Judith Anderson) tells daughter-in-law Maggie (Elizabeth Taylor): "Do you make Brick happy? Something's wrong. You're childless and my son drinks." After three years of marriage, she is still not fulfilling her function as a wife to bear children, with the hint that husband Brick is more attracted to men.

But it was Vivien Leigh in *A Streetcar Named Desire* (1951), as delusional and moth-like Blanche DuBois, who was the template for the lonely older woman. The original Broadway production had premiered in 1947, with Jessica Tandy as Blanche. Vivien Leigh starred in the London run of the play, before being cast in the film adaptation.

Blanche is the definitive "Woman Alone," unable to accept her lost social status and her need to work to survive. She puts on the airs of a genteel Southern Belle, to cover for how she has prostituted herself for money. She still dreams of love, but she's afraid to be seen in harsh light as it would reveal her true age. She's unmarried and desperate, putting on an act of respectability which is uncovered by the brutish, working class Stanley, who torments her and rapes her, pushing her into having a complete mental breakdown.

Another Tennessee Williams character that was reminiscent of the tragic "Woman Alone" was Alexandra in *Sweet Bird of Youth*, which he initially wrote with Tallulah Bankhead in mind. Alexandra is a faded movie star who drowns herself in alcohol and sleeps with younger men to escape from the negative criticism she received for her last performance. She knows that youth and beauty are a prerequisite of her profession, and it sends her spiraling into an abyss. She was both Norma Desmond and Baby Jane, and all the other tragic older women who regret the transience of time.

Crawford played a similarly lonely and regretful spinster, Millie, in *Autumn Leaves* (1956). "This was one of my very favorite pictures," she said. "It was, I think, the best film of its type ever made - the older woman with a younger lover. The loneliness and desperation of her situation came through with no need for melodrama or overacting - in fact, I played it down."

Millie is a typist who is haunted by the regrets of her adolescence, when she turned down dates to look after her invalid father. "Don't worry about me," the young Millie reassures him in a flashback. "There's plenty of time." In the opening scene, as Millie works away on her typewriter, we see how repressed she is by her position trapped at her desk, and the realization that time did indeed pass too quickly for her. As a cautionary tale to young women in the movie theater, we see Millie's own expression of regret at the loss of her youth and her lack of love, as she listens to mournful music at a concert.

That evening she is reluctantly pushed into sharing a table in a busy diner with a young man, Burt, played by Cliff Robertson, even though she prefers to eat alone. They are served by an old, overweight waitress who is a contrast to Joan's elegant suit and neatly sculpted hair, but offers her a vision of her future as an older, working woman. "You know something, you're lonely," Burt says to her. "It's no disgrace to be lonely, nowadays everybody's lonely…you know what I see in your face – fear."

Burt "love bombs" the repressed Millie by complimenting her on her youthful looks, despite her fears of appearing in a swimsuit in front of him, and sweeps her off her feet and into marriage. Yet her honeymoon turns to a nightmare when his ex-wife, and Millie's younger rival, Virginia (Vera Miles), beautifully-dressed in youthful white, arrives on the scene. Burt is schizophrenic, having been pushed to the edge when Virginia slept with his father, and he takes it out on Millie by smashing her typewriter on her hand, and destroying her way of making a living. Despite these depictions of domestic violence, Millie tries to mother him back to health, and in one symbolic shot, she is bathed in light like a statue of the Virgin Mary, while he rests his head on her lap and she comforts him.

With costumes designed by Jean Louis, Joan was dressed more expensively than the character should have been, and director Robert Aldrich struggled to persuade her to ditch the glamor. "I admired her," he said, "but I could not get her to be a drab, aging woman, and that threw off the balance of the picture." While Bette Davis relished realism and embraced a haggard appearance if it was right for the part, Joan Crawford refused to look anything but beautiful in her films.

"*Autumn Leaves* did nothing to embellish my reputation," Robert Aldrich later said. "I quite liked it, thought it was funny. I didn't mind it either - I liked a lot of things in it that were really corny - I'm not unproud of it." It may not have been one of his favorites, but Aldrich's successful working relationship with Joan Crawford led to a further collaboration – *What Ever Happened to Baby Jane?*

The film would also make an impact on another future director. When Curtis Harrington arrived at Columbia Pictures in 1955 to work as an assistant to producer Jerry Wald, he was blown away when he got the chance to watch the dailies of Joan Crawford in a scene from *Autumn Leaves*. He found it a revelation, helping shape his desire to cast iconic stars in his own horror movies. "For the first time, I became aware of what the term "movie star means," he wrote in his memoirs. "The word 'star' in the context of a top movie personality is very appropriate, since astronomically speaking, a star is a body that is illuminated from within."

As the fifties progressed, "The Woman Alone" became increasingly neurotic. Rather than a feasible object of desire, she becomes a grotesque caricature to be pitied, and then feared. By the sixties, "The Woman Alone" in melodrama would morph into the older spinster woman in gothic horror, serving as a cautionary tale to women against being too independent.

As Jackie Byars in *All That Hollywood Allows* (1991) wrote: "Good Girls were traditionally feminine, carefully protected, and ultimately married - not like 'them,' the Flappers, the Bad Girls who grow into Dark or Evil Women Alone. The key word here is, of course, married."

4. "Hundreds of youngsters waiting patiently to have the 'shit scared out of them'"...

When the French thriller *Les Diaboliques*, directed by Henri-Georges Clouzo, was released in the United States in 1955, it became one of the most talked about films of the year. Based on the novel *She Who Was No More* (1951), by Pierre Boileau and Thomas Narcejac, it reinvented the rules of cinema with a narrative that tricks the audience up until the very last moment.

One rainy night, director William Castle was struck by the long lines of teenagers waiting to go into a theater showing *Les Diaboliques*, despite being soaked from the heavy downpour. "Word was around that *Diabolique* was doing great business, but I never expected the excitement that surrounded the theater. Only the very young would venture out on a night like this, or the very crazy - like myself," he recollected. "It was an amazing phenomenon - hundreds of youngsters waiting patiently to have the 'shit scared out of them'. The theater was packed, sold out. All kids - some of them didn't even seem old enough to read the English subtitles for the French film, but it didn't matter. They wanted thrills and chills, and *Diaboloque* delivered in a big way."

The fifties was a tumultuous time for Hollywood, following a 1948 ruling that banned Hollywood studios from owning their own theaters, and the Senator Joseph McCarthy "witch hunts" which targeted alleged communist sympathizers and destroyed many lives and careers in the film industry. As Bette Davis recounted: "It was a terrible decade for Hollywood. The old studio system as we knew it began to crumble. Actors with long-term contracts were let go. They worked in independent films, on television, or they went out of their minds."

Cinema attendance also dropped dramatically following the introduction of television, and as more and more homes boasted their own TV set, there was less need to catch entertainment in the movie theater. To attract young audiences and lure people out of their living rooms, movie studios launched new technologies including 3-D, VistaVision and CinemaScope. Drive-in cinemas also boomed in the fifties, going from 820 outdoor screens in 1948 to 4,063 screens in 1958. They proved particularly popular over the summer months, and because studios tended not to show their big films at that time of year, drive-ins offered the chance to screen B-movie double bills that might not receive a traditional screening. It was at the drive-in theaters, where teenagers crowded into cars, or looked for thrills and laughs on first dates, that cheap horror movies thrived. One popular genre in the fifties was the alien invasion horror movie, such as *Invasion of the Body Snatchers* (1956) and *The Blob* (1958), which is understood to have fed into fears around the communist threat that was felt so keenly in media and politics.

In 1954 Universal introduced *Creature from the Black Lagoon*, which led to a trend in science-fiction horror. Instead of a haunted castle the monster came from the Amazon rainforest, and it was a film that spoke very much of modern concerns around pollution and nuclear power. It even made an appearance in *The Seven Year Itch* (1955) as the film Marilyn Monroe goes to see before her skirt is lifted by the breeze from the subway grate. As Curt

Siodmak, writer of 1941's *The Wolf Man*, once said: "When the war ended, the bottom fell out of the horror film business. When they began testing the atom bomb, it all started again. In times of peace of mind, there's no place for horror films."

In the era of Rock n' Roll, Hollywood's output shifted from Film Noir to content that catered to teenagers, with movies like *The Wild One, Rebel without a Cause, Blackboard Jungle* and Elvis Presley's *Jailhouse Rock*. The themes stirred up emotions in the young audience, who could identify with the teen rebellion of Marlon Brando and James Dean. Culture was becoming much more aligned with youth power, with *American Bandstand* bringing the hottest new music direct to living rooms, and radio stations pumping out the latest rock n' roll hits.

In 1959, John Cassavetes wrote an article titled *What's Wrong with Hollywood*, which began, "Hollywood is not failing. It has failed." There was a sense by the end of the fifties that the traditional notion of movies was unable to hold onto audiences who were drifting away from cinema in favor of watching television. With nine out of ten households in America having their own television set by 1960, going to the cinema was a less-frequent event, saved for special occasions. It was realized that to attract a youthful audience who were unimpressed with mainstream films, cinema had to offer what television, restricted in content by their advertisers, couldn't provide – more sex and violence.

In August 1956 Joan Crawford traveled with her new husband, Pepsi-Cola executive Alfred Steele, to England to film *The Story of Esther Costello*, the last of her three films as part of her Columbia package. "This was my last really top picture," she said. "Why the hell didn't more pictures like this come along?" she later asked. "Why did I get stuck in freak shows?"

The answer to Joan's question was partly to do with changing audiences. Since the 1920s it was known that women made up the majority of cinema-goers, and it was universally accepted that they were responsible for selecting what film to see. By the late fifties there was a major demographic shift as teenagers with disposable incomes became the driving force in box-office revenue. They wanted a different offering from what they could see on television with their parents; they wanted thrills and shocks, and for young people to win out over the stuffy older generation.

Alfred Hitchcock, always with an eye for a good story, had tried and failed to buy the rights to *Les Diaboliques*. To compensate, he purchased another thriller by the writing duo Boileau-Narcejac, *D'entre les morts* (From Among the Dead), which would be the basis for his 1958 film *Vertigo*. While the film, with its theme of obsessive love and voyeurism proved popular in art-house cinemas, it didn't make the impact Hitchcock had hoped for, and so he began to develop a film that would be so shocking in its premise that it would outdo any horror that had come before.

Based on the Robert Bloch novel, and with a screenplay by Joseph Stefano, *Psycho* marked a seminal moment in cinema on its release in 1960, testing the boundaries of the strict censorship codes and transforming Hitchcock into the first blockbuster director. Just as *Les Diaboliques* featured a grisly bathroom scene, Hitchcock chose the shower as the setting for his gruesome, shocking murder, where the streaks of blood contrast with the stark white tiles of the Bates Motel bathroom. He cast Janet Leigh as his murder victim Marion Crane, to confound expectations that he would dispatch a well-loved movie star in the first thirty minutes. Audiences, taken by complete surprise as the shadowy figure of an older woman enters the bathroom, screamed throughout the murder scene. The tension didn't let up until the twist is revealed - that the killer is not the old woman locked up in the creepy, gothic house, but her son, Norman Bates, who has taken on his mother's persona after murdering her.

Hitchcock also copied *Les Diaboliques'* advertising slogan for his own groundbreaking publicity campaign, which implored people not to reveal the ending and warned that latecomers to the theater would not be admitted. The audience came out of the cinema in shock and on a high from the adrenaline-boosting thrills. *Psycho* redefined the horror movie by relating it to an insipid every day setting, with shocking murders taking place in a neon-lit motel run by ordinary people. Hitchcock's decision to shoot in black and white for budgetary reasons further added to this sense of grit and realism. However the gothic mansion behind the motel borrows from Victorian horror, with the madwoman in the basement and the sinister staircase; motifs which Freudian theory connects to sexual repression in the subconscious. As critic Robin Wood wrote, the predominant subject of the horror genre is the struggle against repression, with the monster punishing themselves and their victims for acting out against "normal" family values.

"*Psycho*, in my humble opinion, is the first modern horror film because it so strikingly took horror out of gothic romanticism," said John Carpenter, director of *Halloween* (1978). "It wasn't a vampire or a werewolf. It wasn't an old castle with cobwebs and costumes. It was a motel. You had the motel in the front, and you had this gothic house in the back. It was like passing the torch from old gothic romanticism into modern horror."

Psycho's terror was built around the fear of the everyday, of a seemingly normal man, Norman Bates, who turns out to be a serial killer, and that horror can strike while doing a mundane activity, such as taking a shower. "We all go a little mad sometimes," Norman tells Marion Crane, and it was this concept that changed the face of horror for the sixties.

Hitchcock told director and film critic Peter Bogdanovich: "Well, that's what life is like. Things happen out of the blue. You may say I'm going downtown to the movies, but on the way you might be killed. One must never set up a murder. They must happen unexpectedly, as in life."

Marion Crane pays dearly for both the money she steals from her employer and for her hotel room transgressions with an unavailable man. This sexualized violence against women would become a particular theme of horror films over the next several decades. We might see the victim taking off her clothes, preening in the mirror, having sex, taking a shower; moments which excite and arouse the audience. Her violent murder then causes an equal sense of horror and delight as a form of punishment for her loose morals and vanity. As film critic Robin Wood explained: "The violence against women in movies have generally been explained as a hysterical response to 1960s and 1970s feminism: the male spectator enjoys a sadistic revenge on women who refuse to slot neatly and obligingly into his patriarchally predetermined view of the way things should naturally be."

Another horror film trope that would be fully developed by the early 1980s was the smart, sensible Final Girl, a phrase coined by Carol J. Clover in her 1992 book *Men, Women, and Chainsaws: Gender in the Modern Horror Film* to describe the last girl standing, who is also the most virginal. One of the first Final Girls was *Psycho's* Lila Crane (Vera Miles). Lila's instinct tells her that something terrible has happened to her sister Marion, and after her investigations lead her to the Bates Motel, she survives her terrifying encounter in the basement with Norman Bates.

There is another woman in *Psycho* whose creepy presence shapes the film. Norma Bates, a single mother who controls Norman from beyond the grave. All that's left of her is her mummified corpse, and Norman's imitation of her with the grey wig and floral dresses, but through Norman's descriptions, we believe that her suffocating possessiveness has driven him to his murderous impulses. Because of his mother's fanatical rejection of sex, Norman's repressed sexual desires lead him to punish women who arouse him, and he takes on his mother's persona to do so.

The mother is traditionally the stable force in the family, the person children should feel safest with, and when she is the villain, it shatters our sense of order. Deadly mothers who threaten their own children became a theme of female-led horror from the sixties and seventies onwards. Carrie White in *Carrie* (1976) is so damaged by her religious fanatic mother that she can only use her telekinetic abilities to unleash destruction.

In the 1960s, a decade marked by a sense of violence and uncertainty, the horror film transformed from the classic monsters of the past, into what writer Charles Derry called "the horror of personality," and Norman Bates was the first of these everyday American monsters. As Derry wrote in *Dark Dreams: The Horror Films from Psycho to Jaws* (1977): "*Psycho* and the horror-of-personality films suggested that the world was horrible because it was insane and therefore perversely violent."

Mass murderers like Richard Speck and the Boston Strangler hit the headlines, and there were riots in the streets as people protested injustice. What seemed terrifying was humanity itself, rather than fictitious monsters, as if society itself was showing signs of insanity. With the introduction of the contraception pill, women were also given more control over their bodies, and as more women excelled in the workplace, it seemed that this sense of independence was threatening the position of the man. "Horror films have always reflected man's deepest anxieties about himself," wrote Charles Derry. "In a time where life, or at least man's awareness of it, seems to be increasingly horrible, it is most understandable that elements from the horror-of-personality films (violence, insanity) are now being fed into the mainstream."

Psycho's depiction of horror lurking in modern life paved the way for a new type of movie. It would be one that drew on the fears felt over women's increasing power, and which spoke of the contradictions around young audiences who wished to rebel against the older generation. It would also appeal to women, who looked for thrills to make sense of the fears they were feeling in an increasingly violent society. As Robin Wood wrote in his study of the American horror film: "Since Psycho, the Hollywood cinema has implicitly recognized horror as both American and familial," and what the house of horror, as seen in a wide range of horror films, from *What Ever Happened to Baby Jane?* to *Rosemary's Baby* and *The Texas Chainsaw Massacre*, "signifies is the dead weight of the past crushing the life of the younger generation, the future."

Reflective of this fear of violence at the beginning of the 1960s, Ross Hunter's colorful melodramas became darker and more dangerous. After the success of *Imitation of Life*, he teamed up with 39-year-old Lana Turner again for the neo-noir thriller *Portrait in Black* in 1960, notable as the final screen appearance of Anna May Wong.

He followed it with another thriller, *Midnight Lace* (1960), with Doris Day playing an American heiress in London who is paranoid that someone is trying to kill her. It had a glossy, fashionable sheen amidst the gothic horror, to appeal to both female fans of Doris Day and younger audiences who would enjoy seeing her in peril. Copying the marketing of *Psycho*, the trailer advised audiences to see the film from the beginning, and not to "reveal to your friends the shocking surprise ending!"

Director Robert Aldrich, whose work was so often influenced by the exploration of psychology and humanity, took the concepts of *Les Diaboliques* and *Psycho*, and combined it with the theme of wasted lives and faded celebrity with his seminal horror *What Ever Happened to Baby Jane?* This horror film proved to be Norma Desmond on acid, and with two older female stars cast in the lead, it pushed boundaries in its questioning of how Hollywood, and the patriarchy, not only treated older women, but viewed their place in society.

5. "Sometimes I wonder about the two of them in that big house all alone..."

"Now she saw that it had been a mistake, watching the old movies. They had brought with them a sad disillusionment that, in its own way, had been a kind of dying."

Henry Farrell's *What Ever Happened to Baby Jane*.

In 1962 American soldiers were preparing to fight in Vietnam and the American and USSR space race geared up when John Glenn became the first American to orbit the earth. For twelve days in October the Cuban Missile Crisis threatened to bring the world to the brink of nuclear war, and in August Marilyn Monroe had been found dead from a drug overdose. It was also the year that *What Ever Happened to Baby Jane?* was brought to theaters, marking a new type of horror movie with Grand Guignol thrills and, in a rare exception, with two older actresses above the title.

Bette Davis and Joan Crawford, at one time the most powerful stars of Hollywood's studio system, were cast as the older, unmarried sisters and former actresses who are confined together in their home following a tragic accident. They are trapped in the memories and regrets of their past and slowly driven mad by their frustrations as they live outside societal norms. While Blanche is literally imprisoned in her wheelchair, Jane is imprisoned by her foolish desire to return to her childhood success by recreating her old act exactly as it was, girlish costume and all. When she goes into the outside world, she is an old relic, with every wrinkle exposed under the dazzling Los Angeles sun, as the harsh reality of the outside world contrasts with the gloominess of their prison-like house.

At first no studio would touch a film with two aging stars (Jack Warner, their former boss, called them "washed-up old bitches"), yet they helped to create a winning formula that would be replicated numerous times over the next decade. *Baby Jane* attracted repeated viewings from a youthful audience who enjoyed the Grand Guignol delights of Bette Davis serving up a dead rat on a platter to Joan Crawford, yet were unfamiliar with these two actresses at the height of their beauty.

Director Robert Aldrich later recalled: "In *Baby Jane*, we thought that if you made a movie about the periphery of Hollywood which had something to do with the ancient Hollywood, and put in two stars who were getting old, people would read into that picture a secret show-biz nostalgia. The audience feels that they are privy to real-life secrets about Crawford and Davis."

From early on in their careers, Crawford and Davis were set up as rivals – two movie stars of the thirties who clashed when both were at Warner Brothers in the mid-forties. A May 1946 article in *Motion Picture* magazine announced that: "The hottest feud to hit these parts since they thought up Technicolor, is the one between Joan Crawford and Bette Davis at Warner Brothers. Since Joan's Oscar victory for *Mildred Pierce*, she's been getting pretty much of anything she wants at the studio. All of which leaves Davis sizzling."

They both had four husbands and had been widowed, and later in life both would have their daughters write unflattering accounts of their mothering skills. They were also supposedly the same age, born in 1908, although Crawford's real date of birth is believed to have been in 1904. "Crawford is five years older than me, if she's a day," Bette proclaimed.

There had been previous discussions about the two stars working together. In the fifties producer Jerry Wald had considered pairing them for a film called *Women Without Men*, about a female prison warden who tries to rehabilitate a female prisoner. "I knew of the women's prison picture," Crawford said in 1973. "It was written by Virginia Kellogg and later became *Caged*, with Eleanor Parker and Agnes Moorehead. Certainly I wanted to work with Miss Davis, but from what I recall, the studio did not want to put two of their top stars in one picture."

"Baby Jane was a breakthrough in women's pictures," wrote Bette Davis in her memoirs. "Not in ten years had there been a successful woman's film. Actresses had owned the industry for the previous twenty years and the men were entitled to their turn in the fifties and sixties. By then the world's problems were wars, drugs, crime, political corruption - all the ills that involve men much more than women. And writers write about what's going on in the world. Given that trend, *Baby Jane* was truly a break for both Joan and me."

In July 1961, after the grueling filming of his biblical epic *Sodom and Gomorrah* in Rome and North Africa, Robert Aldrich was on the lookout for a script that could be his second "Hollywood" movie, after the success of *The Big Knife* (1955), a barbed study of a mogul based on Columbia Pictures' Harry Cohn. When Geraldine Hersey, his English secretary, sent him a letter with a copy of the book *What Ever Happened to Baby Jane?* by little-known author Henry Farrell, it immediately piqued his interest.

Henry Farrell enlisted in the US Army in World War II, where he took a creative writing class to make up for his lack of education. After his army discharge, he moved to Los Angeles to try acting, and it was where he met his wife, actress Molly Dodd, whose Anglican minister father was known as "the Padre of Hollywood."

Molly and Henry were entrenched in the Hollywood set, living in a grand home in Pacific Palisades, while he wrote for pulp magazine penny dreadfuls and worked on his ambitions to write a novel. His first, *The Hostage*, was published in 1959, followed by *Death on the Sixth Day* in 1962. He also moved into writing for television, including episodes of *Alfred Hitchcock Presents*, which suited his fondness for Grand Guignol.

When Molly was diagnosed with cancer, Henry sought to come up with a commercial idea for a book to help pay for her treatment. He was inspired by Jane, the young daughter of family friend Yvonne Winslow, who would have tantrums whenever Henry and Molly came to visit. She reminded Henry of the precocious vaudeville child stars, like Baby Rose Marie, later a regular on *The Dick Van Dyke Show*. "I decided on a story so outrageous that it couldn't help but be commercial," he said.

He believed that "The subject of early movies, kiddy stars and movie queens already embodied the camp element just by nature. It had been exploited over and over for years." With this spark of a story, little did he know it would launch a new trend for gothic horror, with a tinge of faded Hollywood excess.

In *Baby Jane's* prelude, nine-year-old Baby Jane Hudson appears to be a delightfully sweet stage star who is adored by her audience of children and adults alike. Her fans buy up her dolls with their glassy eyes and fixed smiles, which belie Jane's real personality. Behind the scenes she is revealed to be a demanding brat who screams for ice-cream and torments her seemingly patient sister Blanche. However, by the 1930s, when they're in their twenties, it's Blanche who has become the successful film star, while Jane is struggling to be taken seriously due to her difficult reputation and penchant for booze. Blanche's film career comes to a dramatic end following a tragic collision which leaves her in a wheelchair, and which has whispers that it was Jane who deliberately drove at Blanche in a moment of rage. Thirty years later the two of them are trapped together in their Spanish colonial home, both living as recluses, with regrets as to how their lives could have been.

In the novel, their neighbor, Mrs Bates, muses to her friend Harriett about legendary film star Blanche and her sister living in the house on their own. "Sometimes I wonder about the two of them over there in that big old house all alone. They don't ever seem to do anything - or have anyone in for company. It must be awful…"

The two sisters are chewed up by the Hollywood system, and over the years they become forgotten relics and bizarre caricatures of the women they once were. The on-screen battles between the two former stars were even more symbolic as audiences considered the real-life parallels of Davis and Crawford. The rivalry between the stars perfectly fitted the theme of the film. Jane tells sister Blanche: "I made a picture in 1934 too. But the studio didn't want to show my film. They were too busy giving a big build-up to that crap you were turning out."

At first Blanche seems like the innocent victim of her demented sister Jane, who is jealous of her success in the thirties, at a time when Jane had been rejected as an adult star. But later, we begin to realize the full toxicity of their relationship and there are hints that it is Jane who is the real victim. In the precredit sequence, we see a close-up of the bitter face of Blanche as a child, and in the thirties, as the studio executives pass Blanche's car, one of them comments: "What do they make monsters like this for?" While it is initially unclear who is driving the car and who is crushed against the gates on the night of the accident, we see the damaged head of the Baby Jane doll, with its broken porcelain and blank eyes.

In the present day, with the showing of Blanche's films as part of a retrospective on television, the past seeps into the present. Blanche is hit with a wave of nostalgia at seeing her luminescent image in the romantic movies that made her famous, and jealousy at the fan letters Blanche is receiving triggers Jane into re-enacting her childhood routines. She places an advertisement in the paper for an accompanying musician, and this brings the hulking presence of Edwin Flagg (Victor Buono) to her door.

There's another unflattering depiction of an older woman in the story; that of Edwin's mother Del, who in the film is a clucking, overweight Cockney, and in the novel, he calls a "stupid old bitch." Similarly, in the novel, Edwin dismisses Jane as a "silly, drunken old woman, got up like a Main Street harlot," but he knows that the money he can earn from the "old girl" can help him escape his mother.

Del fell pregnant with Edwin out of wedlock, and after his birth she denounces all associations with men, considering sex as sinful, and places expectancy on Edwin to be celibate too. Wrote Farrell: "He was frightened of all men, including those younger than himself. Women, generally, disliked him instinctively, sensing his hatred for all womankind which had its roots in his hatred for Del."

For Aldrich, Farrell's novel had all the elements of the type of story that he was interested in telling, with its theme of Hollywood, family feuds, violence and a descent into madness. While Aldrich's most successful films had been male-dominated stories of survival and pressure, such as *Apache* (1954), *Vera Cruz* (1954) and *Ten Seconds to Hell* (1959), this time it would be two women doing battle. It also seemed the perfect story for bringing Bette Davis and Joan Crawford together. "I could never see them working together in anything. Then I read *Baby Jane*," recollected Aldrich.

"I sent the novel to Joan Crawford who, for several years had urged me to find a suitable story to team her and Bette Davis," he wrote in an editorial in *The New York Times* in November 1962. "Inevitably, during the forty day period, speculators had learned of interest in 'Baby Jane' as a film possibility and had moved to cut themselves in on the action. The price was now $61,000."

Joan Crawford remembered the story differently. "I found the book," she later told author Shaun Considine. "I read it and went out and bought three copies. I sent one to Nicholas Ray, one to Alfred Hitchcock, and the third to Bob Aldrich. He was the first to option it. He wanted me for Blanche, and he suggested Katharine Hepburn for Jane. I insisted on Bette Davis. I also brought Mr. Aldrich and Miss Davis together. Then later, for their own selfish, neurotic reasons, they teamed up against me."

It was just after the filming of *Queen Bee* that Joan Crawford met Alfred Steele, the President of Pepsi-Cola, and after a whirlwind romance, they married. As a corporate wife, she was greeted by huge crowds as she traveled the world opening up bottling-plants and attending conferences, and it offered priceless publicity for Pepsi-Cola.

Crawford loved the lifestyle she was carving with Steele, but she was struck a devastating blow when she woke one morning to find Alfred Steele lying on the floor of their luxury Manhattan apartment, having dropped dead from a heart attack during the night. She received a further shock on discovering her husband had been heavily in debt. Struggling to pay the bills, she sold her Brentwood home and made a permanent move to New York. As her movie roles were becoming scarcer, Crawford went with the times and fully embraced television. She acted in twenty dramas, made over fifty appearances on talk shows and variety shows and also appeared as a special guest on game shows. She was able to maintain her ties to Pepsi-Cola when she was appointed to the board, which gave her a regular salary and the perks of private jets and travel. In return she ensured that a Pepsi dispenser was available for cast and crew backstage, and that Pepsi bottles were used as props on every film and television show she worked on.

By the late fifties, Bette's movie career also seemed to have crashed and burned. After *The Catered Affair* in 1956, playing an aged and downtrodden Brooklyn housewife, she didn't receive another film role until Frank Capra's *A Pocketful of Miracles* in 1961 as the street peddler Apple Annie. Like so many other stars of her generation, she relied on the offers of guest roles on television shows like *Wagon Train* for some much-needed finances. In fall 1961 she accepted a role in Tennessee Williams' new play *The Night of the Iguana*, as earthy and voracious bar owner Maxine Faulk, who feels distraught at losing her looks as she gets older. Bette saw her own similarities in Maxine, and began to drink heavily to cover her insecurities about the attention co-star Margaret Leighton was receiving over her. Twenty years before, Bette had declared that "when I retire from pictures, I'm going to be a nice, plump, comfortable-looking middle-aged lady." Now that she had reached that point, it was a difficult reality to accept. She had assumed that she would be cast as Maxine for the upcoming film adaptation, but the role was passed to the younger Ava Gardner instead.

It was while she was performing at the Royale Theater on Broadway, that Joan made a surprise visit backstage to persuade her of the merits of working together on *Baby Jane*. "I was rather surprised to see her," Bette recalled. "She came backstage after a matinee of *Iguana* and told me about a book which had parts for both of us in it. Robert Aldrich had bought it and thought he could get backing if we agreed to be in it. He was in Italy, and he'd asked Miss Crawford to approach me."

Bette was skeptical of the concept of working with Crawford. She saw herself as more aligned with actresses like Katharine Hepburn, who had come from the theater and who prioritized character over appearance. She considered Crawford to be the complete opposite; primarily defined by her glamor rather than her talents. "At times, I was amused by her. Miss Crawford was just not my kind of actress," she added.

But once she'd read Farrell's story, she thought: "Well, it could work, you know. It's all there. Phony Joan and Crazy Bette." A few weeks later, after having sent her the script, Aldrich visited Bette at her townhouse in New York. The first question she asked was which part she would be playing. The answer was, "Jane, of course." After asking for reassurances that he hadn't slept with Crawford during the making of *Autumn Leaves*, as "Miss Crawford was famous for developing a 'meaningful relationship' with either her male star or her director," Davis agreed to the role, on the provision she would be given first billing.

"Without Joan's initial enthusiasm," Aldrich conceded. "There would have been no *Baby Jane*. I never had anyone else in mind but Joan and Bette for the picture. And then Joan talked Bette Davis into being *Baby Jane*."

Now that he had his two stars in place, Aldrich approached the major studios for backing, but he was told the same thing - it was a non-starter unless he recast it with younger stars who would be more appealing to the new generation of cinemagoers. Jack Warner, whose studio had made millions from Joan Crawford and Bette Davis when they were contract players, told Aldrich to forget about "those washed-up old bitches" and that "I wouldn't give a plug nickel for either one of those old broads."

Finally, Elliott Hyman of Seven Arts Pictures expressed interest in the project, but with conditions. He told Aldrich, "I think it will make a fabulous movie, but I'm going to make very tough terms because it's a high risk venture. But I feel that it's a picture that should be made by you and with Davis and Crawford." With the backing of Seven Arts, Warner agreed to distribute it, but refused to provide space on the studio lot, as much of it was being used for the musical *Gypsy*, starring Natalie Wood. Instead, Aldrich filmed at a B-Western movie lot on Melrose Avenue, and at a Spanish-style villa at 172 South McCadden Place, in the Hancock Park neighborhood of Los Angeles.

To drum up publicity for the film, a press call was held for the two stars as they signed their contracts. Hedda Hopper was also invited onto the set to interview Bette and Joan on July 16, 1962. In her notes of the interview she wrote that Bette arrived from rehearsals first, and that she "mentioned she'd never really known Joan – had merely met her – they'd never worked together."

Joan arrived in a dark dinner suit, with her hair held in place with a diamond pin, wearing diamond earrings and a diamond watch, having come from doing multiple makeup tests. Hedda asked what they'd have to drink. Bette took Scotch on the rocks and Joan had vodka on the rocks – she brought her own flask, because she liked 100 percent proof.

And who got first billing? "Bette, of course," Joan replied, sweetly. "She plays the title role – there was no problem about it."

"We don't know what's happening to the picture business – very few story properties for stars like this come along. Of course everybody is expecting us to clash," Joan said.

"Now they write everything for men – westerns – war stories...we've had it for 15 years," added Bette.

"There are scenes in this picture that will tear you to pieces," Joan told Hedda. "When we were rehearsing Bette practically tore the set up...she whirled my wheelchair around and lifted it six inches from the floor. This is a wonderful thing for me...I usually play the bitches. Now I can sit and watch Bette do it. I don't know how to be a clinging vine...a wheelchair is the greatest prop in the world for an actress."

"We haven't had an excitement around here for years," said Hedda. "The hope of your fighting will bring it to life. This is a dead town and you two are going to be the dynamite - the atomic bomb."

While they played down the rumors of any clashes on-set, the difference between the two stars was obvious when they arrived on set each morning. Crawford sailed onto the set on the first day of filming with her extensive entourage, including her hairdresser, makeup artist, secretary, and maid "Mamacita" Brinke, and a cooler filled with bottles of Pepsi. Bette Davis arrived alone, looking, as Aldrich put it, "every one of her years," and immediately creating a contrast between how the two stars conducted themselves. To prevent any disagreements, they were given the same size of dressing room, which were of equal distance from the soundstage.

Davis believed that Crawford took herself too seriously, and she enjoyed poking fun as she knew she could trigger a reaction. As they worked together, Bette came to realize that Joan "had a deep and gnawing need to be liked, loved, admired, appreciated. She could be touchingly generous. She brought gifts for me to the set and presented them in front of the crew."

Working to a low budget, and to a tight three-week production schedule, shooting began on July 23, 1962. To save money on back projections, Bette drove around Beverly Hills dressed up as Jane, with cameraman Ernie Haller in the backseat, shooting over her shoulder. "To this day I smile when I remember the first time 'Jane' drove down Beverly Boulevard in an old Hudson. The expressions on the faces of people in other cars when they saw me were hysterical. Lots of mouths dropped," she recalled.

In the novel, Jane was described by Henry Farrell as "a squat pudding of a woman in a soiled cotton house dress patterned with faded lilacs and daffodils…In the dyed, cherry-red ringlets of her hair was an enormous satin bow of such a vivid blue that even there in the dimness it seemed to generate a radiance all its own."

The image of Bette Davis dressed in her little girl dresses, with a grotesquely made-up face and sausage curls is one of the most unforgettable images from the film. Costume designer Norma Koch not only used Jane's costumes to demonstrate her stunted emotions, but also hinted at who the bad sister really is through color-coding. Blanche wears black, despite her seemingly sweet persona, while Jane is in light colors and girlish styles.

Jane's clothes appear sweat-soaked, as if they date back to the car crash in the 1930s, and she wears adult versions of her child star outfits. Norma Koch recalled that "There were two distinct changes for Bette's character. As Jane, the sloppy housekeeper, when she was slouching around the house, drinking and being miserable to her sister, I tried to come up with the sleaziest outfits possible. Then as Baby Jane, when she was planning her career comeback, I designed grown-up versions of dresses of what a little girl would wear. They were supposed to be extensions of the child star she once was."

On her feet she wore a pair of ankle-strap shoes, the type that was Joan Crawford's signature shoe in the forties. "We found a few pairs in the wardrobe department at Warner's. I'm not sure if they were Joan's, but they fit perfectly," Koch added. During John Springer's conversation with Joan Crawford as part of his 1973 Legendary Ladies of the Movies, at Town Hall in New York City, he asked her the nickname of those shoes. "It starts with an F, and I think if you remember, they held me up a goddamn long time," she said.

Bette was an actress who had always been willing to look grotesque on screen if it enhanced her character. Just as she had painted her face with white makeup in *Mr. Skeffington*, and insisted on aging herself to suit her character, a dowdy teacher, in *The Corn is Green* (1945), she gave Jane Hudson a powdery white complexion, heavy eye makeup and a smear of lipstick, as if she was piling on more each day, without washing her face first. "I wanted to look outrageous, like Mary Pickford in decay," said Bette. "It was my idea to wear the ghastly white base, scads of black eye shadow, a Cupid's bow mouth and the beauty mark."

"Jane looked like many women one sees on Hollywood Boulevard," wrote Bette in her memoirs. "In fact, author Henry Farrell patterned the character of Jane after these women. One would presume by the way they looked that they once were actresses, and were now unemployed. I felt Jane never washed her face, just added another layer of makeup each day."

When Bette presented herself to Aldrich, wearing the heavy makeup and a blonde wig with sausage curls, giving her the appearance of an overgrown Shirley Temple, Aldrich was horrified. It seemed to him that she would be a laughing stock if she appeared on screen in that get-up, but Davis stood firm. If he forced her to change her appearance, then he would have to cast a new actress.

When writing his story, Farrell said that he knew Blanche was "beautiful beyond description, a photographer's dream who, without trying, could project glamour such that few other stars ever could." It was a description that no doubt appealed to Joan Crawford. She envisioned herself looking attractive in her wheelchair, wearing low-cut negligees and sexy dressing gowns that drew attention to her top half. "I managed to talk her out of that by saying they were too lovely and new, that her character should only wear clothes that looked dated," said Norma Koch. "After all, she was crippled, and her sister, Jane, hated her so much she wasn't about to go to expensive stores to buy clothes for her. Joan agreed on that, and then we discussed the day wear."

Joan learnt how to move in a wheelchair from a paraplegic serviceman who had been injured in the Korean War, and he taught her how to hoist her body from bed to chair. But despite this striving for a degree of realism, she insisted on making herself look as glamorous as she could get away with, even as the two characters disintegrated on screen. As Bette witnessed Joan being filmed by a camera on a long-crane from the outside of the house, in the scene where she cries for help through the bars on the window, she couldn't help but laugh. "Joan was wearing lipstick and ludicrously long eyelashes," said Bette. "In her cry for help, my terrified co-star insisted on looking like she was posing for the cover of Vogue."

"I am aware of how Miss Davis felt about my makeup in Baby Jane," Joan said in 1973. "But my reasons for appearing somewhat glamorous were just as valid as hers, with all those layers of rice powder she wore and that ghastly lipstick. But Miss Davis was always partial to covering up her face in motion pictures. She called it "Art." Others might call it camouflage – a cover-up for the absence of any real beauty. My character in Jane was a bigger star, and more beautiful than her sister. Once you've been as famous as Blanche Hudson was, you don't slip back and become a freak like Miss Davis preferred to see her character. Blanche also had class. Blanche had glamour. Blanche was a legend."

Real-life clips of the two stars were used in the film; a detail that would become a common feature of the "Hag Horror" genre. In a scene in which wheelchair-bound Blanche is intently watching one of her old films being played in a retrospective on television, the actual film was *Sadie McKee* (1934), starring a twenty-five years younger Crawford. In the opening scenes set in the thirties, two Hollywood producers watch Jane's outtakes in the screening room. They dismiss her talents ("She stinks!") on the back of these clips, which were from two of Bette Davis's films in 1933, *Ex-Lady* and *Parachute Jumper*. This moment reveals that Blanche is now the bigger star, and has written into her contract that the studio must make a Jane Hudson picture once a year. Further meta moments in the film included the casting of Bette's daughter BD as the daughter of their neighbor, who was named Mrs. Bates as a homage to *Psycho*.

Despite gossip magazines hoping for a full-blown feud, the production of *Baby Jane* went smoothly. "They obviously didn't like each other, but they were totally professional and ladylike," said Aldrich. "Any comments about one or the other they would reserve for the privacy of their own dressing room when the other one wasn't around. I was very careful and very fair. I had to be objective in terms of getting the best picture."

Nevertheless, there were undercurrents of resentment as the two stars wanted to ensure the other wasn't receiving more attention. Each night after filming, both stars would phone their director to let off steam about the other. "First one, then the other," said Aldrich. "I could rely on it every night. They were like two Sherman tanks, openly despising each other."

It was long rumored that Joan would need a vodka pick-me-up on set, and while filming *Baby Jane*, Davis made constant digs that she was spiking her customary Pepsi with vodka. "She had that bottle by her elbow every minute. When one was finished her secretary would bring her another. Everyone knew what was in it."

Bette relished the scene where Jane serves up a rat on a silver platter to Blanche, perhaps thinking of the time as a child when she served a dead rat to her mother's neighbors; a story she recounted in her memoirs. Holding a cocktail party at New York's Plaza Hotel a few months after filming, she asked them to mold pâté into the shape of a rat. "When my guests lifted the serving cover, they were horrified. I laughed myself silly. It was a wonderful idea," she said.

As Jane's cruelty to Blanche reaches a peak, there were moments when the resentments spilled over. In one scene, Jane kicks Blanche repeatedly when she is helplessly lying on the floor, and Hedda Hopper spread a rumor that the kicks were for real. In another scene, where Jane carries a bound and gagged Blanche from her room, Joan wore extra weights under her gown, which made it even more of a struggle for Bette to carry her. When the director yelled cut, Bette screamed out in pain that she pulled something in her back.

The final scenes were shot on Westward Beach, Malibu, with the dazzling white sunlight offering a contrast to the gloom of their prison-like home. In the scenes where Blanche is dying on the beach, it appeared to Aldrich that every time she returned from her trailer to pick up her position on the sand, she appeared to be getting more glamorous. Bette recounted how Joan had "three sizes of her bosoms" in her wardrobe, and used the largest set for when she was lying on the beach. "The scene called for me to fall on top of her. I had the breath almost knocked out of me. It was like falling on two footballs!"

It's on a beach, in the glaring light that Blanche tells Jane the truth – that it was she who drove the car purposely at Jane, but ended up injuring herself instead. Jane replies, "You mean, all this time we could have been friends?" But too much time has passed, their lives have been wasted and all that's left are these two old ladies, who have lost their looks and their future. "I threw your life away, Jane," Blanche tells her in the novel. "Without the guilt, the false guilt I've given you - with the competition between us ended - you could have had a happy life - even a husband perhaps and children. But it was all finished for me, and I wanted it to be finished for you, too…"

Jane goes to buy an ice-cream cone, just as she had wanted to do in the 1917 pre-credit sequence. As she retreats into her own illusions, she dances in front of a crowd of beach-combing teenagers who have gathered out of curiosity at the eccentric old woman. Believing she has an audience once more, she dances in circles with the two ice-cream cones in her hand, oblivious to the two policemen who are pleading with her to show them where the seriously-ill Blanche is.

This final scene was filmed later in the day, as the sun shifted over the ocean. In order to balance the light, the cinematographer, Ernest Haller, used a strong key light which washed out Bette's complexion and smoothed the wrinkles, as if all Jane's troubles had been lifted. "When I danced on the beach in the famous scene that ends the film, and my face seemed to glow as I twirled up to the ice cream stand, people swore I had changed my makeup. I had not changed a thing. I changed inwardly and it reflected on my face," Bette wrote in her memoirs.

After thirty-six days, shooting finished up on September 12, 1962. Aldrich was asked by Warners to edit the film quickly as they had struck a deal with The Theater Owners of America to simultaneously show it at 400 cinemas nationwide, rather than the traditional method of doing phased openings across the United States.

The gimmicky poster, inspired by *Psycho*, noted that there were five things people should know before they bought a ticket to see the movie.

"1) If you're long-standing fans of Miss Davis and Miss Crawford, we warn you this is quite unlike anything they've ever done; 2) You are urged to see it from the beginning; 3) Be prepared for the macabre and the terrifying; 4) We ask your pledge to keep the shocking climax a secret; and 5) When the tension begins to build, remember it's just a movie."

When *Baby Jane* opened on November 3, 1962, it was immediately met with strong reviews. *Time* called it "a brilliant tour-de-force of acting and film-making." *Newsweek* wrote: "As an ugly old hag, Bette Davis with her ghastly layers of makeup and her shuffling-clump walk, is rather appealing. And Joan Crawford is – oh, just Joan Crawford."

While Bette and Joan had both initially agreed to take part in a national tour, Joan got cold feet and pulled out at the last minute, perhaps unwilling to share the stage with her rival. Bette fully embraced the cartoon grotesqueness of Jane, handing out Baby Jane dolls to fans in the audience and relishing singing her jazzy theme song which shared the movie's title. She performed it in her signature raspy voice on stage during the tour and on *The Andy Williams Show*. "I hear tell that you've made a record. Is it a dramatic record?" he asked her, as she sashayed on stage in an aquamarine chiffon dress. "Well, it's not quite," she says. "I think it's more like Chubby Checker."

For her appearance on *The Jack Paar Programme*, Bette Davis told the host: "This is a terrific victory for Robert Aldrich, who had the idea of Miss Crawford and me. And wherever he went with this film, to raise money to make it, the Hollywood people would say, 'those two old broads? I wouldn't give you a dime.' And if it weren't for him, those two old broads would've been recast. We owe him a great deal, and I must say, we are not feeling charmingly victorious. We're a little gloating...You are really only judged by your last film, they don't care if it's good or bad, only if it makes money. So at least finally I'll be on the books as a potential money-maker, and believe me that's a new career for me."

On seeing this interview, Joan followed up with a telegram: "Dear Miss Davis, Please do not continue to refer to me as an old broad. Sincerely, Joan Crawford."

In her publicity drive, Crawford was nothing but sweet about working with Davis. Joan Crawford appeared on the first episode of *The Tonight Show with Johnny Carson* in 1962. She said of Bette, "it was a fascinating experience...She's a great, great lady, fantastic talent. It was just so exciting, I can't tell you Johnny. She's a real pro...even before we got to the coast they were trying to create a feud."

Baby Jane turned out to be Aldrich's first box-office hit since *Vera Cruz*, grossing nearly twelve times its reported cost of $1,025,000. It was also the first of his films to be nominated for an Academy Award. There were five nominations for the film in all, including actor nods for Bette Davis and Victor Buono, and for costume designer Norma Koch. While Warner Brothers promoted both Bette and Joan as potential Best Actress Oscar nominees, only Bette would be shortlisted. Feeling affronted, Joan chose to undermine Bette by offering to accept the award on behalf of the other Best Actress nominees, should they win. Anne Bancroft, who was nominated for *The Miracle Worker*, was unable to attend and so agreed for Joan to collect her award on stage. For Bette Davis, a third Best Actress Oscar meant everything, as she would be creating an historical moment as the first to achieve that goal. When Anne Bancroft's name was announced, and Joan strode onto the stage, glittering from head to toe in a dress created for the occasion by Edith Head, Bette said she was "paralyzed with shock."

Bette bitterly claimed that "Joan did everything she could possibly think of to keep me from winning. She campaigned openly in New York, contacting all the Oscar nominees who were in plays in New York that year." Both Bette and Joan had been invited to the Cannes film festival, but after the Oscars upset,

Bette refused to go with Joan. Because Bette was more beloved in Europe, Aldrich was forced to rescind the invitation to Joan, leading to her threatening legal action.

Despite the irreparable damage to their working relationships, a feud was something they both continued to deny. "A feud? Oh, no. I couldn't ever be bothered with anything like that. Let's just say Joan's not someone I would have any cause to see socially. Or ever did," Bette Davis told *McCall's* magazine in 1974.

The film marked a turning point in the careers of both actresses, who were suddenly seen in a new light; that of gothic horror queens. For a while, this new image extended their careers as above-the-title stars. "*Baby Jane* was such a huge success it proved there was no reason for me or Miss Crawford to ever be on their unbankable list," Bette Davis wrote in *The Lonely Life*. It also opened up new opportunities for other older Hollywood actresses to take their turn in horror movies which followed similar themes - playing to the memories of their past, often using real-life stills from their movies, and serving up Grand Guignol thrills.

Director Curtis Harrington remembered an occasion when he and producing partner George Edwards had lunch with Bette Davis at the Universal commissary. "My producer asked Bette - he wasn't totally serious - if she would be interested in doing a sequel to *Baby Jane*, with Joan Crawford. "'Yes,' Bette retorted. 'And I'll tell you about the first scene. It'll be a scene of this one,' pointing at herself, 'putting flowers on that one's grave.'"

6. "Just what Baby Jane people will adore!"

Bette Davis and Joan Crawford's follow-up films to *What Ever Happened to Baby Jane?* both came out in the first months of 1964, just a few weeks apart, and both borrowed heavily from the hit film's themes. *Dead Ringer* was released in January, and *Straitjacket* in February, and with their mixed reviews, they failed to live up to the standard set by *Baby Jane*. "Joan Crawford with an axe. Tennis, anyone?" *The New York Times* wrote of *Strait-Jacket*, but compared to Davis's star turn in *Dead Ringer*, it was the greater success thanks to Joan's national in-person tour. "She criticized me, for raffling off dolls onstage for *Baby Jane*," said Davis, "and she's got a goddamn axe under her skirt?"

Just after *Baby Jane* wrapped, and with no new offers on the horizon, Bette placed a "situation wanted" advertisement in the employment section of *Variety*, which she later said was a joke. Yet she was all too aware that her age was detrimental to finding good roles in films. "I have always felt Hollywood very instrumental in America's being so wildly youth conscious," Bette wrote in her memoirs. "It does become contagious - this wishing to look years younger."

She had reluctantly agreed to a small role as a brothel madam in Robert Aldrich's next film *Four for Texas*, a Western action comedy starring Frank Sinatra and Dean Martin. She was about to be fitted for her bordello costumes when she received a script for a noir thriller to be directed by her old friend Paul Henreid, with whom who she had co-starred in *Now, Voyager* (1942) and *Deception* (1946).

There was one particular scene in *Now, Voyager* that would forever be memorialized for both actors; when Henreid lights two cigarettes and passes one to Davis. It was the romantic gesture of the early 1940s, and one that would be copied by many aspirant Romeos at that time. Austrian-born Henreid, who had been deemed "an official enemy of the Third Reich," and escaped Germany for the United States, was again blacklisted for his protests against the Senator McCarthy hearings, which cut short his acting career. Ignoring the edict, Alfred Hitchcock hired him in 1955 to direct episodes of his television series *Alfred Hitchcock Presents*, and from there Henreid developed his directorial career, while taking on small acting roles.

Bette Davis told the *Los Angeles Times* in 1977: "The greatest thing about Paul was his courage, to keep going and do all these things to support his family at a time when no one in this town would hire him."

"We stayed good friends over the years," Henreid told a reporter at the *Los Angeles Times* in 1963, during the making of *Dead Ringer*. "I was directing a lot of Hitchcock's works on television and Bette did a Hitchcock and I directed her. This is when our new relationship started. We decided we wanted to do a film together. We bought a book but unfortunately it was impossible to finance a film on her name – or mine, for that matter."

"It's a terribly cruel life and business, isn't it? The ups and downs," he added. "What I mean by cruel is this: The stability of employment has diminished with the various inventions that bring entertainment to the masses...As for me, let's be honest. I wasn't in demand but I think a girl like Bette Davis or Katharine Hepburn – there should be a way to give them continuous employment. They may have a string of bad luck but they remain excellent actors and they prove it time and time again."

Dead Ringer, which had initially been entitled *Dead Pigeon*, was based on a 1945 Mexican film, *La Otra*, starring Dolores Del Rio. The remake was set to star Lana Turner, but she was said to have dropped out over concerns about the challenges of playing a dual role. After being sent the script, which offered her not just one lead, but two, and with her name over the title, Bette Davis quit Aldrich's Rat Pack film and signed up to work with Henreid. Made on the Warner Brothers lot, it marked the first time in fourteen years that she had set foot in the studio that had produced her most fêted films. It was where she had once been known as the "Fifth Warner," before being so casually dismissed by Jack Warner when she was deemed no longer a box office guarantee. Now that she and her fellow "old broad," Joan Crawford, had proved their box office worth, Warner had put his faith back in her again.

It wasn't the first time Bette had been cast as twin sisters. In *A Stolen Life* (1946), she played twins who compete over the same man and she relished the performative challenge it brought in creating two complicated women who come up against one another. In an interview with *The New York Times* in August 1963, while filming *Dead Ringer* on location at Rosedale cemetery in Los Angeles, Bette told the reporter that playing "a dual role is great theater. Audiences love it. It's unrealistic to believe that one twin can assume the identity of the other and get away with it, as I do in *Dead Ringer*, but when audiences see it done well in a play or picture they readily accept it."

By playing the dual roles, Bette could throw herself into being both the good, chaste woman, and the wicked, sexually-aggressive one. She could slap herself in the face and kill herself, and could play both a glamorous, beautiful woman, as well as create a character study of the more downtrodden twin, who holds herself differently due to the circumstances in how their lives have panned out.

In *A Stolen Life*, the "good" sister takes on the persona of her "evil" or more sexually-voracious twin, in the name of her love for Glenn Ford, and twenty years later, in *Dead Ringer*, the motif is to revenge the wrongs of the past, and to punish the evil twin for the sins cast on her sister. The sisters in *Dead Ringer*, Margaret and Edie, have been estranged for eighteen years, until they meet up at the funeral of Margaret's husband Frank. He and Edie had originally been a couple, but Margaret forced the wealthy Frank into marrying her by pretending to be pregnant, which left Edie heartbroken. While Edie, owner of a downbeat cocktail bar, is worn out by life and struggling to make ends meet, her identical twin Margaret is a wealthy, but hard-hearted, socialite who lives in an opulent mansion. She has so many clothes that she tries to give them away to her sister as a supposed act of altruism, and she receives a back rub from a male masseuse as she talks on the phone – a common trope in the genre to show the indulgences of the older woman and their grotesque sexuality, with her middle-aged flesh on display.

The sisters are set up as *Baby Jane*-style rivals, both bitter and resentful about the past. Edie is downtrodden and taken advantage of by her sister, and Margaret is the more domineering and dismissive twin who is shown to have ruined Edie's life all those years before. ("You've never forgiven me in all these years…we're sisters," Margaret exclaims, in a line that could have come from *Baby Jane*.) Both films were set in Los Angeles, in which their mansions protect their older characters from the revealing sunshine, and it's when they are in the modern cityscape that their true selves are exposed. Edie's neon-lit bar, down a seedy alleyway, features black musicians playing jazz to a hip young audience, which offers a contrast to the middle-aged sisters, particularly when Margaret enters in her haunting widow's costume.

Unlike Jane and Blanche, who are single spinsters who have been starved of affection for many years, Edie has a considerate and doting police detective partner, played by Karl Malden, who remembers her birthday and genuinely cares for her. But Edie feels so bitter about the wrong done to her by her sister, that she can't see the positives in her life. When Margaret confesses she tricked Frank into marrying her with a fake pregnancy, Edie feels justified in claiming back everything her wicked sister has taken from her. Margaret visits her apartment under the pretense they'll discuss the past, and Edie follows through with her plan to steal her sister's identity and shoots her in the head. After stripping the dead body, and swapping over their clothes, Edie then takes on the persona of Margaret, leaving behind a suicide note which implies the body is that of Edie. She moves into Margaret's wealthy mansion, where she soon discovers that despite their doppelganger looks, the adoption of her sister's life isn't so straight-forward. Not only is her smoking habit (which Margaret had told her she had given up years ago because "it's bad for your skin"), and the dog's new affection for her, a possible giveaway, but she worries that the maid, played by Henreid's daughter Monika, and Margaret's playboy lover, a turn by Rat Packer Peter

Lawford, will uncover the truth – that she murdered Margaret, and has now switched places.

As well as harking back to *Baby Jane*, there were also similarities to the horror of *Psycho*. The credits, soundtracked with foreboding music by André Previn, feature a sinister graphic of a skull, and it opens onto a panorama of a city scene, like the opening shot of the city of Phoenix in *Psycho*. The final line of the film is also a classic *Psycho* reference – "I'm Margaret DeLorca. Edie would never hurt a fly."

Dead Ringer's advertising campaign was designed to appeal to horror fans, describing the film's "shock, upon shock, upon shock," with a trailer featuring a screaming, shrill Davis in her role as the two sisters. The poster featured Davis's face with a skull superimposed on it, and its slogan, "Just what 'Baby Jane' people will adore," made it clear that it was capitalizing on the phenomenon of her previous horror film, as well as referencing the final shot in *Psycho*, where Norman Bates' face merges into that of his mother's skull.

With the pressure of recreating the box-office success of Davis's last film, *Baby Jane*, Henreid believed that the scene where Davis effectively shoots her own likeness in the head, and then has to lift the dead weight of the body while she strips it of its clothes, would be the shock moment of the film. He wrote to Jack Warner that it "should bring the dollar bills into the box office like the rat in *Baby Jane* did."

In spite of Davis's difficult reputation, she worked well with Paul Henreid. "I understood her temperament and her peculiar gifts. I knew what she thought was effective for her," he recalled. "Bette had to go through extensive makeup. There was a lot of face lifting and that sort of thing, But she was a pro. She was always ready. Of all the actors I've ever worked with, Bette was the most professional. I'm talking about acting ability, being on time, cooperating, her attitude, the whole nine yards. Totally professional."

Bette was equally enamored with Henreid. For many years they frequently corresponded with one another, sharing memories and asking about one another's family. "Saw *Deception* the other night. It was a much better film than I remembered. You were so sexy in it! ☺," she wrote in a letter to Henreid in the mid-sixties.

Having often chosen roles where she underwent a degree of "uglification" to suit the character, Davis took full advantage of the glamor required for playing Margaret. Bette spent three hours in makeup, where her face was taped tightly to smooth out the wrinkles, and she was given subtle makeup contouring to make her look truly beautiful, particularly during the party scene at the DeLorca mansion. She had tried this technique before. In the late fifties she asked makeup artist Perc Westmore to give her the effect of a temporary face lift by taping her face. When she looked at herself in the mirror, she was "enchanted" by her reflection. "A little expressionless but smooth as a baby. I was mesmerized. I was lovely. I rushed home feeling sure Gary would look at me in amazement and wonder what miracle had happened. Quite the reverse. He looked up from the script he was reading and said, 'What in the hell happened to you - you look awful.'"

She was particularly kind to Peter Lawford on the set, knowing that he was going through a number of personal crises, having been linked to the recent death of Marilyn Monroe, and with his marriage to Pat Kennedy, John F. Kennedy's sister, crumbling. He was self-medicating with alcohol, and the heavy drinking affected his performance as he struggled to remember his lines. Bette pushed him as gently as possible to deliver the best performance he could muster. Playing Margaret's best friend Dede Marshall was the comedic actress Jean Hagen in her last film role. She was best known for her Oscar-nominated turn as the nightmare silent screen actress Lina Lamont in *Singin' in the Rain* (1952). Due to technological limitations, a stand-in for Bette Davis was required to play Margaret in her widow's shrouds for moments when she and Edie shared the same shot. Connie Cezan was best known for playing Gertie, the receptionist, on Perry Mason, between 1957 and 1966, and the blonde gold-digger in *The Three Stooges* films, but she also had a close resemblance to Bette Davis, with her large eyes and eyebrows. While there are moments when the audience can see her face through the veil, Davis was so impressed with her impersonation, that she and Cezan remained close friends afterwards.

While the shoot for *Dead Ringer* went smoothly, Paul Henreid worked hard in post-production to bring it up to his standard, often arguing with Jack Warner over the final cut and asking for a larger budget for publicity. Henreid wanted the film to be scored with ominous music throughout, and he successfully campaigned for André Previn to be hired to create the eerie soundtrack. He was particularly pleased with Bette's dual role, gushing that hers was "a performance that is quite extraordinarily, brilliant and fascinating. If your superb work does not earn you an Academy Award I will resign from the Academy. The film is exceptionally effective, rich looking and full of fine performances."

Davis didn't receive an Oscar nomination for her performance, and while reviews were positive, critics didn't take the film as seriously as perhaps she and Henreid had hoped. Eugene

Archer at *The New York Times* offered praise that the film was an "uncommonly silly little film, but it is great fun to watch," and that Davis evoked "sheer cinematic personality on the rampage, in a performance that, while hardly discreet, is certainly arresting. Deadly as her films may be, Bette Davis, the star, is very much alive."

The reviewer for *Time* on February 7, 1964, was unkind in his description of Davis. "Exuberantly uncorseted, her torso looks like a gunnysack full of galoshes. Coarsely cosmeticked, her face looks like a U-2 photograph of Utah. And her acting, as always, isn't real acting; it's shameless showing-off. But just try to look away."

In the UK, the film was retitled *Dead Image*, and in its film review, *The London Times* in March 1964 praised Davis for her "superb" performance which was "sometimes acute, often extravagant to the verge of self-parody, always riveting. No one else gets much of a look in, and the film is a bit dull in the rare moments when Miss Davis is not on the screen. But no fan can afford on any account to miss it."

Davis, however, was thrilled with the film, and excitedly wrote back to Henreid in October 1963, from London, that she heard from top Warners executive Steve Trilling "a most glowing account of their reactions to our film – think is so great they want 'us' to do another right away – what about Stubborn Broad 2."

She may have been keen to do a follow-up with Henreid, but one thing she wasn't so keen on was to work with Joan Crawford again. The sense of rivalry was still in the air, and Crawford's almost simultaneous follow-up to *Baby Jane*, didn't quite offer the same challenges as *Dead Ringer* had provided for Davis.

7. "When I look in the mirror, it's hard for me to believe that twenty years have passed."

"I get very frightened of people rather than monsters. I think people are more fun to work with than monsters anyway."

William Castle.

Joan Crawford was willing to embrace the roles that were coming her way after *Baby Jane*, even if she knew that they were a little lacking in quality. "There were gossips who speculated on why I didn't retire gracefully after my long career," she said. "There were two reasons. The first was I genuinely loved working. The only problem was that there weren't so many parts, and I didn't have much choice at my age. Stars of my age weren't in constant demand. If it was a good part that suited my talents, I took it. I felt lucky to be asked, though I did feel I was being asked more often for my name value of the past than for my talent in the present."

She acted in an episode of the television crime drama *Route 66* entitled *Same Picture, Different Frame,* and for her appearance in the movie *The Caretakers* (1963) she was given less than ten minutes screen time as Lucretia Terry, authoritarian head nurse at a mental hospital. In their review *Variety* described how "Miss Crawford doesn't so much play her handful of scenes as she dresses for them, looking as if she were en route to a Pepsi board meeting."

She coordinated television appearances with her business trips around the world as a corporate executive for Pepsi-Cola, bringing the Crawford glamor to the opening of bottling plants. Despite keeping up with the latest styles, with her hair in a beehive, and dressed in Chanel suits and oversized sunglasses, she was annoyed at being introduced as "the legendary Joan Crawford." She wasn't a *legend*, which suggested *retired*; rather she was very much still working in the business.

Baby Jane had demonstrated how older actresses could still bring in the audiences with horror roles, and Crawford further embraced the genre when she teamed up with William Castle. He was the shock director known for his ever-inventive gimmicks at film screenings, and who was desperate for his own *Baby Jane*-style hit after watching the movie fifteen times. "I saw *Baby Jane* and I was amazed at the business it was doing, how good the film was, and at seeing two great superstars playing in this shocker. It was just an amazing phenomenon."

One of William Castle's earliest memories was of being taken to see a horror play, *The Monster*, with his father, which was so scary that he wet himself with fright. At the age of thirteen, in 1927, he took $1.10 from his sister's purse for a balcony seat to see the stage performance of Bela Lugosi as Dracula. He returned again and again, and rather than solely concentrating on what was happening on stage, he eyed the audience with fascination as they screamed in terror. One night he managed to bluff his way backstage where he found himself in Lugosi's dressing room, in front of the man himself. Lugosi invited Castle to watch the play from backstage the next night, and it was at that moment Castle realized that he had found his calling. "I knew then what I wanted to do with my life - I wanted to scare the pants off audiences."

When Castle turned twenty-five, he inherited $10,000 from his parents, who had both died when he was a child, and which gave him the freedom to pursue a career as a filmmaker with his vaudeville sensibilities. Castle's easy charm and gift of the gab led him to producing plays for Orson Welles' Stony Creek Theater in Connecticut in the summer of 1939, and into a contract with Columbia Pictures. His first film as director was the B-movie horror *The Whistler* (1944) starring Richard Dix, followed that same year by the thriller *When Strangers Marry*, starring Robert Mitchum and Kim Hunter. "The low-budget B picture in the 1940s, before the advent of television, was a training ground for talented young directors who were forced to use their imagination in lieu of money. Many famous producers and directors graduated from this school," he said.

After churning out B-movies at Columbia Pictures for the next ten years, it was the audience reaction to *Les Diaboliques* that sparked his fascination with horror movies. He bought the rights to Theo Durrant's novel *The Marble Forest*, about the desperate attempt by a man to locate his daughter, buried alive in a cemetery by an unknown madman. In a surprise *Les Diaboliques* style twist, the doctor himself is revealed to have been the culprit all along.

He renamed it *Macabre*, and on its release in 1958 Castle came up with a headline-grabbing concept to give every audience member an insurance certificate from Lloyd's of London, which guaranteed a $1000 payout if they died of fright. The film was a huge hit on its release, with lines of teenagers around the block of every theater, lured in with the giant insurance policy hanging over the theater marquee.

Distributors Allied Artists wanted another picture immediately, and he followed with a classic ghost story, *The House on Haunted Hill* (1959) about a millionaire, played by debonair Vincent Price, who invites six people to spend the night in a haunted house. To further excite young audiences, he came up with a stunt called "Emergo" which featured a skeleton on a wire hurtled over the heads of the audience.

For his next, film, *The Tingler* (1959) made at Columbia Pictures, Castle earned his reputation as "King of Gimmicks," when he installed buzzers under selected seats in every theater to administer a shock when The Tingler gets loose. He told an interviewer in 1960: "I've modeled my career on (P.T.) Barnum. Exploitation's the big thing in the picture business today. Stars and contents don't mean much at the box office any more…Gimmicks, surprise, shock - that's what draws the crowds."

When he witnessed how successful *Psycho* was for Hitchcock, Castle created his own version, *Homicidal* (1961), where the killer has also been masquerading as his own wife, and in which he cast an actress, Joan Marshall, in the lead role. To create further gender ambiguity, he changed Marshall's name to the neutral name of Jean Arless. Wanting to top Alfred Hitchcock's killer publicity that no one was allowed into the theater after the film started, Castle decided that during the last two minutes of *Homicidal*, he would interrupt the show on screen, offering a refund to those who felt too frightened to see the rest of the film. For those who chose a refund, they would then have to sit in "Cowards corner."

After meeting Castle at a Hollywood party, Crawford read the script for *Strait-Jacket* with interest and Robert Bloch, the writer of *Psycho*, was hired to work on the screenplay. Crawford invited Castle, Robert Bloch and Columbia's Leo Jaffe to her New York apartment for lunch, where she greeted them at the door in her apron. Over quiche Lorraine and Pepsi, she told them she liked the script, but that it would have to be completely rewritten for her. She insisted that they make the character younger; in her forties rather than in her fifties. She also requested a percentage of the profits, along with a salary of $50,000, which gave her an incentive to throw herself into a publicity blitz for the film. Castle agreed to her terms, and she signed on.

While she took immense interest in all aspects of shaping the character and the production, and despite Castle's wooing of her, the script hadn't in fact been tailor-made for Crawford. Joan Blondell had been offered the role first, and Crawford was lambasted by both gossip queen Louella Parsons and Bette Davis for taking it from her. "*Strait-jacket* was supposed to star Joan Blondell," said Bette, "until Crawford stepped in and stole the role."

"Joan Blondell was set for the lead and had been fitted for her costumes," Parsons confirmed. "Then out of the blue, producer William Castle signs the other Joan. And then he proceeds to turn his picture upside down to please her. Even the crew has been revamped, with a new cameraman, makeup man, hairdresser, costumer – even a switch in the publicity man. No one involved is talking."

As teenage audiences in 1978 watched *Grease* in the cinema, they were unlikely to have realized there was an extra layer to the fifties nostalgia. Playing kindly waitress Vi, in what would be one of her final roles before her death, was Joan Blondell, the perky, wise-cracking blonde of Warner Brothers musicals like *42nd Street* (1933) and *Gold Diggers of 1933*. As one of the most popular musical comedy stars of the thirties, she had a warm effervescence and accessible, blowsy sexuality.

Born in 1906 in New York to a vaudeville family, Blondell was signed up to Warner Brothers in 1931, just before Bette Davis arrived at the studio. She worked tirelessly throughout the thirties by acting in over fifty films, helping to lift the spirits of audiences during the Great Depression, and forming a hugely popular pairing with James Cagney in films like *The Public Enemy* and *Blonde Crazy*, both in 1931. In real life she married Dick Powell in 1936, her co-star in a number of Busby Berkeley musicals, and after their divorce in 1944, she entered into a short-lived marriage to Mike Todd, which was marked by his physical and emotional abuse.

Despite being one of the highest-paid and most popular actresses of the Depression years, Blondell found that once she'd reached her late thirties, she suffered the typical fate of actresses. For the first time in fourteen years, she was billed below the title in *Adventure* (1945) starring Clark Gable, and the hot new star Greer Garson, who was in fact two years older than Blondell, but possessed a British self-possession and prestige from having won the Best Actress Oscar for the wartime morale-booster *Mrs. Miniver*. Blondell received rave reviews as Aunt Sissy in Elia Kazan's *A Tree Grows in Brooklyn* (1945), but she was disappointed that some of her scenes were cut and she was overlooked for an Oscar nomination. Instead, Warner Brothers continued to give her uninspiring roles, such as *Don Juan Quilligan* (1945) and *The Corpse Came COD* (1947).

One great role that came her way was in the film noir *Nightmare Alley* (1947) playing a con-artist, Zeena, where she used her older looks and street-wise image to full advantage. While the film failed to set alight the box office, *Hollywood Reporter* described her as a "dramatic actress of considerable power."

By 1950, she was desperate to find work. With a serious lack of offers for films, she was concerned enough about her finances that she moved into a Malibu trailer. But her fortunes changed when she was sent a script for the drama *The Blue Veil* (1951). Initially she was offended by the word "faded" to describe her character, an older musical actress, Annie. "When I saw the word it turned me off," she said. "But I could see the 'faded' just around the corner. I knew my cute little glamour girl days were over. I quickly went into character roles and beat them to the punch."

The Blue Veil earned Blondell an Oscar nomination for Best Supporting Actress, and it encouraged her to embrace the older roles, rather than clinging onto the affirmation of her youth. "The only tight thing I ever did was when I looked at myself in the mirror in 1951 and the rosebud lip weren't quite as upturned and there was that line between the eyes," she said. "I told my agent to get me anything that said 'aged.' I'm not going to have anything lifted so, why not, I might as well play the fallen-faced dames."

Despite this new strategy, she wasn't offered another film role for five years, and instead moved to New York where she could focus on stage work. In *Crazy October*, she played a middle-aged waitress in a seedy roadhouse, and found her co-star Tallulah Bankhead difficult with her drink binges and arguments with the director.

By the sixties, there was a growing appreciation of the stars of the Golden Age. While Blondell was of the same era as Crawford and Davis, she did not share the name recognition until arthouse cinemas began showing reruns of her old films like *Gold Diggers of 1933*. Beat writer Seymour Krim described Blondell as "the last of the great troupers" and having "slung that marvelous ass and those fantastic breasts around long enough on celluloid to enter every straight American male's mental nightlife."

With this new interest came opportunities for guest appearances on television. She moved back to Los Angeles to focus on small-screen work, and was cast in an episode of *The Untouchables* in 1961, *The Virginian* and *Wagon Train* in 1963, and as Aunt Win in three episodes of the TV show *The Real McCoys* in 1963.

On Hedda Hopper's radio show Joan revealed she was in talks with CBS for a series about a former actress who runs a Hollywood Boulevard restaurant, but ultimately it didn't progress further. While she was getting by with television roles, there was one film offer she was particularly excited about. She had been in discussions with William Castle about *Strait-Jacket*, a film he thought could be as successful as *Baby Jane* and help to revive her career. "It's a fantastic acting role," said Blondell at the time. "So far we have had only a handshake on the deal. But I would like to do it."

Blondell had been fitted for her costumes and was preparing to start shooting, when it was said that William Castle cast Joan Crawford instead. Bette Davis was angry on Blondell's behalf, having known and liked her since the twenties, when they studied acting together in New York. "It stinks," she proclaimed. "There is an unwritten law in this town. Once an actor is signed for a part, it's his until they die or drop out voluntarily. Miss Crawford knows this and should be ashamed of herself."

Blondell remembered it differently, insisting that she dropped out after slashing her leg when stepping through a glass partition at her home. "Nothing was said in the newspapers, because of the insurance, but Joan Crawford did not steal the role. Someone had to do it."

It may well have proved fortuitous to her, because she made what was likely to have been a more impactful comeback in

The Cincinnati Kid (1965) as shrewd poker player Lady Fingers, earning her a Best Supporting Actress Award from the National Board of Review, and a Golden Globe nomination. Because of her arthritis, she was concerned about how she could play and deal poker, so instead the filmmakers found a hand double for her, and she threw her all into the performance. "When she entered and had a few lines here or there, there was this great energy, this strong presence on camera," said director Norman Jewison. "We had lots of fun together. She was worried about the part."

Crawford's character in *Strait-Jacket*, axe-wielding killer Lucy Harbin, was partly inspired by Lizzie Borden and her notorious murders. Several years after being locked up in an asylum for the murder of her cheating husband and his lover, Lucy is released and sent to live with her grown-up daughter. But when murders start happening once more, suspicion falls on Lucy, who wonders if she can trust her own mind.

While *Baby Jane* had touches of Grand Guignol, *Strait-Jacket* was pure William Castle in its camp shocks and thrills. Always with a twinkle in his eye, Castle had a good-natured enjoyment in bringing gore to the screen, and one of his favorite props was his not-entirely-realistic model of a decapitated head, which would be put to good use in *Strait-Jacket*. "We used the same old dead head in every movie," he said. "We bought it for $12.50. That was the head that was used in *Psycho*. They rented it from us for a hundred dollars a day."

Even though she may have thought a script was poor, Crawford would give everything to the production, ensuring perfection over all aspects of her performance and the film itself. As Castle wrote, "During the ensuing weeks of preparation, I found her demands excessive. Crawford was a perfectionist and usually is right, and I was starting to worry about directing her."

He was particularly concerned about her demands to hold rehearsals first, as he preferred to go straight into filming. But he yielded to her requests and they began rehearsing on an empty stage. Anne Helm, initially cast as Lucy's daughter Carol, recollected that Crawford had invited her for a meeting at her Los Angeles apartment, where she was warm and welcoming, and insisted she call her Joan, rather than Miss Crawford. At the rehearsals, when Helm addressed her as Joan, she was immediately reprimanded by the star for not calling her Miss Crawford. The younger actress also made the fatal error of arriving with a Diet Coke, and as Helm recalled, Crawford "took a personal affront to that. She didn't like it, she made a point of it and she said that she would have an entire case of Diet Pepsis for me."

As they acted together in rehearsals, Helm became more nervous as she found Crawford losing patience with her and chiding her for missing a beat in the script. "It was obvious that she did not like me," said Helm. "She was just very cold toward me. There was no warmth." When she made the decision to speak with Crawford and ask if there were any reasons for tension in the air, Joan denied there was an issue. Later that day Crawford summoned Castle to her dressing room, and told him to fire Helm and find another actress. Not willing to argue with Crawford, he suggested Diane Baker, and Crawford, having acted with her in *The Best of Everything* (1959), agreed.

As the episode demonstrated, Crawford was very much in control of the production, considering herself on an equal footing with Castle. She requested a chilled temperature on set to keep her skin firm, she hired her own makeup artist and hairdresser, and her dressing room was to always be stocked with brandy, 100 proof vodka and beluga caviar. She also dominated all of her scenes in the film, dialing up the emotions for every passionate, violent, camp moment as she believed an over-the-top performance could guarantee a hit film.

"She was the boss in every way on that picture," Diane Baker recalled. "She saw to it that the set was kept very cold, for the sake of her makeup, and she placed bottles and cans of Pepsi-Cola everywhere she could in the movie's scenes."

Crawford may have been almost sixty, but she was putting in a performance of a woman twenty years younger, reenacting those moments from the films of her golden-era. Just as her real film clips had featured in *Baby Jane,* the bronze bust of Joan that features in the film as the work of Lucy's daughter was a real film artifact of Joan's. It was created by Yucca Salamunich for *A Woman's Face* in 1941, further highlighting the new trend for the cross-pollination of real Hollywood lore with 1960s modern.

The film begins with a piercing scream, the news that Crawford's character Lucy Harbin was declared insane, and a flashback scene that opens with the pulsating sound of jazz on the juke-box. It reveals the situation leading up to Lucy murdering her cheating husband and his lover, by lobbing off their heads with an axe, and leaving two very fake decapitated heads on the pillow. We first see Joan, making an entrance to sexy music, looking much like her version of Sadie Thompson in *Rain* (1932), all hooped earrings and rattling bangles, with heavy eye-makeup, a pageboy hairstyle, and curves accentuated in a skin-tight dress. In the voice-over, Lucy is described as "very much a woman, and very much aware of the fact."

Twenty years later, after being released from the asylum, Lucy must live on her family's chicken farm with her now grown-up daughter Carol, who witnessed the murder as a three-year-old.

She may be drab and afraid coming out into the world again, but slowly her confidence grows as Carol encourages her to dress just as she did before the murders, with a flower-print dress, the page-boy wig and the chiming bangles. She is described as a woman who is trying to recapture her past, and as she tells her doctor, "When I look in the mirror, it's hard for me to believe that twenty years have passed."

In a particularly camp Joan Crawford moment, she knocks back several drinks before flirting with Carol's boyfriend, looking at him as if she wishes to devour him and even placing her finger in his mouth. Diane Baker later said: "What word could I use in lieu of camp? The way she seduced her daughter's boyfriend who was half her age is wonderful. Classic."

Lucy is haunted by memories of the past, and is treated like an invalid by her family. After axe murders begin happening again on the farm, she starts to believe that she might be responsible. In the final scenes, it's discovered the real killer is Carol, who is dressed exactly as Lucy and is wearing a creepy plastic mask over her face. One of the "shock" moments is Joan Crawford wrestling with a younger image of herself, as Lucy tries to take the axe from Carol, just as Bette Davis fights the more glamorous image of herself in *Dead Ringer*. The lessons learned by the film is that having an easy, flirtatious mother has repercussions on the stability of Carol. As we see in many horror movies, the sins of the mother pass to the daughter, and just like Norman Bates, Carol takes on the persona of her mother to commit her deadly crimes.

The demands of an original Hollywood diva were fascinating to the public in 1964. As well as plugging "a very bad movie about an axe-murderess called *Strait-Jacket*," an article in *Life* detailing her publicity tour for *Strait-Jacket* described how Crawford carried with her 28 pieces of luggage, which contained "picnic hampers, a supply of liquor, two knitting bags and an axe with a three-foot haft, which all of the photographers en route found irresistible as a prop."

The publicity tour was a well-oiled machine, with Crawford put up in hotels across the United States, and rushed briskly to each interview with newspaper and television reporters, checking her lipstick and eyelashes on the way, answering questions sweetly, and informing them, as a spokesperson for Pepsi, that "it's wonderful at eight in the morning. I drink it for breakfast." A room was booked in every hotel for her wardrobe, and was set out with hat boxes, racks of gowns and day dresses and furs, and with her maid, Mamacita, stationed at the ironing board, to allow for Joan to change ten times a day. Sometimes there were mishaps, such as a giant Coca-Cola sign visible from her Philadelphia hotel room, or an east coast blizzard grounding her plane to Boston, which forced her to take a train. When the lights and heat went out in her train carriage, according to the report in *Life,* she was undaunted, as she knew she had the right equipment in her luggage to get through it.

"From the hampers she produced an elegant picnic of roast chicken, hard-boiled eggs, salad (with her own home-made dressing), pickles and 100-proof vodka. Afterward, snuggled in her minks, Joan Crawford – still unmistakably the movie queen – explained the seemingly miraculous process by which the picnic had materialized. 'It's all in the organization,' she said. 'If you have an organized mind you can do anything.'"

While the critics enjoyed the full Crawford publicity treatment, the film was considered almost laughable. Bette Davis's *Dead Ringer* had noir-esque style and substance, but Crawford's follow-up left them squirming. David Toor, film critic at Oregon's Eugene *Register-Guard* wondered why Crawford "doesn't spend more of her time selling Pepsi Cola, instead of doing such other things." He added that "the boys in Hollywood, anxious to get some of the TV audience back into the film houses, have taken the sturdy (and often entertaining) mystery-thriller type movie and larded it with gore, probably on the assumption that the biggest popular attraction (after plain filth) is blood and dismembering."

In lieu of a quality film, Crawford threw everything into the publicity tour, and this dedication paid off. The film may have been ridiculed by critics, but audiences lapped it up and it was a hit. For William Castle, it was everything he had hoped for, and instead of using his inventive stunts to thrill the audience, Joan Crawford proved to be all the attraction he needed.

"*Strait-Jacket* had been a dazzling success at the box office, and a star name over the marquee had completely spoiled me," Castle wrote in his memoirs. "I was not yet in the big time, but damn well knew that I wanted to be. I longed to play someday at Radio City Music Hall. Critics around the country had grudgingly admitted that I could make a picture without a gimmick, and while the reviews on *Strait-Jacket* were mostly favorable, they considered it another horror exploitation picture."

He fantasized that one day he might be the recipient of an Academy Award, and despite the schlockiness of his horror films, this ambition would turn out to be not too far away.

"Many of the films are being taken very seriously today at the universities where they study them," William Castle reflected in the mid-seventies. "I never expected that they would put under the microscope pictures that I made in the fifties and sixties and look for hidden meanings. Nevertheless, that's what is happening. One of the questions I had from one of the students who called me from one of the universities was: 'When you were doing *Strait-Jacket* with Joan Crawford, and she stepped off the train and the smoke enveloped her and just completely fogged her out, was the feeling that you were trying to get that she was going back to the fetus position in her mother's womb? Is that true?' You know, you didn't want to say that actually it was merely that you were trying to make time and the smoke didn't work."

After his success working with Crawford, William Castle had his eye on another veteran star to cast in his next film, which would once again be penned by Robert Bloch. *The Night Walker* is a psychological chiller about a woman trapped in her vivid dreams, and when Castle sent the script to Barbara Stanwyck, she was immediately intrigued. Stanwyck, at one time the highest-paid woman in the United States, was determined to continue working in both film and television, despite the offers having dried up since the fifties. "I'm not giving up. I'm ready to work anytime and I'll take any part that comes along. I don't care about the money or the size of the role. All I care about is working," she said.

Born Ruby Stevens in Brooklyn in 1907, Stanwyck created an incredibly varied range of work over the decades since her film debut in *Broadway Nights* in 1927. Having worked as a freelance actress, rather than being committed to one studio, she had certain freedoms in comparison to other contracted actresses in being able to play the complicated but gutsy women of her films. As Frank Capra once said, "Stanwyck doesn't act a scene.

She lives it," and she brought conviction and earthiness to every performance, where she felt more accessible and real than many of her contemporaries.

She earned her first Academy Award nomination as the ambitious, sacrificing mother in *Stella Dallas* (1937) who is vulgar and flawed. She played a charming con-woman in *The Lady Eve* (1941), a striptease artist in *The Lady of Burlesque* (1943), and the ultimate villainous femme fatale in *Double Indemnity* (1944). At a 1981 tribute to Stanwyck at the Film Society of Lincoln Center in New York City, Walter Matthau commented: "She played five gun molls, two burlesque queens, half a dozen adulteresses and twice as many murderers. When she was good, she was very, very good. When she was bad, she was terrific."

Like Joan Crawford, Stanwyck had grown up in poverty, having been punted between foster homes after her mother died and her father left, and she began her career as a dancer in the twenties before making it as a Hollywood star in the 1930s, first attracting attention as a social-climbing hustler in *Baby Face* (1933).

She later demonstrated longevity in the business by adapting her career to changing trends. Stanwyck's Oscar-nominated role in the film noir *Sorry, Wrong Number* (1948) could be considered an early "Hag Horror." In her powerful performance, she played the haughty invalid wife of Burt Lancaster, who overhears a murder plot against her. Trapped in her bedroom, much like Blanche in *Baby Jane*, she is terrorized by the fear that someone is coming to kill her while she desperately tries to get help from the telephone company, the police, and her husband.

Despite the career highs in the 1940s, by the mid-fifties she was ready to admit that her film career was likely over. "I couldn't stay up there forever. It's a man's world and it's getting worse," she said. "They aren't writing beautiful adult stories any more. Oh, I know stars who say they can't find anything they want to do in films, but I wouldn't be like that. I just haven't had any offers, period!"

After filling in for Loretta Young on her weekly television show in the 1950s, Stanwyck had her eye on doing her own show. Television was a hugely popular medium for aging Hollywood stars in the fifties, offering them a chance at a career revival, first sparked by Gloria Swanson's 1948 lifestyle show. NBC's *The Barbara Stanwyck Show* aired in September 1960, and which earned her an Emmy for Outstanding Performance by an Actress. Yet despite her win, the show was canceled by NBC shortly after, due to poor ratings and lukewarm reviews.

In 1961 she signed up for the film *Walk on the Wild Side*, as the madam of a brothel who becomes possessive of the new girl, played by model Capucine. She also relished a co-starring role in an Elvis Presley teeny-bopper film, *Roustabout* (1964), playing the owner of a struggling carnival who hires Elvis to shake it up. "I want to be exposed to the younger generation who have probably never heard of me," she said of the reasons she took the role. "I had worked with producer Hal Wallis many times so when he called me about a part in an Elvis Presley picture I was naturally curious about the script, I liked it."

During her meeting with William Castle to discuss *The Night Walker*, the director suggested that her ex-husband, Robert Taylor, act opposite her, which would give him not one classic Hollywood star, but two. "I think it's a wonderful idea, but you'd better ask Mr. Taylor how he feels about it. And Mrs. Taylor," she replied.

Robert Taylor was furious when his agent accepted the role on his behalf, as he wasn't keen to work with his ex-wife again.

Since separating in 1951 they'd gone through an acrimonious divorce, and he was bitter that he was still paying her spousal support. "I might have gotten out of it, but then Castle offered me a percentage of the profits, and I couldn't turn my back on that," he said. "Anyway, Barbara and I don't have many scenes together."

When Castle announced the pairing of the two exes to the press, it became too late for Taylor to back out. The *Los Angeles Times* reported in April 1964 that "Barbara Stanwyck and Robert Taylor aren't going to let an unsuccessful marriage spoil a good working relationship. The famous film couple, divorced in 1951 after an 11-year hitch, have signed to play opposite each other in a suspense shocker, *The Night Walker*."

Castle said he was apprehensive about approaching Stanwyck and Taylor for the roles, but they were both receptive and they "liked the script." Taylor diplomatically told reporters: "Any actor who would turn down a chance to play opposite Barbara Stanwyck, under any circumstances, would have to be out of his head. She's certainly one of the pros in the picture business."

William Castle held a party in the Universal cafe to celebrate the start of filming in May 1964, attended by the Hollywood crowd, including Stanwyck and Taylor, who sat on tables at opposite sides of the room, Taylor beside his young wife, Ursula Thiess. *Associated Press* reporter Bob Thomas commented, "Where but in Hollywood would they give a party for a divorced couple?"

The *Journal-American* described both Stanwyck and Taylor as "coming out of semi-retirement," which was news to them. Rather than having opted to be less prevalent on screen, it was more the case that the roles just weren't coming in as they had when they were younger.

Using Robert Bloch's reputation as the author of *Psycho*, *The Night Walker* borrowed from a number of Hitchcock films, from the dream sequences of *Spellbound* to the creepy gothic house of *Psycho*. It told the story of an older woman, Irene Trent, who is in an unhappy marriage to a blind millionaire inventor, Howard Trent, and who is haunted by her erotic dreams of a fantasy lover. Howard makes her life a misery due to his jealousy of her dreams, and her attraction to the only visitor to the house, her husband's attorney, Barry Morland, played by Robert Taylor. When Howard is killed in an explosion, Irene inherits his fortune, but she is haunted by nightmares that he'll come back and take his revenge on her. She tries to convince the attorney her dreams are real, and as they become more vivid, she begins to question her own sanity, or is she a victim of gaslighting?

Irene is atypical as an older female character, as she is shown to still have sexual desires outside of her marriage, while also remaining dignified throughout. This was testament to fifty-six-year- old Stanwyck's own strong persona, bringing a sense of noble sophistication to the character of Irene. She appeared slender and glamorous, but embraced her age by keeping her hair streaked with gray. Stanwyck believed that "all the fretting, fussing, stewing, lying and dying, all the tensions created by wanting to be forever young, age one faster. They look what they are - battle-scarred veterans of their lost war against time. I decided not to enlist in that war three years before I turned forty."

Despite the novelty of the formerly married couple starring together, it didn't prove to be a big enough pull for young audiences who were not old enough to have any sense of nostalgia for their real-life love affair, and the box office for *The Night Walker* struggled as it played to almost empty cinemas.

The *Los Angeles Times* described Stanwyck as "looking trim and chic after some seasons off the screen" and the film as one of "the better horror efforts now screening locally. Robert Bloch's screenplay provides more punch and plausibility than regularly offered in these amusements." In his review, Bosley Crowther, of *The New York Times* wrote: "The whole thing would not be worth reporting if it didn't have Barbara Stanwyck and Robert Taylor. Miss Stanwyck, silver-haired and seasoned, does lend an air of dignity to the otherwise unbelievable woman in this totally unbelievable tale. And Mr. Taylor, lean and wrinkled, does at first make the lawyer seem something more than the spurious character he finally turns out to be."

The Night Walker marked the end of Stanwyck's film career, but she continued on television with parts on *The Untouchables* and in the popular western series *Rawhide* and *Wagon Train* - a genre that she loved and wished to star in. "In all the westerns these days...the women are always left behind with the kids and the cows while the men do the fighting. Nuts to the kids and the cows!" said Barbara. "There were women who went out and fought, too. That's what I want to do. People say it's not feminine. It isn't! Sure, those women wore guns and breeches. But don't kid yourself. They were all females!"

Finally she won her own Western moment when ABC-TV offered her the role of Victoria Barkley in *The Big Valley* (1965 – 1969), a tough but feminine widow who runs a cattle ranch with her sons. It was a grueling schedule, with each episode filmed in six days, and Barbara was up at 4am, working until 9pm, despite suffering from emphysema and a bad back. Sixty-year-old Barbara had little patience for the younger actors who she said "were always running to their makeup tables. That's the most important part of their performance - their hairdos! After that, their makeup and their wardrobe and lastly their performance."

While *Big Valley* never reached the popularity of *Bonanza* or *Gunsmoke*, Barbara won an Emmy for her performance, but it suffered the same fate *as The Barbara Stanwyck Show*, and was canceled in 1969. After Robert Taylor's death in June 1969, stories of the Stanwyck and Taylor romance appealed to a curious younger generation who only knew Barbara from *The Big Valley* and Taylor from his show, *Death Valley Days*. There were half-truthful stories printed of how Barbara, now painted as the crazy widow, was so devastated at his death that she wore the nightgown from her honeymoon, watched his films over and over and hung his photos in her house. By 1970 Barbara was also mourning the end of the Golden Age of Hollywood. She said to friends, "I want to forget the past but the future in Hollywood looks bleak."

After *Night Walker*, Castle's next film, *The Spirit is Willing*, starring Sid Caesar, also failed to light up box offices, and he blamed these failures on the power of television, which was capturing a greater audience than cinemas, and forcing a decline in audience numbers at theaters.

"My small empire was beginning to collapse, and by 1967 I was ready to throw in the towel. I had tried everything, from insurance policies, flying skeletons, and buzzing the audience, to money-back guarantees, bloody cardboard axes, big stars, and big telephones...Desperately I started to search for the miracle that would save my career. I had to find something – anything - or I'd be out of business."

8. "The sounds of an uncaring world..."

Both *Baby Jane* and *Strait-Jacket* had proved the box-office appeal of horror films that cast older, recognizable actresses in perilous, degrading situations, and Luther Davis's *Lady in a Cage*, which he wrote and produced, sought to do the same. With its simple concept and literal title, *Lady in a Cage* was way ahead of films like *Phone Booth* (2002) and *Snakes on a Plane* (2006), by telling the story in one simple soundbite.

A writer for stage and screen, Luther Davis won a Tony Award in 1954 for his musical *Kismet*, and screenplay credits included *The Hucksters* (1947) starring Clark Gable and Ava Gardner. Davis had been planning a play about a power failure in the suburban Midwest, leading a group of residents to fight for survival. Inspired by the New York blackout of August 1959, he turned his attention to a situation that would convey the claustrophobia of a New York City elevator. While researching, Davis realized his story was hindered because New York law stated that all private elevators were to be equipped with a telephone, so instead he shifted the story to an unnamed city during a hot and sweaty summer, populated by marauding youths and desperate opportunists.

Davis's story came to the attention of Martin Rackin, head of production at Paramount Pictures, who saw its potential as "a picture somewhat in the *Baby Jane* category," particularly if there was a grande dame of cinema attached to it, and he agreed to distribute it.

The production was first announced in the *Los Angeles Times* in August 1962, with a report that the role of Mrs. Hilyard had been initially offered to Joan Crawford. The *London Times* on August 4, 1962, reported that the project was called *Woman in a Cage* and "in which Miss Crawford gets trapped alone, overnight, in a lift, from which, while unable to make herself heard, she can see all sorts of extraordinary things going on around her."

When Crawford took too long to decide whether to accept the part, Rosalind Russell was considered, but by the beginning of December 1962 it was announced that Olivia de Havilland, who was residing permanently in France, would step into the role.

Hedda Hopper reported in the *Los Angeles Times*: "When Livvy got a call from [Luther Davis], she was under the dryer at Elizabeth Arden's in Paris. Said she, 'I must read the script before I give you an answer.' They flew it over and within 24 hours she had read it and told them yes. This is the one Roz Russell turned down because she doesn't want to do another drama."

It was true that Olivia was suffering from a dearth of decent roles now that she was in her fifth decade. Famed for her role as Melanie in *Gone with the Wind* (1939) and for her pairing with Errol Flynn in a number of swashbuckling movies including *Captain Blood* (1935) and *The Adventures of Robin Hood* (1938), Olivia was a two-time Best Actress Academy Award winner for *To Each His Own* (1946) and *The Heiress* (1949). As one of the most in-demand actors in the forties, she brought a sense of lady-like dignity to the screen, and she challenged herself with more complex characters, such as the good and bad twins in *The Dark Mirror* (1946) and the mentally-wrought schizophrenic in *The Snake Pit* (1948).

Following her marriage to screenwriter Marcus Goodrich in 1946 and the subsequent birth of her son Benjamin in 1949, she turned down film roles whilst she devoted time to motherhood. In early 1953, Olivia made an appearance at the Cannes Film Festival, where she met and fell in love with the French publisher of Paris Match, Pierre Galante, and following their marriage, she made a permanent move to Paris. She recounted her time in France in her humorous 1962 memoir *Every Frenchman Has One*, where she looked back at her Hollywood career. "I have happy memories of Hollywood, where I grew up...But life in Paris, the 'capital' of Europe, is so much more rich and colorful than the Hollywood way of life. There's nothing like the French joie-de-vivre."

Her last leading role in a film had been in *Libel* (1959) in which her biographer Charles Higham noted that she "unfortunately adopted a style that was to become the mark of her later career: she became excessively haughty and dignified, reading her lines with a pause between her words, her vowels excessively orotund." At the beginning of 1962, she performed on Broadway for the third time, appearing in *A Gift of Time*, with Henry Fonda, playing a wife whose husband is dying of cancer. Having been separated from her husband and children, who were still in Paris, she returned to France to begin divorce proceedings. It was under the strain of a disintegrating marriage that she accepted the offer to film *Lady in a Cage*, her first to be made in Hollywood in six years. The deal offered her 10 percent of the gross receipts, along with a reduced salary of $20,000.

Olivia had a particular ritual whenever she traveled from Paris to Los Angeles. She always flew on Air France on a Friday, and always stayed at room 275 at the Beverly Hills Hotel, where there was a lemon tree outside the window, and a small terrace where she could eat her lunch. When she flew into LAX airport at the end of January 1963, Luther Davis greeted her with the novelty of a cage full of flowers to welcome her to the production, and waiting at the Beverly Hills Hotel to take her to dinner was her friend Bette Davis. Excitement was building around Davis's potential Oscar win for *Baby Jane,* and Olivia told Hedda Hopper: "Bette's got to be the first actress to win three Oscars. She's the greatest and should have the award for *Baby Jane.* The industry owes her this."

What appealed to Olivia de Havilland when she was sent the script was the exploration of being incapacitated while being surrounded by people who are too detached and oblivious to offer help. Mrs. Hilyard is a wealthy widow with a broken hip, who becomes trapped in the private elevator of her townhouse following an electrical fault and finds herself at the mercy of a couple of down-and-outs and a trio of marauding youths. The film played to the moral panic around wild, out-of-control "hipsters" and "beatniks" whose behavior is blamed on the welfare state, much like *The Wild One* (1953) and *The Desperate Hours* (1955) a decade before. The opening of the movie also took its cue from *Psycho,* as the camera pans over a cityscape and comes through the window of the house of Mrs. Hilyard. It was a method that had been picked up by directors inspired by the realism of Hitchcock, as if the story could be about anyone, anywhere; of how we're anonymous entities who are victims of modern life, consumed by the vast cityscape.

"The most horrible thing is the detachment of the bystander, isn't it? People who watch and do nothing," De Havilland said on her press tour for the film. "Luther Davis, our writer producer, told me he based the script on an incident here in New York during an electricity breakdown, when vandalism erupted within a matter of hours and two boys rescued a woman from an elevator by flashlight and proceeded to rape her. He thought we think of ourselves as so civilized, so technologically advanced, yet the minute there's a flaw in the system, we revert to the primitive. He's right, too."

Olivia's character, Mrs. Hilyard, is not mad and deluded, like other older women in the genre, although her failure to have a warm relationship with her son suggests that she is deficient in what is considered the most important role of a woman. In the opening scenes, we discover Mrs. Hilyard has had a falling out with her son, Malcolm, with hints that it's because she can't accept that he's gay.

"In essence, the part is a stunning, tour-de-force, with real dimension," said Olivia. "That's what appealed to me. You see this trapped woman, supposedly sensitive, educated and tasteful, finally exposed for what she is, a selfish mother who robbed her son of his young manhood. But I liked this: she has character. She recognizes the truth about herself."

Mrs. Hilyard has an authoritative glamor, and her sculpted hair and low-cut negligee makes her far-removed from the stereotypical grotesque woman of horror. Yet Olivia also allows herself to be degraded, becoming sweatier and grimier the longer she's trapped in the stifling lift. The group of hoodlums who terrorize her, particularly the leader, Randall, played by James Caan in his first role, treat her disdainfully because she's a representation of the older generation who fail to understand them.

Cast as the alcoholic prostitute, Sade, was Ann Sothern, the comedic actress best known for her television shows *Private Secretary* and *The Ann Sothern Show*, and as the star of the hugely popular *Maisie* series of films at MGM throughout the forties. As Hedda Hopper reported: "Luther Davis had a brainstorm and asked Ann Sothern to play a shady lady in his 'Lady in a Cage.'

Since she's been dying to get away from those sunny characters ('producers won't let me grow up – they forget I started as a dramatic actress'), I'll be darned if he didn't get her."

Born Harriette Lake on January 22, 1909, in Valley City, North Dakota, she was first discovered by Columbia Pictures when performing on Broadway. Signed to a Columbia contract in 1934, she was given a new identity by the studio, who renamed her Ann Sothern and dyed her hair platinum blond. She churned out eighteen films between 1934 and 1936, but frustrated at being relegated to B movies, she switched to MGM to further her career. Jean Harlow had been set to play a street-smart Brooklyn chorus girl in *Maisie,* but when she tragically died at the age of twenty-six, Sothern stepped in, and on the film's release in 1939, it would become a phenomenon. Follow-ups included *Congo Maisie* (1940), *Gold Rush Maisie* (1940), *Ringside Maisie* (1941), *Swing Shift Maisie* (1943) and *Undercover Maisie* (1947).

Feeling locked into this cycle of films, she begged Louis B. Mayer to give her other roles, but she recounted that he refused, because, in his words, "Your movies pay for our mistakes." She was able to show her singing talents in MGM musicals including *Lady Be Good* (1941) and *Panama Hattie* (1942), and was praised for her dramatic turn as a waitress who is pressed into joining the war effort as a nurse, in the woman-centered World War II drama *Cry Havoc* (1943).

After a long battle with hepatitis, which she contracted in 1949, MGM canceled Sothern's contract, despite the success she had yielded for them. In order to pay her debts and hospital bills, she reluctantly moved into television as Susie McNamara, secretary to a New York talent agent in *Private Secretary*, which ran from 1953 to 1957, and in which she struck a chord with the women who were entering into employment across America. Following contractual disputes with producers as she campaigned to earn a share of profits, she left the series with several million dollars from selling her rights, and returned to CBS with *The Ann Sothern Show* from 1958, where she played the assistant manager of a luxury New York hotel. While it had been an initial success, the show was canceled in 1961 following a drop in ratings.

Once she reached her fifties, Sothern found it increasingly difficult to keep her weight at the level she liked, partly as a result of the debilitating hepatitis, and following a car accident which had left her struggling to walk. With the cancellation of her self-titled show, she found herself unemployed, owing a million dollars in back-taxes, and even being sued by her mother for monthly support. During this tough time, she was forced to move out of her Bel Air mansion, and moved into a suite at New York's Plaza Hotel, taking what television work she could. She shot an unsuccessful NBC pilot, *Atta Boy, Mama*, directed by Ida Lupino, and guested on *The Andy Williams Show* in January 1963, where she danced the bossa nova. She was cast in *The Best Man* (1964), in a co-starring role opposite Henry Fonda, her first since Fritz Lang's *The Blue Gardenia* in 1953. She also took part in a summer stock tour of *God Bless Our Bank* in 1963, where she performed opposite Jeff Corey, an actor and director who had been blacklisted in the fifties. It was her friendship with Corey that led to her being offered a part in *Lady in a Cage*.

Corey was cast as the down-and-out drunk who first discovers Mrs. Hilyard's plight but decides to rob her rather than help her. When Maureen Stapleton, who had originally been cast as Sade, couldn't make it to Los Angeles in time for the start date of production, he suggested Ann.

As part of their research into their destitute characters, Sothern and Corey drove to Skid Row in downtown L.A to observe the look of the people there. Ann was shaped into the alcoholic prostitute, with dark shadows under her eyes, a dark auburn wig with a hair band to add a touch of girlishness, like the stunted adolescence of Jane Hudson, and cheap bangles and a straw handbag as a finishing touch. "When she took the part of a blowsy dame in *Lady in a Cage*, she was out to change her image, and from what I hear she sure succeeded," wrote Hedda Hopper. "Nobody on the set recognized her in a dark auburn wig and dress right out of Skid Row."

While she called motion pictures "her first love," Sothern wasn't impressed by her return to Hollywood. "The studios look so tacky. A coat of paint would help, you know," she told a reporter in 1963. "I was spoiled rotten during my twelve years at Metro. In those days money was something for the studios to spend lavishly. *Lady in a Cage* is on a tight budget."

Hedda Hopper also recounted that de Havilland "loves her part. Tells me she's approaching it from a psychological viewpoint, whatever that means. I know one thing. If Davis shoots the story the way it's written, he may not get it past Paramount's front gate."

Because of the gritty realism of the film, which culminates in a gruesome showdown on the street, Luther Davis was forced to make cuts to get past the censors, including a scene where James Caan chokes Ann's character to death. The scene was so realistic that James Caan was horrified when Ann blacked out for real. The film's nihilism and violence struggled to earn approval from certification boards around the world, and was so controversial in its violence that it was refused an initial cinema release in the

UK, as well as in Australia, where it wasn't available until the 1990s.

While Olivia received ten percent of the profits, the film was not a commercial success, and so she didn't reap the rewards she had hoped for. She was frustrated at the response from film censors around the world, and from critics who attacked the violence, as she had considered the film to be a critique, rather than a promotion of it.

In a stinging review in *The New York Times*, the film critic Bosley Crowther wrote that while "there will never be total agreement on the social responsibility of the screen...what is irresponsible about it - what is downright dangerous, indeed - is that it tends to become a sheer projection of sadism and violence for violence's sake."

Luther Davis addressed Crowther's review in a letter to the editor of *The New York Times*. "I would like to deny as forcefully, as quickly, and as publicly as possible his allegation that this film is socially hurtful or irresponsible. As a critic, he should consider what I, as the writer and producer, tried to do, which was to dramatize and make emotionally comprehensible one of those seemingly inexplicable outbreaks of violence which are the hallmark of our times."

Ann Sothern was singled out for praise for her performance, with the *Los Angeles Herald Examiner* declaring that she "will surprise all with her acting as the blowsy gal of the streets." She was nominated for a Golden Globe for Best Supporting Actress for her role, but because the film had been banned in some countries, not all members of the Foreign Press had been able to see it. Olivia and Ann had also been tipped for Oscar nominations, but ultimately they were overlooked, possibly as a result of the controversy.

Life's Richard Oulahan wrote in his film review in June 1964 that "the only member of the cast who is left with any solace is the prostitute, played by Ann Sothern…I also hope that she manages to avoid what seems to have become the standard fate of other cherished film queens of yesteryear. The charming ladies who once lit up the screens with their talents are now consigned to ugly roles in cheap bloodbaths and sensational horror films. What Ever Happened to Baby Jane, indeed? Whatever happened to Joan Crawford? (*Strait-jacket*, that's what). To Bette Davis? (*Dead Ringer*). The movies are big enough to provide these durable ladies with roles commensurate with their abilities and their years, without making them into monsters. I sincerely hope that Olivia de Havilland will in the future stay out of snakepits like *Lady in a Cage*."

Oulahan's review triggered a debate on the letters page of *Life* magazine. One reader, David I. Roose, from Atlanta, Georgia, defended the film. "For your critic to compare a fine, perhaps great, allegorical film like *Lady in a Cage* to old schnitzels like *What Ever Happened to Baby Jane?* is like comparing *Moby Dick* to *Flipper*…we're all going to die, as she nearly does in the picture, hearing the sounds of traffic, of airplanes passing over, of ice-cream venders – the sounds of an uncaring world."

In another letter, Gene D Phillips, from West Baden Springs, Indiana, lamented "that such great stars of yesteryear as Academy Award winners Olivia de Havilland, Bette Davis and Joan Crawford have recently been wasted in a succession of horror films filled with aimless sadism."

The random violence in *Lady in a Cage* was influential on films like *Targets* (1968), directed by Peter Bogdanovich, and based on the Charles Whitman killings at the University of

Texas. It starred Boris Karloff, the Frankenstein monster of Universal horror movies in the 1930s, as an out-of-touch actor who comes face-to-face with a shooter, Bobby Thompson, who has targeted his wife, his mother, the delivery boy, and members of the public from on top of a drive-in theater. He is only stopped when confronted by Karloff on the screen and as his character in real-life. There's no explanation given as to why Thompson goes on a murder spree, reflecting the sense of horror of random violence in the 1960s. Similarly in *Pretty Poison* (1968), it's not Anthony Perkins who turns out to be murderous, despite audience expectations from having watched *Psycho*, but rather, sweet, pretty Tuesday Weld, an all-American high school drum majorette. It was reflective of the sense of fear around young people at the time, of the feckless hippies who seemed so different from the generation that came before. In the film's conclusion, Perkins feels safer going back to the asylum rather than being in society.

Lady in a Cage was groundbreaking in capturing the apprehensive mood, that violence was at the heart of society, and it accentuated the chasm between young and old – reflective of the traditional stars, represented by Olivia de Havilland and Ann Sothern, battling with the up-and-coming stars like James Caan, who would come to represent New Hollywood.

Despite Luther Davis's intention, to make a film that commented on the degradation of society, his work was lumped in with the camp horrors starring older actresses that were gaining a reputation. *Time* magazine on June 19, 1964 wrote that the film added de Havilland "to the list of cinema actresses who would apparently rather be freaks than be forgotten ... a grande chance to go ape. Attagirl, Ollie.

9. "A frazzled, night-gowned wraith..."

"Oh, Charlotte, why have you stayed here like this all these years? Why have you thrown your life away?" Henry Farrell's *What Ever Happened to Cousin Charlotte*?

After the disappointment of his rat-pack Western *4 for Texas*, which Bette Davis had left in favor of *Dead Ringer*, Robert Aldrich hoped to recreate the *Baby Jane* magic by asking its author Henry Farrell to develop a new story, specifically for Joan Crawford and Bette Davis. With a creepy gothic mansion, a severed head and hand, a treacherous staircase, and flashbacks to the past, *Hush, Hush Sweet Charlotte* was an unofficial sequel to *What Ever Happened to Baby Jane?* that amped up the Grand Guignol horror. Rather than a black comedy on the fickle nature of Hollywood, or a comment on the grotesque realities of modern life, as with *Lady in a Cage*, it was more aligned with Gothic fiction and the axe-wielding horror of William Castle's *Strait-Jacket*.

Aldrich had a burning desire to create good stories, but after a number of disappointments, he was after a film that would be profitable. He commissioned Henry Farrell to work with him on another crowd-pleasing thriller, and he was inspired by the stories of the Lizzie Borden murders, as well as *Baby Jane* and by *Les Diaboliques*, to create a narrative of a demented older woman, Charlotte, who is stuck in the memories of her past, while being manipulated by her glamorous but wicked cousin Miriam.

Not only did it feature a lament for a lost life, an older woman who is stunted in her development, and a battle between two female relatives, Farrell also tentatively titled it *What Ever Hap-*

pened to Cousin Charlotte? to further reinforce it as a follow-up to *Baby Jane.* Once more Bette would play the haggard and lonely woman, fully embracing the grotesque styling and makeup, to immerse herself in character.

In Farrell's short story, he describes Charlotte Hollis as "Once strikingly pretty, there was still about her traces of the aura of a lively beauty that in the distant year of her coming-out made her one of the most celebrated debutantes in the country - and perhaps even the world." When her cousin Miriam ("a woman of 'achieved chic'"), arrives at the faded Hollis plantation, she now sees Charlotte as "a frazzled, night-gowned wraith" who is a victim of the passage of time. Charlotte is trapped in the past as she creaks around her gothic mansion, following the rumors that many years ago she beheaded her married lover with an axe.

"I really had a marvelous relation with Davis and she hadn't done anything worthwhile in between," said Robert Aldrich on his decision to follow up *Baby Jane* with another female-led horror. "I had made a terrible picture with Henry Farrell called *4 for Texas,* and he had this other book, not yet published, which he brought to me. I sent it to Davis and she liked it. I thought it would be a marvelous vehicle for her. It really didn't disturb me, it would be different enough from *Baby Jane* so I couldn't be characterized as only a horror-film director. *Charlotte* is a bigger kind of movie and the marketplace was very anxious for that kind of movie."

Because of the success of *Baby Jane,* 20th Century-Fox gave Aldrich a budget of $1.3 million for his much-anticipated follow-up, and as well as reuniting cast and crew, Aldrich also doubled up on the old Hollywood flavor by casting veterans Joseph Cotten, Agnes Moorehead and Mary Astor, in her last film role.

Audiences may have remembered Astor's regal villainess in *The Maltese Falcon*, but in *Sweet Charlotte* she seems a lifetime apart as a decrepit old lady, Jewel Mayhew, who's at the end of her life. A contract player at MGM, Astor had struggled with alcoholism throughout her career, and by the 1950s she sought treatment in sanatoriums, while taking on the television work that was available to her, including episodes of *Alfred Hitchcock Presents* and *Rawhide*. In a 1960 episode of *Boris Karloff's Thriller* anthology series, titled *Rose's Last Summer*, she played a character that was close to home; an aging film star and washed up drunk who would do anything to find the success she once had twenty years before. For Astor, *Hush, Hush Sweet Charlotte* was designed as her swan song to the movie industry; the last role she would take before retiring from acting.

While Aldrich, and the studio, was keen to reunite Bette Davis and Joan Crawford, the issue was persuading them to both work together again. They may have been civil to one another during the short production schedule for *Baby Jane*, but the debacle around the Academy Awards and Joan's rescinded invitation to the Cannes film festival had caused lasting damage to their relationship.

As Bette wrote in her autobiography, *This n That*: "I was offered another part in a Robert Aldrich movie - co-starring Joan Crawford. I told him I would not work with Joan again. The film was originally called *What Ever Happened to Cousin Charlotte?* - a title I very much opposed. I don't believe in repeating successful titles and this was clearly a copy of *What Ever Happened to Baby Jane?*"

While the studios insisted on Davis and Crawford as a package, Aldrich was also considering Ann Sheridan to play Miriam, if Crawford proved too difficult to persuade. Aldrich met with Joan to discuss the script, highlighting how Miriam was a glamorous character with the potential for some fabulous wardrobe opportunities, much more so than Blanche had been, and this naturally appealed to her vanities. She may well have appreciated Henry Farrell's description of Miriam as a woman who is "noticeably smart, compellingly turned out, commandingly beautiful—a kind of woman to be seen in all the smart restaurants, clubs and hotels in all the great cities of the world." She accepted the role, but this time insisted that her name come before Bette Davis's in the credits.

Davis believed Crawford was "wrong for the part" of cousin Miriam, but she agreed to sign on to *Charlotte*, with second billing after Crawford, if she received a salary of $200,000, more than double what she received for *Baby Jane*, and also insisted that the title be changed to *Hush, Hush, Sweet Charlotte*, after the film's theme song. Aldrich was reluctant to switch a title that he believed was part of a winning formula, but grudgingly, it was changed to follow Bette's stipulation.

As with *Baby Jane*, the film opens with a prologue set in 1927 that flashes back to the childhood of Charlotte and Miriam, showing conflict with Big Sam Hollis, the omni-present, but stifling, father who Charlotte adores. At a party at the Hollis plantation, Charlotte plans to elope with her married lover, John Mayhew, but Sam intercepts, and tells John that his wife Jewel has discovered the affair, and he must end his relationship with Charlotte. However, John is confronted by a mysterious assailant and axed to death in the summerhouse, with Charlotte discovering the body, and leading to suspicion falling on her that it was she who murdered him.

In the same way that *Baby Jane* used real-life film clips of Bette Davis and Joan Crawford, on the wall of the mansion is a painting of Charlotte in a white dress, which has a striking similarity to Bette Davis in *Jezebel* (1938). Even though the dance sequence is set in the 1920s, the styling of the guests is very much of the 1960s, perhaps as a way of appealing to the teenage drive-in audiences.

Thirty-seven years later, Miriam arrives at the plantation to persuade reclusive spinster Charlotte that she needs to pack up her belongings, as the house is set to be bulldozed to build a new interstate highway. She uses her city sophistication to torment her cousin Charlotte by staging haunting reminders of the violent death of John. Her plan, with the help of her former lover, Doctor Drew Bayliss (Joseph Cotten), is to drive the emotionally-vulnerable Charlotte further into madness so that Miriam can claim the inheritance from Big Sam.

Aldrich pushes the boundaries of points of view, at first leading us to believe that the mysterious goings-on, such as the French doors blowing open, and the appearance of a mysterious meat cleaver, are all a result of her psychosis as she imagines her house is haunted. It's later revealed, in a *Les Diaboliques* twist, to be an elaborate plot. By killing those who have been gaslighting her, Charlotte is finally able to depart the house in modern clothes, leaving behind her music box, as she eradicates the haunting memories of her past.

20th Century-Fox held a press conference to announce the reunion of director Aldrich with his two stars. "This isn't going to be Baby Jane strikes back. It's altogether a different picture," Aldrich said. Joan noted how she wouldn't be in a wheelchair in this film. "I will be very active and appear more attractive I might add. My character works in public relations in New York, which means I will get to wear some beautiful, expensive clothes."

Bette insisted she would be singing the theme song for the film, accompanied by a harpsichord. "It will be quite lovely," she said.

Costume designer Norma Koch, who won an Oscar for her work on *Baby Jane*, was again tasked with designing costumes for Bette and Joan. Just as Baby Jane Hudson's refusal to move on from her childhood is reflected in her blonde curled wig and girlish dresses, Charlotte still wears her hair in pigtails and dresses in white crinolines, as if she is trying to remain the little girl who her father loved. Yet because of her age, this look takes on a grotesque quality – the older woman trying to be young. In contrast, her cousin Miriam is a modern woman of the sixties who works in PR. It offered Joan the opportunity to wear a more glamorous wardrobe that suited the sophisticated character.

The maid Velma, played by Agnes Moorehead, suffers the same fate as Elvira in *Baby Jane*, in that her suspicions lead to her being killed to ensure her silence. Moorehead was a character actress who had been a principal player at Orson Welles' Mercury Players, and was cast by Welles in his first two films *Citizen Kane* (1941) and *The Magnificent Ambersons* (1942), for which she earned an Academy Award nomination.

At the same time as being cast in *Charlotte*, she was also lined up for a new television show, *Bewitched*, as Endora, Elizabeth Montgomery's flamboyant, twisted mother. She was relying on the production of *Charlotte* finishing up on time, so she could begin filming her episodes of the show.

Moorehead hated the way she looked in *Sweet Charlotte*, a marked difference between her real-life image and the glamor she would project on *Bewitched*. She felt ashamed to appear on the Fox lot as a "slob, a blob of sagging flesh in a shapeless house dress that had seen better days." She recounted that "I looked so awful that I refused to eat in the studio commissary, and I'd suppose I'd have starved if not for Debbie Reynolds who invited me to join her for lunch each day in the privacy of her dressing room."

Several years later, Moorehead would take the lead role in another "hag horror," *Dear, Dead Delilah* (1972), which was a cheap copy of *Charlotte*, *Baby Jane* and *Strait-Jacket* combined. She played the controlling Southern matriarch of a dysfunctional family living in a Nashville plantation, who takes on as house-keeper a woman just released from prison for killing her mother with an axe. Because Moorehead was suffering ill health, and would die just two years later, her character was in a wheelchair, which further served to fit the character trope.

Following the rehearsals in Hollywood, the *Charlotte* production moved to Baton Rouge, Louisiana, where filming was to begin on May 31, for a ten day location shoot. "I hope we live through it," Aldrich wryly commented.

Joan Crawford arrived three days later with twenty pieces of luggage, her maid Mamacita, hairdresser Peggy Shannon and makeup artist Monty Westmore. To her dismay no one came to meet her at the airport, and so she made her own way to the Belmont Motel, on the outskirts of the city, where cast and crew were already settled. Bette Davis had claimed the larger bungalow for herself, and Crawford was further upset to find her room was positioned next to the bins.

Joan rose early to ensure she had time to do her exercise routine, for Monty Westmore to apply her false eyelashes, which took two hours, and to then paint on her trademark heavy mouth and eyebrows herself. Bette was amused at the extensive luggage Joan had brought with her, the "mounds of hairpieces" and her chiffon clothing all needing to be pressed in the heat. There was a marked difference between Bette's relaxed manner on sat, where she could laugh with the crew, and Joan, who kept herself isolated. To travel any distance on location, Joan moved by golf cart, while Bette walked.

As Bette wrote in her memoirs: "She knew I was not likely to be friendly to her, as I had been during *Baby Jane*. Not after helping me lose the Oscar. Also, Agnes Moorehead and Joseph Cotten were in the cast this time, not just I."

On location in Louisiana, Bette went for dinner with Aldrich and with Agnes Moorehead to see Phyllis Diller perform in a Baton Rouge nightclub. She held parties in her bungalow, including a special celebration for Mary Astor, where she invited the director and cast, bar Joan. The principal actors were close to one another; Moorehead knew Mary Astor and fellow Mercury Players alumni Joseph Cotten, and she had a friendship with Davis, having both been at Warner Brothers in the forties. In contrast, Joan spent the evenings on her own, with her vodka and Pepsi for company. As gossip columnist Sheilah Graham reported: "Bette lets her hair down but Joan surrounds herself with the aura of a great of yesterday. Times have changed and she doesn't seem to realize that."

Because of the tensions between the two stars, Aldrich began by shooting the scenes with the other actors, before bringing Bette and Joan together for their first exterior scene, where Miriam arrives in a taxi at the mansion. Despite their differences, Bette spoke of her admiration for Crawford's ease at handling the continuous shot of her arrival, where she steps out of the cab, pays the driver, lowers her sunglasses and looks up at the balcony to see Charlotte with a shotgun aimed at her. It was a complicated series of directions, but she carried out the movements seamlessly and without missing a beat. It would be the only scene she would shoot for the film.

After location shooting, the production returned to the Twentieth Century-Fox studios for the interior shoot, and Davis was unrelenting in her treatment of Crawford, which unnerved the more sensitive star. Still angry at Joan's behavior at the Academy Awards, Bette had tried to provoke her by always holding a bottle of Coca-Cola, and in retaliation, Joan insisted that a Pepsi-Cola machine be installed on the Hollywood lot. "When Crawford brought back the Pepsi machines," Henry Farrell recalled, "Bette had the crew gather all the Coke bottles on the lot and line them up in the path outside Crawford's door."

Despite being the more glamorous character, Joan began to feel that Miriam was really second fiddle to Charlotte, and that Bette was sure to steal all the scenes. She insisted to Aldrich that her part be bulked up with more dialogue. When these demands weren't met, Crawford asked her lawyer to find her a way out of her contract. While Davis was called to reshoot some scenes for the drama *Where Love Has Gone* (1964), Crawford checked into Cedars-Sinai Hospital for pneumonia.

Aldrich rescheduled scenes around Joan while she recovered, but he was skeptical as to her illness as she had called in sick during both *Johnny Guitar* and *Strait-Jacket*, as a way of wielding power to force changes to the script. This time Joan had a list of demands for Aldrich, which she dictated from her hospital bed. She wanted Miriam to have a number of male love interests, and she wanted a welcome ball for Miriam, which would give her the chance to wear a show-stopping gown.

Once Aldrich had run out of scenes to shoot without her, production was temporarily shut down to save money. On her first day back after being discharged from hospital, Joan was scheduled to shoot a scene with Moorehead, where Miriam tells Velma she's dismissed. Crawford gushed that working with Moorehead was "One of the greatest professional thrills I've had", but the next day, when Davis was back on set, Joan again began to feel affronted as Davis insisted on scoring out pieces of Miriam's dialogue, and she was rushed to hospital once more.

"The rest of the cast and I kept up with her condition by reading Hedda Hopper, who received frequent bulletins from Joan's hospital room," said Davis. "She had clothes fitted every day. The Brown Derby catered her food. Her recovery was a slow one, for reasons that I suspected were not entirely medical."

Aldrich questioned whether she was faking pneumonia, but he also knew that the insurance company wouldn't pay out if he revealed his suspicions. "I was very hurt," Joan said, "that anyone could imply I was pretending to be ill. I understand that's what happened. It was, for anyone who knew me, totally contrary to my character to agree to make a film and then fake an illness. I had given my word, signed a contract, and my word was more important to me than a piece of paper."

The insurance company insisted that Crawford be replaced so that production could get back on track as quickly as possible. "I would have done anything I could to keep Joan," Aldrich said. "But my backers were nervous. Joan saw her part as playing second fiddle to Bette Davis, and whether that contributed to her not feeling well, I don't know."

To recast Miriam, he went through a list of older actresses including Loretta Young, Barbara Stanwyck, Katharine Hepburn, Ann Sheridan and Vivien Leigh. "Obviously the ideal candidates would have been Vivien Leigh and Katharine Hepburn, but there are deep-seated personal and historical reasons why [Bette] didn't want them," said Aldrich. Bette Davis dug in her heels and refused to work with Leigh, despite a threat of suspension by Fox if she didn't agree to a co-star. She was still bitter that Leigh won the role of Scarlett O'Hara in *Gone with the Wind*, when it had originally been planned for her at Warner Brothers. She dismissed both Leigh's acclaimed performances as Scarlett and as Blanche DuBois in *A Streetcar Named Desire*, insisting that as a quintessentially British woman, she couldn't authentically play a Southern belle. "I felt she would be as temperamental as Joan. I told Aldrich this would be like jumping from the frying pan into the fire," Bette wrote.

Aldrich sent a telegram to Leigh's London home to ask her if she'd be interested, but she threw it straight in the wastebasket. When he followed up with a call, she told him she was just about prepared to work with Joan Crawford, but there was no way she could face seeing Bette Davis at seven o'clock in the morning.

Both Loretta Young and Barbara Stanwyck were friends with Crawford, and out of loyalty, turned down the offer. With time running out for a replacement, Bette suggested that her friend Olivia de Havilland might be perfect as manipulative Miriam. While Olivia was known for her seemingly sweet persona, despite the long-standing feud with her sister Joan Fontaine, she had played against type in both *The Snake Pit* (1948) and *The Dark Mirror* (1946), in the dual role as a good and bad twin sister. Like

Crawford, she was shrewd and tough, and continued to exude Hollywood glamor, which made her perfect for Miriam.

Aldrich couriered Olivia the script to her Paris apartment, and on receipt, she immediately turned it down. Jaded from the outraged reception around her previous horror, *Lady in a Cage*, she also found the characterization too simplistic. Determined not to give up, Aldrich immediately flew to Switzerland, where she was now vacationing, and sought to persuade her by offering to fix any of her concerns around the duality of Miriam. "That isn't the problem," Olivia told him. "It's that the writing lacks ambivalence and subtlety. Miriam is all coloured in black. Solid black, with no relief!"

Olivia suggested that Miriam be rewritten to be a gracious Southern belle, with her superficial charm disguising her danger, and Aldrich agreed to whatever she wished. "I spent four terribly difficult days with all the persuasion I could command," he recalled. "I don't believe half of the things I said myself; but I knew there was no other place to go. If I came back without de Havilland, we wouldn't have a picture, because we had gone through all the other people that Fox would live with."

Finally, it took a phone call to Bette to persuade her to take the role. "Livvie, you must," Bette said. "You would be wonderful in this."

"I'm glad for Olivia, she needs the money," Joan Crawford said, on hearing the news.

Davis and de Havilland had previously worked together in *It's Love I'm After* (1937) and *The Private Lives of Elizabeth and Essex* (1939), where Olivia initially found working with Davis to be daunting. But it was during the filming of *In This Our Life* (1942), with Bette playing the bad sister, and Olivia as the good

sister, that the two became friends. In 1971, on Bette Davis's episode of *This is Your Life*, Olivia rushed up to her former co-star
to give her a big hug. Olivia said Bette scared her "nearly to
death" the first time she met her. "We had to make three pictures
together for her to warm up to me." Bette seemed flummoxed by
her statement, confessing she didn't remember it that way. "I feel
I've always known and loved Olivia...I was probably jealous of
you being so damned good-looking."

After being convinced by Davis, de Havilland finally agreed
to a salary of $100,000 and expenses, and flew into Los Angeles
on her preferred Air France flight, with Bette meeting her at the
airport in the early hours of the morning.

Joan was devastated that she had been replaced, perhaps hoping that she could shut down the film entirely and deprive Bette
of her role. "I looked forward to working with Bette again," Joan
Crawford said several years later. "I had no idea of the extent of
her hate, and that she planned to destroy me.… I still get chills
when I think of the treachery that Miss Davis indulged in on that
movie."

Years later, Olivia told author Charlotte Chandler that "I
did it to please Bette and not disappoint her. Given the choice, I
wouldn't have deprived Joan Crawford of the honor."

Production started up again on September 9, 1964, with
Olivia and Bette toasting their working relationship with bottles of Coke. While the atmosphere on the set was much more
congenial with Olivia present, she was steadfast in refusing to be
drawn into the games that Bette liked to play. Olivia told Charles
Higham in 1964 that despite their friendship, Bette saw her as she
saw other actresses – a challenger she must destroy. During one
scene, where Olivia was simply to walk up the stairs, and then

pause, Bette sat on a chair off camera, dragging on a cigarette and giving her a hard stare. "That was something no actress should do," said Olivia. "Unlike Bette I'm not a competitive person. If I am attacked, I simply refuse to fight back. I never said a word to Bette. I just did my scene. The next day I was on the set while Bette was working, and I knew she expected me to retaliate. I didn't. I just looked at her, but I'm sure the look said what I didn't verbalise: 'I will not fight you; I will not accept your challenge.' Bette understood."

Later, during the scene where Miriam gives Charlotte a hard slap, Bette was afraid all Olivia's pent-up annoyance at her from over the years would come out in that smack. She announced she couldn't do it, and a stand-in had to come in place instead.

"I liked de Havilland. Oh, she was wonderful. She was better than Crawford would have been. Oh, much better," said Aldrich. "I think probably the casting damaged the picture commercially, but it helped the picture enormously in believability. Crawford was Crawford and very good, but she'd never have given that kind of role the nuances de Havilland did."

He also felt "that de Havilland seemed intrinsically more of a bitch somehow." Olivia wasn't as sweet as she appeared in public. She was tough with her two children, who had both come to Los Angeles for a holiday during filming, but got easily bored while waiting around on the set of *Charlotte*, which frustrated her. At the 20th Century-Fox studio commissary, Benjamin knocked over a bottle of sauce while looking at the murals of stars of the past, and furious at this stunt, and other bad behaviors, she canceled their vacation and sent them back to Paris.

Bosley Crowther in his review in *The New York Times* called it "Grossly contrived, purposely sadistic, and brutally sickening ...

grisly, pretentious, disgusting and profoundly annoying.... Davis accomplishes a straight melodramatic tour de force. Moorehead is allowed to get away with some of the broadest mugging and snarling ever done by a respectable actress."

Variety praised the acting in its review of the film. "Davis' portrayal is reminiscent of *Jane* in its emotional overtones, in her style of characterization of the near-crazed former Southern belle, aided by haggard makeup and outlandish attire. It is an outgoing performance, and she plays it to the limit. De Havilland, on the other hand, is far more restrained but nonetheless effective dramatically in her offbeat role."

With mostly positive reviews, the film proved to be another success for the Grand Guignol genre, appealing to a young audience who enjoyed the gothic horror and the camp performances. The film received seven Oscar nominations, including Best Song, Best Editing for Michael Luciano and Best Supporting Actress for Agnes Moorehead. With strong notices for her performance as Velma, and a Golden Globe win for Best Supporting Actress, and with *Bewitched* as the highest-rated new program on its debut, Moorehead was now elevated to star, at the age of sixty-four.

Bette and Olivia made a number of media appearances together to promote the film. On *Hollywood Palace*, with Bette dressed in black and Olivia in white satin, the presenter told them: "I wish I could have been on the set to watch you two make *Hush, Hush Sweet Charlotte* together. Boy, it must have been exciting seeing you two stealing scenes from each other."

Olivia: Stealing scenes?

Bette: Oh Gene, that's just an old wives' tale. You know, most actors never resort to such tactics.

Olivia: No, most performers wouldn't dream of doing a thing like that. They just couldn't be bothered.

At the New York premier, the crowds had to be held back with a police cordon, and Olivia told reporters, "The fans are so young! Their parents could hardly have been born when Bette started out!" Bette playfully retorted: "Olivia, you were wonderful! Even when I was not on the screen, you somehow managed to hold the audience's attention!"

The production of Charlotte proved to be so stressful that Aldrich was briefly hospitalized for exhaustion. When asked by Peter Bogdanovich about the problems on *Hush, Hush Sweet Charlotte*, he said diplomatically, "As long as I've been around - almost twenty-five years - I've never been on a picture that there wasn't a beef."

After the female-centric *What Ever Happened to Baby Jane?* and *Hush, Hush, Sweet Charlotte* (1965), he said he was relieved to go back to an all-male cast for the survival drama *Flight of the Phoenix* (1965), his production company Associates and Aldrich's second picture with 20th Century-Fox. "We only had one bit of trouble on the whole picture - it was the day we had the one female in front of the camera. So, it is different: there are certain latitudes you can take with men. It's just not possible to wake up and say, 'I think the whole thing stinks - let's reverse the scene and go off to the other side.' Not very many women are capable of that kind of inversion - they like to stick to what they've practiced and rehearsed."

Charlotte was Bette's fourth box-office success in three years, and despite her reluctance to be pigeon-holed, it further added to her growing reputation as the grande dame of horror films.

"I must admit, the public liked the movie more than I did," Bette confessed in her memoirs. She also damned her director with faint praise. "I was fond of Robert and enjoyed being directed by him, but he had strange lapses of taste. I thought the scene in *Charlotte* in which the head bounces down the stairs was a bit much. *Baby Jane* had some shocks and high drama, but no heads bouncing down the stairs."

For older actresses, a hit film with Oscar nominations wasn't an automatic guarantee they would receive more film offers. Even after the success of *Charlotte*, de Havilland found her career struggling as she approached fifty, and like many of her contemporaries, she turned to television. In 1967 she was directed by Sam Peckinpah for ABC's *Noon Wine*, and she starred in *The Last Hunters*, about a group tracking down Nazi war criminals, for *The Danny Thomas Hour* on NBC.

That same year she received the devastating news that son Benjamin was suffering from lymphoma. During this difficult time, she reluctantly accepted the part of Mother Superior in *Pope Joan* (1972) as she needed the money to pay for his treatment. With difficulties in meeting her living expenses, she asked to borrow money from her sister Joan Fontaine, despite their strained relationship. Fontaine advised her that older Hollywood actresses could profit from the dinner circuit, by regaling anecdotes from their film days to an appreciative audience. As society seemed to have completely shifted from the world depicted in old movies, it allowed for a sense of nostalgia for simpler times.

10. "The most sensational case of the aging process being unkind"...

When Eugene Archer of *The New York Times* interviewed Tallulah Bankhead in her Manhattan apartment in 1964 to publicize her new film *Fanatic*, he recounted her conversation as she purred down the telephone to a friend. "Darling, I'm talking to the nicest gentleman from *The New York Times*, and I'm trying to be tactful as hell about the film."

An international co-production between Columbia Pictures, Seven Arts and Britain's Hammer Films, *Fanatic*, later renamed *Die! Die! My Darling!* in the United States, was based on the novel *Nightmare* by Anne Blaisdell, with a script adapted by American writer Richard Matheson. Tallulah played Mrs. Trefoile, a former theater star turned religious fanatic, who goes to increasing extremes as a reaction to her grief following the death of her son. To keep his memory alive, Mrs. Trefoile imprisons his beautiful fiancée, Pat, locking her in the attic of her gothic home, located in a small English village, and threatening her with a pair of scissors and a gun, while she prepares to sacrifice her. The cast of oddballs who also live at the house include the lecherous servant (Peter Vaughan), his bitter wife, Anna the maid (Yootha Joyce), and the simple-minded gardener, Joseph, played by Donald Sutherland in one of his first roles.

"Seven Arts is confident that her appearance in *Fanatic* will be the most bloodcurdling thing since Bette Davis terrified Joan Crawford in *What Ever Happened to Baby Jane*? - and will do for Tallulah what that hit did for Bette. Miss Bankhead had no comment on that," wrote another article in *The New York Times*, following the announcement of the production in July 1964.

The film's Canadian director, Silvio Narizzano, later told *House of Hammer* magazine, "The original script was about this little old Welsh lady, living in a tiny Welsh village, who had never been out and was an extremely religious woman. It should have been played by somebody like Flora Robson. But we were confronted with Tallulah playing it…So we made up a whole new story that she had married a Welsh seaman who had brought her back and she was a convert."

In the 1950s, Hammer Films revitalized the horror genre with their color productions that showed blood and gore in all its vivid glory. *The Curse of Frankenstein* (1957), co-produced by Eliot Hyman and distributor Warner Brothers – the same pairing as *Baby Jane* - cast Peter Cushing as Baron Frankenstein, and Christopher Lee as the monster. Their follow-up, *Dracula* (1958), used the debonair Lee to inject a sense of erotica into the story. While they were also producing war films, police dramas and comedies, it was their gothic horror, with heaving bosoms and plenty of blood, that was bringing in the audiences.

Terence Fisher, director of Hammer's version of *The Mummy*, said: "We don't go in for monsters from outer space, man-devouring vegetables, or killer spiders the size of locomotives. Our monsters are always human, or near-human – like Dracula, Frankenstein's Creature and the Mummy. They are believable, and for that reason far more terrifying."

As they grew their horror output in the late fifties, Hammer Films hoped that they could replicate the international success of films like *Psycho* and *Les Diaboliques* by creating a series of psychological horrors that were grounded in realism, beginning with *Taste of Fear* in 1961, *Maniac* and *Paranoiac* in 1963 and *Hysteria* (1965). They also looked to the success of *What Ever Happened to Baby Jane?* in their decision to reach out to aging American movie stars to persuade them to take up the mantle of the demented older woman in a formula that was proving so successful.

"I'm the fanatic," said Tallulah gleefully, before she was due to begin the production. "You might say, 'Tallulah joins the ghouls.' Really, though, I do hope this will be more serious, a bit better than the usual. The script, you know, is rather well written. I have the star part, of course, I'm always on, there's almost no one else in the picture except the girl I prey upon."

Tallulah Bankhead was one of the most outrageous actresses of her generation. She was known for her fondness for alcohol and cocaine, her affairs with both men and women, including Billie Holliday and Marlene Dietrich, and for her complete lack of inhibitions. She was led by a strong desire to shock, by throwing off her clothes and prowling naked, or by making wry proclamations in that deep whisky-soaked voice. "My father warned me about men and booze, but he never mentioned a word about women and cocaine," she once declared.

Born to a prominent political Alabama family in 1902, Tallulah's beautiful twenty-one-year-old mother died just two days after she was born, giving her a ferocious drive to look after herself. Her father, William Brockman Bankhead, was a Democrat member of the US House of Representatives and Speaker of the House from 1936 to 1940.

Desperate to perform from a young age, Tallulah left Alabama for New York at fifteen to launch herself as an actress. She checked into the Algonquin Hotel on 45th Street, which had a growing reputation as New York's theatrical and literary meeting place. Tallulah was an exhibitionist who thrived on being the center of attention, and she desired not to just be famous, but to be infamous. "Hello, my name is Tallulah Bankhead," she told one writer when she was still in her teens. "I'm a lesbian. What do you do?"

She had just turned twenty-one when she arrived in London to star in *The Dancers* and it would mark the start of a hugely successful career on the London stage. Tallulah immediately enchanted the theater district and was soon in high demand as a name to bring in crowds of devoted fans. She described her cartwheels and unpredictable antics on stage as "doing a Tallulah" – "You know, dance and sing and romp and fluff my hair and play reckless parts."

In 1930, Walter Wanger, an independent producer at Paramount Pictures, persuaded Tallulah to transfer her talents to the movies, and after a dazzling run, she left the London stage for Hollywood where she was signed to a $5000 a week contract. Built up by Paramount as the American Marlene Dietrich, she was first cast in *Tarnished Lady* (1931), a Park Avenue melodrama directed by newcomer George Cukor. "A fine actress made her screen debut in a poor picture," Regina Crewe reported in the *New York American*. After four further flops, there were doubts about her suitability in film, and she made her escape from Hollywood to return to theater in New York. "Put me on a lighted stage before a crowded house," she told *Silver Screen*, "and I'm myself."

She was due to star in *Jezebel*, a new play by Owen Davis, but she was forced to drop out after being hospitalized following excruciating abdominal pain, eventually diagnosed as gonorrhea.

It had caused so much damage to her reproductive system that she had to undergo a hysterectomy. While she recovered from the operation, she was replaced by Miriam Hopkins.

Tallulah's hysterectomy would have been physically and emotionally devastating. As well as immediately going into menopause, she had to face the prospects of never being able to have children. She upped her drinking and drug use, including cocaine and amphetamines, to cope with the trauma, and it would become a habit that lasted a lifetime.

David O Selznick was in the opening night audience of George Kelly's *Reflected Glory* in San Francisco in July 1936, and awed by her performance, which was written specifically for her, he immediately pegged her as his Scarlett O'Hara in his adaptation of Margaret Mitchell's novel *Gone with the Wind*. While Tallulah was in the running for almost two years, and her 1938 screen test was considered superb, ultimately, she was thought too old at thirty-six. As consolation, Selznick offered her the role of older prostitute Belle Watling, but she turned it down.

In 1939, Tallulah brought her most electrifying performances to the stage, playing the ruthless Regina in Lillian Hellman's *The Little Foxes*. When the film rights were sold to Samuel Goldwyn, Bette Davis was cast as Regina, once again taking Tallulah's stage role to the screen. As well as having been set to be the original *Jezebel*, Tallulah had starred as doomed socialite Judith Traherne in *Dark Victory* on stage in 1934, which would become one of Bette's best-loved screen performances. Tallulah enjoyed playing up to the feud with Bette Davis, particularly after she supposedly copied Tallulah's image and persona for *All About Eve*. Tallulah later insisted that she turned down Bette Davis's breakthrough role in *Of Human Bondage*, because she was afraid of the reaction of her friends in England to her attempts at a cockney accent.

In 1944 Tallulah returned to the screen for Alfred Hitchcock's wartime drama *Lifeboat*, playing a high-maintenance reporter, Connie Porter, who finds herself cast adrift in the Atlantic with a motley crew of fellow survivors after their ship is torpedoed by the Germans. "Isn't a lifeboat in the middle of the Atlantic the last place one would expect Tallulah?" Hitchcock said, but she had been reluctant to play up to her real-life persona. She had told Hitchcock, "Don't make me say Darling, they'll say I'm playing myself", but her pleas went unheard. She returned to Hollywood in 1944 for *A Royal Scandal*, as Catherine the Great, but she would find that, as a woman in her forties, it would be her last role as leading lady for twenty years.

After dramatically announcing 1948's smash-hit Broadway play *Private Lives* would be her last stage performance, she was approached by NBC to host her own 90-minute radio variety show, *The Big Show*, which launched in November 1950. Attracting a roll call of famous guest stars, including Ginger Rogers, Marlene Dietrich, Groucho Marx and her friend Billie Holliday, Tallulah's show was received enthusiastically by the public, who enjoyed her blunt words, her bluster and her self-deprecation.

Four years after her last performance in *Private Lives*, she agreed to go on stage again with the drawing room comedy *Dear Charles* in 1954, as Blanche DuBois in *A Streetcar Named Desire* in 1956, and opposite Joan Blondell in *Crazy October* (1958) as the West Virginian owner of a roadside honky-tonk. One of her most beloved television appearances was on *The Lucy-Desi Comedy Hour* in December 1957, in the episode *The Celebrity Next Door*, where she played up to her reputation as a heavy-drinking diva. Her opening line, "Hello, Darling," as she answered the telephone, received an immediate laugh, as it had become the catchphrase that defined her.

As she entered into her sixties, as well as contending with the disappointments of her career, she was gripped with insecurities around her appearance. Suffering from emphysema, she struggled for breath, and sucked on a portable oxygen tank between the cigarettes she smoked. Orson Welles cruelly described her as looking like "an old quilt. She was the most sensational case of the aging process being unkind. I'll never forget how awful she looked at the end and how beautiful she looked at the beginning."

Heavily dependent on alcohol and drugs as she struggled with insomnia, she suffered regular injuries as she bashed into things and stumbled over. She relied on her loyal following of gay men, some of whom she would employ as her "caddies," to assist with her lifestyle and to ensure she always had company.

Tallulah was visiting her friend Dola Cavendish at her home in British Columbia when she was sent the script for *Fanatic*. She'd had a number of recent stage disappointments, including the short-lived *Midgie Purvis* in 1961, which had earned her a Tony nomination for best actress, and Tennessee Williams' *The Milk Train Doesn't Stop Here Anymore*, which only lasted a few performances on Broadway. Williams had based the character Flora Goforth on Tallulah – an unflattering portrait of a decaying ex-Follies showgirl, now a wealthy widow living out her final days in a haze of booze.

Despite her doubts as to the quality of the story, she accepted the role in *Fanatic* not just for the $50,000 salary and ten percent of the profits, but because she wanted to keep working, and it offered her the opportunity to return to the UK for ten weeks of shooting. "I love those British crews; they have to quit every evening promptly at six. It's supposed to be because of unions, but I think they just need their tea," she told Eugene Archer.

Jane Fonda was considered for the role of Patricia Carroll, the victim of Mrs. Trefoile's fanaticism, but ultimately the part was given to Stefanie Powers. She had been signed to a seven-year contract with Columbia Pictures at the age of sixteen, just as the studio system was disappearing, and had been cast in roles in the neo-noir suspense thriller *Experiment in Terror* (1962) and *Love Has Many Faces* (1965), with Lana Turner and Cliff Robertson. "It was an extraordinary experience to work with Tallulah," remembered Stefanie. "She was nervous. This was the first film she had done in twenty years."

Tallulah arrived in London on August 20, 1964 and was picked up from the airport in a Rolls-Royce and taken to the Ritz Hotel, where her suite on the fourth floor had flowers and a bucket of champagne waiting for her. Tallulah, accompanied to London by Dola Cavendish's niece Laura Mitchell, was thrilled to return to the Ritz Hotel, where she had first stayed in 1923 when it was the luxury place to be. However, at this point in the sixties, it was more representative of a faded glamor, as if some of the gilt had worn away. As Tallulah made her way to the lobby, she tripped on a loose part of the steps leading up to the entrance, and stumbled backwards onto the street. A group of photographers, who had been waiting for her arrival, captured her mid fall, as she landed on her rear on the sidewalk. The photographs were splashed in newspapers the next day with headlines like "Tallulah slips into the Ritz."

Naturally she was mortified, and according to Stefanie Powers, seeing those photos "put her immediately to bed. She got a terrible case of laryngitis; the doctors were called. It was a dramatic reaction. She really, really felt terrible, and she was already nervous about doing the film, and this was the straw that made her go to her bed."

These early delays in the production caused worry for director Silvio Narizzano, who was conscious that it was his first film, and Tallulah was his first star. "My director was terribly sweet," Tallulah recounted. "But we were rushed. My contract provided a month for rehearsals, but I was prostrate with the flu the moment I arrived, and by the time I was acclimated, or acclimatized - oh, the hell with it, I just plunged right in."

A rehearsal was planned to help Tallulah adjust to working on the film, and Powers remembered her making an entrance in a floor-length mink coat, with two young men on either side of her to support her. She made exaggerated movements to indicate that she still couldn't talk because of the laryngitis that she was afflicted with.

The script had been adjusted to suit Tallulah and her theatrical persona by including an old archive of photographs and mementos that Mrs. Trefoile keeps in her basement, along with her secret stash of booze and makeup. Tallulah was asked to bring her own stills from her younger days, and she took pride in going through them and selecting which ones would be used in the film. "Oh, my, wasn't I beautiful? And look at me now!" she lamented. "It all goes, doesn't it? You can't hold on to it."

In 1930, at the height of Tallulah's beauty, Britain's leading artist Augustus John had painted her portrait, but rather than hiding it in the basement, like Mrs. Trefoile, she kept it in pride of place in her apartment in New York. In comparison to the pictures from her youth, Mrs. Trefoile was to look monstrous and severe, and Tallulah reluctantly allowed herself to be shown without makeup, and with her grey hair pulled back in a severe bun. While top designers like Coco Chanel and Elsa Schiaparelli had provided costumes for her stage roles in the twenties and thirties, for this production she was dressed in the dark, austere clothing of a religious extremist. Narizzano told *House of Hammer* magazine: "She was very miserable about having to take all the curl out of her hair and knot it back. The makeup man, Roy Ashton, had an awful time. He just couldn't get Tallulah's lipstick off." In one scene, as a way of purging herself after shooting to death one of her employees, she takes out an old lipstick and smears it over her face – a creepy moment replicated by Diane Ladd's crazed mother in David Lynch's *Wild at Heart* (1990).

Despite being pleased to be back in London, Tallulah groaned to reporters about the lack of excitement during the shoot – a far cry from when she was living it up in the Roaring Twenties. "I was up at 5:30 every morning. I didn't go anywhere in London. When I'd get home from the studio I'd go to bed. At the Ritz, of course; I always stay at the Ritz, though I don't know what they've done to the food there."

To prepare Tallulah for her scenes, Laura Mitchell made sure to receive the next day's lines from Narizzano, running over them with Tallulah at the Ritz that night and in their car on the way to the studio the next morning. "She was very easy, very amenable, always ready to rehearse," Narizzano recalled in 1982. In the evenings, Tallulah would phone Narizzano out of loneliness from her hotel suite, sharing old anecdotes and discussing the next day's filming. But sometimes he found himself getting frustrated at all the questions she asked about her directions for each set-up. "I don't know, Tallulah. I'm just the director. You're the actor," he told her one day. "I am not an actor," she replied, "I am a star."

In one of the first scenes to be shot, Tallulah brings a bowl of porridge to her captive, Patricia, who is being kept in the attic, but she was confused as to the directions of having to also carry a gun at the same time. "I feed her the porridge?" Tallulah asked Narizzano. "Oh, yes, that's right, Laura told me something about the porridge…I have to carry the porridge and the gun? How am I going to do that?"

Regular Hammer Films script supervisor Renee Glynn also recalled some of the frustrations of working with Tallulah. "When Tallulah had to sit on a chair, hold a gun, hold a bible and suspend her very dainty, short legs, not reaching the ground… she got really angry and she said, 'I can't do this, I can't do this,' and (the director) said, give me the gun and the bible, and I'll do it. And because he'd used a profanity, she leapt up and said, 'Don't you use that word with me again.' She refused to come back on unless he kissed her passionately in front of the crew, which he found very difficult to do, and which he did do."

It was a daily struggle to collect Tallulah from her dressing room to bring her onto the set to begin shooting each day. Narizzano sent his first assistant director to collect her, but he wasn't persuasive enough to match Tallulah's forceful personality and would end up being caught in conversation with her. The second assistant director tried a different method - taking her by the hand and gently leading her back to the set, giving her the chance to try out her Tallulah charm on him.

As Stefanie Powers remembered: "My dressing room was next to her dressing room, and she always had a tradition of calling people by their character name, so that she wouldn't forget that as they were working together. She'd pound on the wall, and that meant to come in to see her. But unfortunately sometimes coming in to see her was a bit shocking, because on occasions she'd be sitting naked on the toilet, and with the door open. She was quite a character."

At 4pm every day, Laura brought Tallulah a seemingly innocent cup of tea, but Narizzano began to have suspicions about its contents. After insisting on taking a sip, he discovered it was bourbon, and mortified that she had been caught out, she implored that it wasn't affecting her work. Instead of cracking down on her drinking, the director decided they'd both have a cup of bourbon for their afternoon tea-break.

Decades later, Powers drew on her experience on *Fanatic* when she played Tallulah in *Looped*, a 2009 play based on Tallulah's frustrating experience trying to deliver one line of dialogue during a redubbing session for *Fanatic* in the summer of 1965. It recounted how she had turned up to the session inebriated, and the longer it took, and the more mistakes she made, the more flustered she got. Several hours later, she finally managed to deliver that one line.

Throughout the making of the film, Tallulah jokingly referred to it as "this piece of shit we're doing," and justified that she was solely there for the paycheck, although in reality she was comfortably established with savings. In an interview with the BBC from her suite at the Ritz, she joked that she'd taken the role for the "Money, darling, what else? You've got to live, you know, and I'm not a very good chambermaid."

Despite Tallulah's protests, *Fanatic* was retitled *Die! Die! My Darling!* for its American release in the spring of 1965, to take advantage of her most famous expression. All those "darlings" may have dripped from her tongue, but she loathed being stereo-typed for her trademark expression. Nevertheless it was played up to in the film's publicity book. It claimed that "everyone, from director Silvio Narizzano to the coffee boy, was using the word with Tallulah-like indiscrimination. A term of endearment in most people's book, the word takes on a different usage, Tallu-lah-style. It is an excellent way of covering up the fact that you don't know, or have forgotten, someone's name."

Posters for the film featured a hand brandishing a gleaming pair of scissors, and a terrified Stefanie Powers, with the tagline "The ultimate in sheer shock! The ultimate in stabbing suspense!" The publicity book also gave some interesting suggestions to cin-emas to publicize the film by playing up to the "shocks," such as constructing a huge "animated pair of scissors" on top of the marquee, or sticking scissors, "the largest and shiniest you can borrow!" to wall displays so they appeared to be cutting up stills of Stefanie Powers.

The change in title and the promise of gruesome stabbings wasn't enough to encourage audiences to see the film. Dora Jane Hamblin in *Life* magazine offered a positive review, describing Tallulah as "the saving grace of the film, and she may well be launched – at 60 or 65 – on a new career."

The *Los Angeles Times* similarly praised Tallulah's "unforget-table portrayal" as "worthy of an Oscar nomination," but the film did minimal business, and disappeared quickly from cinemas. When Tallulah went to see *Die! Die! My Darling!* in New York, she winced at her first close-up. "I want to apologize for looking older than God's wet nurse."

In the last few years of her life, Tallulah made guest appear-ances on *The Andy Williams Show* and *The Red Skelton Show*.

Producer Paul Gregory, married to Janet Gaynor, had plans for Tallulah, Gaynor, and Agnes Moorehead to star in a horror movie together, but for Tallulah, *Fanatic* had been quite enough of an experimentation of the genre.

Her last acting performance was for the television series *Batman*, with a character written especially for her. The Black Widow has turned to a life of crime after the death of her husband, Max Black, and despite suffering from poor health and breathing difficulties Tallulah threw herself into the camp role.

In early December 1968, she came down with flu, which turned into double pneumonia. Admitted to intensive care, she was placed on a respirator. Her last words were to ask for codeine and bourbon, and she passed away on December 12, 1968 at the age of sixty-six. An autopsy reportedly revealed that she had died of malnutrition in addition to pneumonia and emphysema.

Her final appearance on television was on NBC's *Tonight Show*, alongside Paul McCartney and John Lennon in May 1968, where she jokingly asked them for tips on how to meditate. As Tallulah's career had flitted from the days of vaudeville to the countercultural 1960s, it was a fitting end for her to be mixing with the new icons of youth culture.

11. "A lonely old lady, in a house up on a hill..."

"It is foolish of the actress to cling to youth," Bette Davis lamented in her 1962 autobiography, *The Lonely Life*. "But somehow an actor, damn him, can be attractive at any age without cosmetic aid. A woman - certainly an actress - clings to those things which first made her desirable. It is only when she insists on remaining eighteen that she becomes a bore."

As she approached her forties, Bette had been fearful that she would "wind up as a lonely old lady, in a house up on a hill." By her late fifties, she was beginning to feel like a relic of the past, without being offered the strong roles that had once been her bread and butter.

"They don't make them like Bette Davis any more. She belongs to that vintage era when all a marquee had to do was advertise, 'Nobody's as good as Bette when she's bad' and fans would flock to see," *The New York Times* wrote in March 1965, as if paying tribute to an icon who was no longer relevant. One could imagine her retaliating in the manner of Margo in *All About Eve*. "I admit I may have seen better days, but I'm still not to be had for the price of a cocktail – like a salted peanut."

After the camp thrills of *Hush, Hush Sweet Charlotte*, Bette tried to break away from gothic horror. When Warner Brothers bought the rights to Edward Albee's play *Who's Afraid of Virginia Woolf?* she campaigned hard to be cast as Martha, particularly when one of her own lines, "What a dump," from *Beyond the Forest*, was immortalized in the script. She was horrified to discover the role was being given to Elizabeth Taylor, who she thought was far too glamorous for the part, and twenty years younger than the age the character was written as. "Miss Taylor is a darling, but, my dear, they must be obviously making another picture," said Bette. She was devastated at losing what she described as "the right role," and snapped to a reporter that there had been no other decent parts coming her way. "Except for *Baby Jane* and *Charlotte* – nothing."

With a lack of serious film or television offers in 1964, she was convinced that television saved her career, not only by offering her the ability to make witty guest appearances on shows like *What's My Line?*, but with her classic movies now being syndicated on television, and enjoyed by new and nostalgic audiences. "Warners was the first to release their oldies in the 'fifties, and there I was, everything I ever did, over and over. They couldn't forget me if they tried," she said.

Her movie drought in the mid-sixties was broken by Hammer Films. One of the British production company's regular contributors, Jimmy Sangster, who served as director, production manager and writer, was tiring of the gothic horror films he had helped to create, and inspired by *Les Diaboliques*, he came up with a domestic thriller, *Taste of Fear*, released in 1961 and directed by Seth Holt. Considered to be in the same style as *Psycho*, its success triggered a series of films that Hammer's founder James Carreras called "mini-Hitchcocks," which proved to be a mainstay for the studio in the sixties.

Carreras commissioned Jimmy Sangster to adapt Evelyn Piper's novel, *The Nanny*, for the screen, which would be co-produced by Seven Arts. It was a domestic thriller about the antagonistic relationship between a young boy and his nanny, who may or may not be the killer of his little sister. It shared similar themes to the British film *The Servant* (1963), starring Dirk Bogarde as a butler who slowly begins to hold dominance over his employer. The overarching plot of *The Nanny* is the after-effects of a botched abortion which killed the Nanny's daughter, triggering her mental breakdown. It would have been a shocking theme in the fifties, but was less so by the more progressive sixties, as women's reproductive rights were being discussed more openly.

The Nanny would be the last Hammer film to be shot in black and white, further creating the air of a gritty domestic melodrama, rather than purely as a horror film. It also marked the beginning of a new distribution pact between Hammer and 20th Century-Fox in the United States and ABPC in the UK. Seven Arts was able to connect Hammer to the sought-after Hollywood stars that would normally have been out of their reach.

When it came to casting an older actress in the role of the Nanny, Sangster went to Santa Fe, New Mexico, to speak with Greer Garson, who had expressed interest. She hadn't made a film since *Sunrise at Campobello* in 1960, but when faced with the thought of starring in a horror film, she hesitated.

"I went out to see her, and she read the script," recounted Sangster. "And I came back to England and we heard she didn't want to do it because it was bad for her reputation. I didn't like to say she didn't have a reputation in those days, because she hadn't done anything for about four or five years."

It was Ray Stark from Seven Arts who suggested Bette Davis would be ideal for the part, and so Sangster traveled to LA with director Seth Holt to meet with her. Warming to the Brits, she agreed to sign on to the project. Six weeks later Davis arrived in the UK on board the Queen Mary, and Sangster met her at

Southampton and took her to her rented house near Elstree Studios, where she would stay for the duration of filming.

For Davis, *The Nanny* would be a continuation of the disturbed older lady roles of *Baby Jane* and *Charlotte*, but rather than being pitted against a female rival, this time it would be age battling against youth. She informed *The New York Times* of her plans to make *The Nanny* – "another horror film, I'm sorry to say."

Despite it being her fourth horror film, she rejected the idea that her career was on the same career trajectory as Joan Crawford in pigeon-holed in the genre. "*Hush, Hush, Sweet Charlotte* was not a horror film," said Bette. "It was the study of a very sad woman who had a terrible thing happen in her life."

The Servant's Wendy Craig was cast as Virginia, a mother who is more in need of care from her nanny than her children, following the bathtub drowning of her daughter Susie, which has been blamed on her son, Joey. The film opens with the news that Joey is to come home after being sent to a children's home, and we first see him hanging from a rope. He's playing a sick prank on his teacher, but immediately triggers the audience into wondering whether he did kill his sister Susie, or if it was the Nanny, as he insists.

The plot also shares similarities to Roman Polanski's *Repulsion* (1965), released the same year, capturing a feeling of agoraphobia and claustrophobia within a London apartment as a young woman descends further into madness. *Les Diaboliques* and *Psycho's* influence was also evident in *The Nanny* with the use of the bathtub as the spot where death occurs. Just as *Psycho's* bright white bathroom becomes a place of horror, it's here that the Nanny accidentally kills Susie, when she turns on the water tap without looking in the bath first. The high camera as she walks into the bathroom to find Susie drowned was also reminiscent of Hitchcock's camerawork in *Psycho*. As part of his plan to torment the Nanny and drive her away, Joey uses a doll to scare her by placing it in the bath, so that it resembles the body of Susie. As used to effect in *Baby Jane*, the waxen face and glassy eyes of dolls were a common feature in horror; the impenetrable stare of the doll, and its fixed smile, implies that there's something more sinister behind its supposed innocence.

Another *Les Diaboliques* touch was for Virginia's sister Penelope, played by Jill Bennett, to suffer from a weak heart. As soon as it's mentioned that she could die if given a bad fright, the audience knows that it won't end well for her. As Penelope suffers a heart attack and staggers into the bedroom, the low camera, operated by Kelvin Pike, who would go on to do the camerawork for *The Shining* (1980), creates a sense of claustrophobia. Nanny follows behind her, picking up shoes as she goes, as she calmly acts the servant while watching Penelope die.

Bette told the BBC she was proud of *The Nanny* because it was "a complete departure from anything I've ever played. It is very easy to say, 'Well, you know, she's always the same.' This is not true. This I will never accept from any critic… One of the things over the years that critics have repeatedly referred to have been my 'mannerisms.' Well, that depends on what part I'm playing. I can show you just as many parts where I don't flutter one eyelid, ever!"

Shooting began on Bette's fifty-seventh birthday, in spring 1965. In 1951, when Bette traveled to the UK to make *Another Man's Poison* with then husband Gary Merrill, the notoriously hostile press referred to Gary as Mr. Davis, and Bette as a "middle-aged matron." She reflected in her memoirs that it is "very different making a film in England. There is a great contrast in technical equipment, wardrobe and all the amenities. Plus the lack of comforts the American actor has grown accustomed to."

Rather than having a large entourage, Sangster remembered that "She had one person with her, who was a middle-aged ex hairdresser, I think. Violla Rubber. She was quite a dear lady. That was the only entourage, although she did bring her son with her."

In Sangster's script, the Nanny is described as being about "sixty-five-years-old, wearing the traditional blue topcoat, hat, and sensible flat-heeled shoes. No makeup, and hair under her hat done neatly but above all, functionally. Everything about NANNY is functional." While younger audiences were mostly aware of Bette Davis as *Baby Jane*, the Nanny was a different type of old spinster. Baby Jane Hudson was an overly-made up grotesque, but the Nanny is so drab that she becomes almost invisible, with a hat pulled over her gray hair and with her black dress and white apron marking her as the servant class.

Davis insisted on wearing her padded costume during early rehearsal run-throughs around the table, as she wanted to experience the sensation of wearing the repressive clothes to aid her understanding of the character. Despite her choice of costume, she found it difficult to see herself dressed as a middle-aged matron. The film's director, Seth Holt, recalled that Bette refused to watch the day's rushes because "she hated to look at herself. I'd ask her what did it matter since she was made up and dressed to be a frumpish, unattractive, middle-aged nanny anyway - and she was fifty-seven or so…but I couldn't get her to look at those rushes. If I had, I might have made her realize that she was pouring it on too much."

"He's a mountain of evil, but he's a super director," said Bette of Holt, and they got on well, despite some disagreements. The first scene on the shooting schedule was between Wendy Craig and Bette Davis, who complained that Wendy was given the first close-ups. "We didn't know about this star thing," recalled Sangster. "That you'd always do the star's close-up first. She told me, and I had to tell Seth. So we just watched it after that…She was quite a difficult lady and she asked for difficult things, but they were always for the good of the picture. Never for her own pleasure or selfish needs. She wasn't always right, and in those cases you could talk her out of it, and if she would agree with you it would be fine, but she was a difficult lady."

Script supervisor Renee Glynn recollected that Bette Davis displayed little diva behavior on set, apart from insisting that cast and crew follow her example by arriving promptly, and keeping the noise down on the set. "She wanted the set very quiet, and if there were any noises, off she'd be, angry. But she was really very co-operative and professional throughout."

While there were rumors that Bette nipped into the pub in Elstree with Violla Rubber for a quick Scotch before filming each day, Sangster recalled it a little differently. "She frowned on any of the cast in the studio restaurant if anyone had a beer on the table. She didn't like that at all, because in America the studios were dry," he recollected. She did, however, enjoy a drink in the evenings. When Jimmy went to Bette's rented house to discuss the scenes for the next day, he said, "I must admit, she could put the booze away, but she didn't drink on the job. I'd take her out to places in London occasionally and she would sink a few drinks but nothing…I never saw her fall over drunk or anything…. She came to dinner at our house a couple of times, and we went to dinner at her house a couple of times. And we went out two or three times in London. My wife was a bit intimidated by her because she was a bit of a bully. But, you know, she behaved herself."

Carry On actor Frankie Howerd was a huge fan of Bette Davis, and Sangster recalled that Howerd called him up to ask if it would be possible to meet the star during filming. "I invited him down to lunch, and said to Bette, there's this guy, Frankie Howerd coming to have lunch with us…he's a very well known comic. She says 'fine', so we go and have lunch, and he's at the table. Then she comes in, I introduce them, and she says, 'Oh, Jimmy tells me you're a comic…well, make me laugh.' And I don't think he said another word. That was Frankie Howerd. Poor man."

In an interview on the set of *The Nanny*, *Kinematograph Weekly* wrote: "Bette Davis, unlike the creatures she has played in films (particularly latterly: Baby Jane, Charlotte, now Nanny) seems to be a perfectly normal human being. True, she did protest that *What Ever Happened to Baby Jane?* and *Hush, Hush Sweet Charlotte* are not horror films ("They are films about people"), but she also told me she likes custard – and what could be more normal than that?"

The Nanny received good reviews, with particular praise for Davis's restrained performance when compared with her other horror roles. *Time* magazine described Bette as "moviedom's Ace Bogeywoman" who "now goes about her grisliness with quiet, unruffled efficiency. The Nanny is her definitive essay on the servant problem, and may be taken as an antidote by those who found Mary Poppins too sweet to stomach."

Howard Thompson, in his review in *The New York Times*, said *The Nanny* was "the quietest, tightest and most lifelike Davis film in a cavalcade of gory jamborees that started with *What Ever Happened to Baby Jane?*"

Despite the success of *The Nanny*, it was another two and half years before Bette Davis would accept another part. In the meantime, Hammer Films continued with their profitable formula of casting a Hollywood actress in a horror role when they courted Joan Fontaine for another home-grown thriller.

Throughout most of 1959, Joan Fontaine suffered a debilitating illness, bed-bound with flu-like symptoms, and going through custody battles over her daughter Debbie with ex-husband William Dozier, as well as problems with her adopted daughter Marita. "To pay my income, I spent summers in stock, made a horrendous film for Irwin Allen with Walter Pidgeon, *Voyage to the Bottom of the Sea*," she wrote in her memoirs *No Bed of Roses*. "I invested in oil drilling, bought citrus groves in Florida, an apartment building in Beverly Hills. Now that I was comparatively free of financial obligations other than to Martita and my now-widowed mother, I could begin to think of my own future."

The start of the 1960s was marked by her divorce from her third husband, producer Collier Young, and dealing with the aftermath of her Brentwood home going up in flames after being caught in the path of a wildfire. Yet her life continued to be a whirl of cocktail receptions and dinners at embassies around the world, of attending White House dinners with the Kennedys, and holidaying abroad on expensive yachts. She also had a short-lived marriage to golf writer Alfred Wright Junior in 1964, but she felt restless when tied down to domesticity. Having suffered all her life with chronic illnesses, she flitted through marriages, and through life, with a sense that she wanted to embrace her freedom to the full. "With friends on Broadway, at the UN, in Washington, New England, New Jersey, my new life was gayer than it ever had been during my twenty-five years in Hollywood," she wrote.

According to her biographer Charles Higham, Joan Fontaine was quite different from sister Olivia de Havilland, who lived a regimented existence as a working mother living in Paris.

"Joan, as always, lived a life that was the exact opposite of Olivia's cramped, grim, and disciplined existence," he wrote. Fontaine told the *Times* in 1966: "We have a number of similar traits and characteristics. I think it would be disastrous if we were ever to make a film together."

As Olivia told the *Associated Press* in 2016, she often called Joan "Dragon Lady," because she was "a brilliant, multitalented person, but with an astigmatism in her perception of people and events which often caused her to react in an unfair and even injurious way."

In 1963, when Olivia was planning a trip to New York, Joan organized a cocktail party for her as a welcome. Fifteen minutes before the guests were due to arrive, Joan received a note informing her Olivia had canceled, sending with it a gift of a Japanese quince tree. When the guests arrived Joan introduced them to her "guest of honor," the quince tree. "They all agreed Olivia had never looked lovelier", Joan slyly wrote in her memoirs.

Born Joan de Beauvoir de Havilland in Tokyo in 1917 to British parents, Joan Fontaine began her film career in the 1930s after signing on with RKO Pictures. It proved to be a slower start than her elder sister, who was riding high in Errol Flynn swashbucklers, and was, at that time, considered the big success in the family, which helped fuel the resentment between the two. Joan had a supporting role in the all-female ensemble *The Women* in 1939, and she was catapulted to fame with Alfred Hitchcock's *Rebecca* (1940), for which she was nominated for an Academy Award. She has the honor of being the only actor to win an Oscar for their work in an Alfred Hitchcock film, playing another insecure, tormented wife in *Suspicion* (1941), and was nominated for a third time for *The Constant Nymph* (1943). Over the next decade she earned a reputation for dramatic, emotionally-wrought roles, such as *Jane Eyre* (1944) and as an alcoholic actress in *Something to Live For* (1952).

She continued to act throughout the fifties and into the sixties, and as she found movie roles were becoming scarcer, she turned to theater and television. Her co-starring role in *Tender is the Night* (1960) with Jason Robards and Jennifer Jones was one of only two films she acted in that decade. "People come up to me and say they've seen *Wuthering Heights* five times, which is very nice apart from the fact that I wasn't in it: or they say how marvelous I was in *What Ever Happened to Baby Jane?* and what hard work it must have been to make," she told a reporter in 1966.

On television she had a starring role in a 1960 episode of *Startime* called *The Closed Set*, playing an imperious movie star in the guise of Joan Crawford. She also made guest appearances in episodes of *The Dick Powell Show*, *Kraft Mystery Theater*, *Wagon Train* and *The Alfred Hitchcock Hour*, in a 1963 episode called *The Paragon*. "My mysterious illness returned. As I sat under the hot TV studio lights doing panel shows such as *To Tell the Truth* and *Match Game* my clothes would be soaked, the fever would flush my face under the pancake makeup. The vertigo, the flu-like symptoms returned with a vengeance," she wrote. After visiting numerous doctors to find out what was wrong with her, she was eventually diagnosed with toxoplasmosis.

With a lack of movie offers coming in, Fontaine began searching for her own material which would capture the lucrative youth audience. She came across a novel called *The Devil's Own* by Norah Lofts, and after buying up the rights, brought it to the attention of Seven Arts and Hammer Film Productions. The role of a timid teacher who is caught up in witchcraft in a quiet village in Cornwall was, according to Charles Higham, "The antithesis of her nature in every way." Like Bette Davis, Joan Fontaine dictated her terms to Hammer and personally selected director Cyril Frankel, who had previously made the controversial 1960 Hammer film *Never Take Sweets from a Stranger*. "It is neither horror nor Grand Guignol. If anything it's really a detective story," Fontaine insisted to a reporter for *The London Times* during production.

Joan arrived in London in April 1966 for three months' filming at Hammer's compact Bray Studios, sitting on the edge of the River Thames in Berkshire. Bray Studios had a strong reputation for the quality of its technical staff and the food served up in the canteens. But its small size was a drawback in making high end productions, and several months after filming was completed, Hammer vacated Bray Studios.

For her extended stay in London, Joan had agreed to apartment-swap with Vivien Leigh, who was staying at Joan's luxury 160 East 72nd Street apartment while performing on Broadway in *Ivanov*. The two had an amenable acquaintanceship despite the rivalry in vying for the lead in Hitchcock's *Rebecca* back in 1939.

As soon as Joan moved into Vivien Leigh's grand antique-filled Belgravia apartment, at Eaton Square, she complained that there was an overwhelming stench of cat litter and the musk of

Vivien's Siamese cat, Poo Jones, and despite her best efforts, she couldn't eradicate the smell.

Joan wasn't discreet about these complaints, later writing in her memoirs about her experience. "When the housekeeper, with whom the cat slept, brought my 5.30am breakfast each morning, I could scarcely force down the food. Her white uniform sent waves of odor toward my bed. I gagged my way to the Elstree studio in a hired Daimler. Arranging a protracted holiday for the housekeeper and the cat, I sent for Mother and my personal maid, both of whom stayed in Vivien's flat as I spent long days on location outside London."

American columnist Radie Harris rushed to defend Leigh against Fontaine's complaints. "Not only me, but all of Vivien's close friends know how outrageous these accusations are," she said.

Joan was also affronted that Vivien wouldn't let her use the garage to park her own car. "Since I had left Vivien with my excellent Jamaican housekeeper in New York, had left out all my linens and silver for her use, I saw no reason why I should leave the Alfa Romeo in the street in Euston Square when her garage was unoccupied. I rang the New York apartment and explained my problem to Vivien, asking for housing of my convertible. 'You are not to use my gar-rahge,' she regally commanded, and hung up the phone. My phone! This was not the last encounter I was to have with Lady Olivier."

Vivien stayed on at Joan's apartment after her show had closed, with Joan having to insist that she vacate the flat. When Vivien claimed that some of the watches that Laurence Olivier had given her had gone missing from Eaton Square, Joan, her mother and her maid were interrogated by the FBI. Tragically Leigh would pass away in the apartment a year later, on 8 July 1967, after suffering chronic tuberculosis for many years.

Driven to the studio by chauffeured car early in the morning, Fontaine would take the opportunity to lie down on the back seat with her hair in rollers, while reading the morning's newspaper. "People who peer in are very surprised indeed. If the twentieth century has produced anything worse than the woman in slacks, it's the woman going to work in her hair rollers," she told *The Times*.

Bray Studios was small and cramped in comparison to the studios she was used to working from, and she grumbled at the size of her dressing room where she rested between takes. "Nobody ever forgot that she was a star, even in this modest effort," wrote Charles Higham. A feature on Fontaine in *The Times* 1966 reported: "After the monolith dream factories of Hollywood, this tiny rural studio provides a restful contrast. On the debit side she finds it somewhat lacking in facilities; but after a take, she has only to walk a few yards to her hardboard and timber dressing, sparingly furnished and about 10ft by 7ft., and lie full length on the couch."

Despite her effusive praise for her time in England to the press, highlighting her love of "horses, old houses and fireplaces," she struggled to adapt to the levels of comfort she was accustomed to. "The director was a dream, understanding that fever kept me lying in my dressing room, coming out only when I was needed, then returning to a prone position whenever possible," she wrote. "I was ill again, homesick, and loathed the union's grip on the studios: the deliberate delays, the mandatory coffee breaks which would interrupt every scene just as it was going well."

Playing opposite Fontaine was Kay Walsh, as the villainous Stephanie Bax, and the two clashed off-camera. "Kay deplored the fact that I made sure Joan Fontaine was well photographed," remembered Cyril Frankel. "I had to tell Joan to take notice, but at one point I was worried Kay would attack her!"

While the film was released as *The Devil's Own* in the United States, in Britain the title was changed to *The Witches* and was slapped with an 'X' certificate, partly due to its mild orgy scene, where it was shown as a double bill with the crime thriller *Death is a Woman*. "There was nothing in the film to justify (the X certificate)," said Frankel. "But it was in Hammer's interests." The production company often courted the X certificate from the classification board, as it provided a publicity opportunity and attracted audiences who were looking for bigger kicks.

While sister Olivia had struggled with finances, particularly when her son was critically ill in the late sixties, Joan had made shrewd investments in oil wells, cattle, Florida citrus groves and property, and as a result was a wealthy woman, so much so that she had the freedom to reduce her acting work to focus on her Manhattan social life. She told the *Hollywood Reporter* in October, 1978: "I married first, won the Oscar before Olivia did, and if I die first, she'll undoubtedly be livid because I beat her to it!"

Bette Davis returned to Britain for another co-production from Hammer Films and Seven Arts; a connection made easier because her daughter BD was married to Jeremy Hyman, nephew of Seven Arts owner Eliot Hyman. *The Anniversary* was written and produced by Jimmy Sangster, and was adapted from the 1966 stage play by Bill MacIlwraith. Bette plays a domineering mother, Mrs. Taggart, who holds a fortieth wedding anniversary in honor of her long-deceased husband. She invites her three sons and throughout the course of the evening manipulates her children to assert her authority over them. Bette makes her entrance down the staircase of her old mansion in vibrant pink crepe, a chic bob and an eyepatch – no longer the dowdy and decrepit woman of *The Nanny*, her appearance is like that of a deranged flapper.

The story spoke of the trauma that mothers can pass onto their children. Mrs. Taggart can be held up alongside Mrs. Bates as one of a line of terrible mothers who drive their children to extremes, and rather than just one son, she had three to influence. She was named "bitch of the year" by *The People*, "the woman you love to hate," by *The Guardian*, and "Malignant, malicious, magnificent...Bette Davis at her most viperish," by the *Daily Mirror*. Her role played into a degree of misogyny in the enjoyment of watching a hateful harridan on screen, and desiring for her to be punished, not just for her vicious tongue, but for being an older woman who refuses to slip into the background.

"My character, Mrs. Taggart, wore an eye patch," wrote Bette in *The Lonely Life*. "I had them made in New York before I left for London. The eye patches were made of the same material as each costume I wore. Very chic indeed. Twentieth Century-Fox was the producer in America. I guess our film *The Anniversary* was too much for them as it was never released here. There's no doubt about it, the mother which I played, was a wicked woman."

Despite Bette's claims that it wasn't released in the United States, it was in fact given a small run in the spring of 1968. *The New York Times* review described it as "not a distinguished example of the Terrifying Older Actress Filicidal Mummy genre, but it isn't too heavy. And the genre isn't that distinguished after all."

Filming began at Elstree studios on May 1, 1967, and almost immediately Bette clashed with thirty-eight-year-old director

Alvin Rakoff. Eight days into filming, with shooting behind schedule, Bette announced that she could no longer tolerate his strict directing style and demanded that he be fired. She wrote in her memoirs of her annoyance at his direction when he told her to "count to five while looking in the mirror, pause two beats, turn and walk away. One hardly gives performances while counting!"

Davis's assistant, Violla Rubber, described as Vice-President of BD Productions, wrote a letter to Hammer Film Productions on May 9, 1967, informing them that "Miss Davis is sorry but she's not prepared to continue rendering her services for the above film as she is not in accord with the director. She regrets that she cannot continue until a director more sympathetic to her method of working is found."

Forced to resign, Rakoff was paid his full salary and replaced by Roy Ward Baker, who was a personal friend of Davis's, and who made her feel more comfortable. "We have reluctantly agreed to release him," said a spokesperson for Hammer. "This is entirely due to a conflict of personalities and in no way is a reflection on Rakoff's ability as a director."

On its release the film was billed with the slogan "What shall we do for Mum on her anniversary..? Kill her!" Davis's characterization of a misanthropic matriarch was so to-the-bone that some reviews considered it quite nauseating. In a *Los Angeles Times* review, Kevin Thomas remarked that "After a studio preview of *The Anniversary* a colleague remarked 'I want to go home and take a bath.'"

He continued: "Indeed the latest Bette Davis shocker is made with such intelligence yet is so overwhelmingly nauseating that on first viewing it's hard to tell whether there's any point to its savage cruelty. On the basis of a second look the answer is no. For in creating his portrait of the most possessive woman imaginable, playwright Bill MacIlwraith, who has got to be the world's champion mother-hater made a fatal flaw: he forgot to make her human."

12. "Your mother will never grow old, she has the gift of eternal youth."

"All the pictures I did after Baby Jane were terrible," Joan Crawford admitted, not long before she passed away in May 1977. "I made them because I needed the money or because I was bored, or both. I hope they are never heard of again."

From the mid-sixties until her death, Joan Crawford was frustrated at the lack of decent roles that were being offered to her, despite her strong desire to work. Like Blanche Hudson, isolated in her mansion, she knew that the glamorous ingénue roles were a thing of the past. It wasn't just about needing the money. She liked to have the structure in her life, and she enjoyed her status as an important, working, movie star.

By taking on these horror roles, no matter how creaky the script, and how poorly produced they were, they reinforced her survivor-status; that she always continued to work, even as cultural tastes shifted. But in her autobiography, she dismissed this concept of her longevity. "What has always bored me is the harping of the length of my career and my damned durability. So I've had the longest career in Hollywood. Mine was an early start, personal unhappiness and good health."

One month after being fired from *Hush, Hush Sweet Charlotte* Joan was offered a supporting role in another William Castle film, *I Saw What You Did* (1965). She was only required to do four days of filming, as her character would be dispatched quickly after being stabbed to death by villain John Ireland, with whom she'd previously worked on *Queen Bee* (1955). "I think the film will have a terrific identity with parents and audiences," she said at the time. It was a cautionary tale about the teenage trend for making prank phone calls, and featured a gory shower scene that aimed to top *Psycho*. Based on a novel by Ursula Curtiss about two teenage girls who make a crank call to a murderer, with terrifying results, William Castle considered that "the telephone was the star." He chose two unknown teenage girls, Andi Garrett and Sarah Lane, who had never ever acted before. To counterbalance this, Universal-International insisted Castle cast a major star in a cameo role, and he called up Joan Crawford to ask for a favor. "She graciously agreed to help me out," he said.

Crawford's character Amy is desperate for her neighbor Steve, played by Ireland, to marry her, offering him an ultimatum. Yet she's unaware that he's just knifed his wife to death in the shower, in a scene that's a blatant mimicry of Hitchcock, and he soon turns his murderous attentions to her. Crawford's death was played out as a shock twist like that of Janet Leigh being killed off in *Psycho*, and in another horror film trope, he must now deal with her body, just as Norman Bates has to dispose of Marion Crane, and Jane Hudson of Elvira.

Howard Thompson in *The New York Times* called *I Saw What You Did* "a generally broad and belabored expansion of a nifty idea," and it proved to be another modest hit for Crawford. But it would be a couple more years until she managed to find a leading role.

She followed it up with a television pilot called *Della*, filmed at Universal, where she played a wealthy woman who holds her daughter, again played by Diane Baker, captive on her estate. While the television series wasn't picked up, the pilot was later released as an hour-long film called *Fatal Confinement*. She continued to make appearances on television talk shows, quizzes and game shows, with multiple appearances on *The Merv Griffin Show* as well as publicity tours and promotional duties for Pepsi-Cola, which gave her the chance to travel the world with five-star treatment, such as to Rio de Janeiro to open a bottling plant.

While she made a spectacular entrance at the 1965 Academy Awards, to present George Cukor with the Best Director award for *My Fair Lady*, movie offers from Hollywood were proving non-existent. Her reputation was tarnished by stories about her drinking, and her costly behavior during *Hush, Hush Sweet Charlotte* had made her uninsurable in the United States. She did have another option, though. Just as Bette Davis, Tallulah Bankhead and Joan Fontaine had discovered, British-made films were keen to use the status of an American star to boost publicity. In 1966 she received an offer to make a thriller in England for Columbia Pictures and Herman Cohen, a producer of gory horror movies targeted at teenagers, including *I Was a Teenage Werewolf* (1957), *I Was a Teenage Frankenstein* (1957), and *Blood of Dracula* (1957), and who would be credited as an early pioneer of the slasher flick.

Having already worked well with horror impresario William Castle on her last film role, Crawford described *Circus of Blood* as "a good gutsy melodrama," but she hated the title and convinced Cohen to change it. "They wanted to call it *Circus of Blood, Circus of Fear*, but I got my own way in the end," she said. The film's director Jim O'Connolly had a long resume of experience in the British film industry, working his way up from third assistant director on *The Lavender Hill Mob* (1951) to the writer and director of low-budget crime films like *The Hi-Jackers* (1963) and the science fiction film *The Night Caller* (1965).

Crawford was cast as Monica Rivers, the ballsy, forthright owner of a circus which is struggling for business as a result of a series of grisly deaths amongst her workers. A high-wire artist is garroted on his own rope, the business manager is spiked through the head, and the blonde magician's assistant is sawn in half, when the classic trick goes wrong. The story also carried with it a depiction of the tawdry side of entertainment. "There's nothing certain in show business," Monica laments; another line which seemed prophetic to Joan's own life. "We've eaten caviar and we've eaten sawdust."

The film wasn't her first circus-themed horror. One of her early lead roles was in a bizarre 1927 horror tale, *The Unknown*, by *Dracula* director Tod Browning, where she played opposite Lon Chaney, star of Universal horror films *The Hunchback of Notre Dame* (1923) and *Phantom of the Opera* (1925). Chaney played a Spanish circus performer and fugitive known as "the armless wonder," who has been faking his deformity in order to hide from the law. He's in love with his assistant Ninon, played by Joan, but she has an unusual phobia of being held in men's arms. To secure her love he has his arms amputated for real, yet despite his sacrifice for her, he is horrified to discover she has overcome her fears and has agreed to marry someone else, in possession of their arms.

In publicity for *Berserk!* she joked with a reporter that *The Unknown* was "my last circus film – 40 years ago. Then I was the girl who stood against a board while they threw knives at me. This time at least I get to crack the whip. I guess that's promotion!"

Just as *Strait-Jacket* revealed the killer to be Crawford's daughter, so did *Berserk!* and both were driven to murder as a substitute for their mother's affection. This theme had also been played out to great success in Crawford's Oscar-winning turn in *Mildred Pierce*, but it would be a prophetic reflection of the real-life clash with her own daughter, Christina Crawford, who famously penned her ruthless memoir *Mommie Dearest* after Crawford's death. Just as Angela is expelled from her expensive ladies' boarding school, in *Mommie Dearest* Christina is forced to leave her private school after being caught cavorting with a boy, which leads to an explosive meltdown between mother and daughter.

On hearing of Crawford's latest film offer, Christina, who was in her mid-twenties and trying to make it as an actress, was hopeful she could be cast as her daughter, but Crawford refused. When asked by a British interviewer about this, Joan snippily replied, "Because she is much too old for the part." Instead, British actress Judy Geeson was cast as Angela, bringing a blonde innocence to the part, which would defy audience expectations when she is revealed to be the killer.

As Monica, Joan ensured she retained her signature glamor and insisted that she would be age-defying and irresistible to the opposite sex. Daughter Angela is told that "Your mother will never grow old, she has the gift of eternal youth," and goes unquestioned that Monica will be having affairs with much younger men. Crawford, aware the film was on a low budget, handpicked from her own wardrobe a range of brightly-colored suits and styled her hair into a tight braid. She did however have one exception to using her own clothes - legendary costume designer Edith Head created as a gift for Crawford a black leotard, black tights and red jacket to wear as the circus ringmaster. The outfit showcased Crawford's famous dancer's legs, which she was still rightly proud of.

Crawford checked into Park Lane's Grosvenor House for the duration of filming, where she was collected every morning at 5am, and driven by chauffeur-driven car to Shepperton Studios. In an interview with the *Los Angeles Times* from her luxury London suite, Joan told reporter Sally Marks that Monica is "mistress of the ceremonies, lock, stock and barrel. She's colorful, she's exciting, she's the most definite dame I ever played. She knows what she wants and she gets it."

The article described how Joan's "whole being exudes efficiency" and in "the British press she has been referred to as 'Her Serene Crawfordship', an acknowledgement of the type of star personality which only Hollywood seems able to produce, and which Miss Crawford epitomizes with every regal pore of her body."

The making of *Berserk!* proved to be the most enjoyable experience on set in her final years, particularly as Herman Cohen treated her with the respect she expected as a star, and she was given reverence in the British press who lapped up the presence of a bonafide Hollywood icon. As she did on American sets, Joan made sure she got to know the British crew, even hosting a party at Grosvenor House for the crew and their partners.

Nevertheless Joan was known for her use of vodka as a crutch to the loneliness she felt, and she would phone Cohen in the night to discuss a script point. "She did that because she was lonely, staying up at night, sipping her vodka, going over her lines for the next day," he said. Aware that she had arrived in the UK with four cases of hundred-proof vodka, Herman Cohen set out ground rules that she wouldn't drink before noon, or without his permission.

"In spite of her sipping the vodka, she was very professional during *Berserk!*, and she never took a drink unless I okayed it," he remembered. "She always knew her lines and she was always on time - in fact, she came in very early in the morning to cook breakfast for anyone who had an early call. She was strong-willed and tough - but tough as she was, she could be reduced to tears at the drop of a hat, and there were scenes in our movie when she had to do just that."

Judy Geeson, who played daughter Angela, recalled that: "Joan Crawford said she was lonely, and I could see and feel that she was. She wasn't easy, but I think *Berserk!* was hard on her precisely because it was a B-movie. And there was something very likable about her - after all, when people show their vulnerabilities, it's hard not to forgive them for other things."

Acting alongside Joan in a supporting role as the magician's assistant was Diana Dors, considered Britain's Marilyn Monroe in the 1950s. At that point in her life, Diana had moved into rented accommodation, was struggling to pay her bills and had creditors on her trail, and so she gladly accepted the small role in *Berserk!* for lack of anything else. "During the making of *Berserk!*, her creditors tried to track her down, but her colleagues put a protective wall around her at Shepperton Studios," says Dors' biographer, Shar Daw. "Diana got along with Joan Crawford very well, and when Diana was diagnosed with meningitis in 1973, Joan telephoned regularly to ensure she was updated on how Diana was doing, and to send her best wishes. Later, Diana recognized that the book *Mommie Dearest* tarnished Joan's reputation, but Diana found it difficult to accept that the woman she knew would be capable of being such a monster to her children."

Diana found Joan to be a "superstar" when it came to her work, and that she even went so far as to install Pepsi-Cola machines at Shepperton Studios. But she could tell underneath the strong exterior that Joan was "a frightened lonely woman," and that there was some semblance of truth to the rumors she was an alcoholic. "From the various situations I witnessed on the set of the film we made, I'm inclined to feel they are true," Diana said.

Author and critic John Russell Taylor described in the *Times* in November 1967 his meeting with Crawford to publicize *Berserk!*, when he made the mistake of referring to it as a horror film, despite the gruesome deaths.

"With a flash from those enormous eyes which have made many a strong leading man turn pale she snapped back: 'No, it's not a horror film. Not at all. It's just...a good, gutsy drama.'"

He added: "Still, stars do not like to feel typed, and presumably after *Whatever Happened to Baby Jane*, *Straitjacket* and *I Saw What You Did* Miss Crawford felt that the very word 'horror' applied to her latest suggested a limitation in her talents...each of her films now, it seems, has to have one sexy scene and one where we see the simple, yielding woman underneath. And, of course, the total effect is grotesque, if unforgettable. Presumably the film's makers know this, and bank on it to sell the film."

Berserk! wasn't released until January 1968, where it received a tepid reception. Howard Thomson at *The New York Times* described Crawford's Monica as operating the circus like "a four-star general," and "even a last-minute, mother-love injection doesn't thaw Miss Crawford's portrayal of a ruthless iceberg who, one feels, gets what she deserves. However, she is professional as usual and certainly the shapeliest ringmaster ever to handle a ring microphone."

Immediately after the eight weeks of grueling filming, Crawford's schedule was filled with plans for lunch with Paul Getty, a trip to Dublin on behalf of Pepsi-Cola, and as guest of honor at the Variety Club luncheon in London. "You can't be organized in any job unless you have an organized mind and frankly I was born with it," she told the *Los Angeles Times*. "The way I discipline myself is pretty rigid."

Back in America, Joan kept busy with invites to dinner at the White House, fundraising dinners in New York, and with guest appearances on television shows. In early 1967 she was invited to star in a two-part episode of *The Man from U.N.C.L.E*, called *The Five Daughters Affair*, and this would be stretched into a film called *The Karate Killers*, released in August 1967.

Joan's daughter Christina was a regular on the CBS soap *The Secret Storm*, but when she fell ill and required emergency surgery, the studio was faced with a big problem in how to cover for her absence. Joan offered to fill in for her, despite being more than twice her daughter's age. It made for dubious optics with her four appearances on the show, particularly as she appeared inebriated from sneakily drinking vodka, but it reflected her need to still be considered youthful and vivacious.

In 1966, ambitious young writer director Michael Reeves approached Hammer with a script called *Crescendo*, which he had co-written with Alfred Shaughnessy. It was placed on Hammer's schedule for the next two years as James Carreras tried to persuade distributors to back it and for Joan Crawford to star. When he failed, the project was dropped, and Reeves went onto create *The Sorcerers*, an interesting 1966 horror with Boris Karloff and Catherine Lacey as the sadistic hypnotist and his "hag" wife who mind-control a young man into committing murders, and 1968's historical horror *Witchfinder General*, starring Vincent Price. By the time *Crescendo* made it to the screen, Reeves had tragically died of a barbiturate overdose at the age of twenty-five, and Stefanie Powers was cast in the lead, rather than Crawford.

Crawford returned to the UK in July 1969 to make another film for Herman Cohen, which would be an even greater climb-down for her, and a sad footnote as her final movie. Crawford played Dr. Brockton, a celebrated anthropologist who has neglected her daughter, Anna, for her career, but strikes up a relationship with a cave-dwelling troglodyte. "It was my chance to do a science fiction film," Joan said. "I'd never played a scientist before."

The New York Times noted that *Trog* "proves that Joan Crawford is grimly working at her craft," and despite the cheap effects and terrible script, she was absolutely sincere in her acting, treating her performance as she would any other film. While she felt embarrassed at having lowered herself to a schlocky sci-fi horror, she later insisted that she "refuse to apologize for this movie." She added that "one never intentionally makes a bad picture. Besides, I like to work. Inactivity is one of the great indignities of life. Through inactivity, people lose their self-respect, their dignity. The need to work is always here, bugging me. In this case, I had never played a scientist or a doctor, so I thought this would be fun to do."

Author Peter Shelley called *Trog's* plot, about an older woman in love with a prehistoric creature, "a rather bizarre comment on the desirability of leading ladies of a certain age." It was directed by Freddie Francis, known for his B-movie horror shockers like *The Skull* (1965), *The Deadly Bees* (1966) and *They Came From Beyond Space* (1967).

Trog was filmed on a very tight budget, and Crawford was dismayed to find out that in place of her own dressing room, she was required to share a van with other actors. She was, however, carried in a chauffeur-driven Rolls-Royce between her luxury apartment at Grosvenor House and location shooting in Berkshire and interiors at Bray Studios. As with *Berserk!*, she supplied her own wardrobe, carrying with her thirty-eight pieces of luggage to take on location, and had her face taped back by her hairstylist, Ramon Guy, to smooth out her complexion.

"*Trog* is a low-budget picture," she told the reporter. "I supply most of my own wardrobe. You see these boots? I had them made for *Johnny Guitar*. But the character I play in the film, Dr. Brockton, wears pretty simple things. Nothing fancy. I thought about her, how she'd behave, how she would look. I decided she'd have short hair, and at the time I was wearing mine very long, So I took two Bufferins, and one Gelusil, and a stiff drink, and said, 'Right, baby, cut it all off.'"

Crawford developed a close relationship with the crew during filming. Every morning she was up at 4.15am, cooking breakfast for her dresser and hairdresser and reporting on set for an 8am rehearsal. In the evenings she returned to Grosvenor House, where it was reported she "sheds her makeup, takes a bath and cooks dinner. She is adamant about the routine." That routine also included copious amounts of vodka.

"In this scene I'm going to cry," she told a journalist from the *London Times*, who was reporting from behind-the-scenes and who recounted that she looked trim in her jacket and slacks, and that one take was all she needed to get a scene right. "I didn't want them to roll like this. They have to roll in the next scene too," she said of her tears. "I like to keep a reserve. Not like money in the bank, but a reserve. I need an emotional trigger to get them going."

In the first weeks of filming she suffered from a cold that turned into bronchitis, resulting in her losing five pounds in weight. Freddie Francis found that despite her professionalism, when it came to directing Crawford, she struggled to remember her lines, and he had to use cue cards to help her. He also claimed to have bulked out the film with footage from the 1956 documentary *The Animal World*, because she slowed down the schedule. It could be debated whether this was due to the illness she was suffering from, a lapse of getting older, or from the increased drinking that Herman Cohen observed. "She had a huge frosted glass marked Pepsi-Cola, but inside was hundred-proof vodka. I had to reprimand her a few times," he remembered.

In a review of the film in 1971, *The Times* praised Crawford in being able to elevate *Trog*'s camp nonsense, while looking "devastatingly attractive." He wrote:

"I feel quite ashamed of myself, with so much glum distinction around this week, for finding *Trog* the only occasion for positive enjoyment. Needless to say this is entirely Joan Crawford's doing. It is the effect of having, however ludicrous the circumstances, a real, full-time, unmistakable, 100 per cent star in the lead – which is perhaps the most potent reality the cinema has ever known. It is nostalgia to some extent: just think Joan Crawford is the only star who can top the bill and carry a film single-handed in the 1970s who was a star in the silent cinema."

On her return to the United States, Joan made a glamorous appearance at the opening of a Pepsi bottling plant in southern Illinois, where she was greeted by a 400-strong crowd and briefly mentioned her work on *Trog*. "Society screams and yells but society is the real monster," she told reporters. In discussing increasing obscenities in films, she put the blame on foreign producers. She also spoke of it being "delicious" to be the only female on the Pepsi board, and that "as more doors open for women in business, it can still get rough." When she turned sixty-five she was devastated when Pepsi-Cola forced her to retire, taking away one of her main fulfillments in life.

In autumn 1969 Crawford travelled to Los Angeles to star in the premiere of a new supernatural horror television series called *Night Gallery*. Presented by Rod Serling, creator of *The Twilight Zone*, it featured three different stories in the two-hour pilot, each with a recognizable name from the Golden Age of Hollywood.

In her segment, called *Eyes*, Joan plays a blind woman who buys the eyes of a man to give her just a few hours of sight. However it coincides with the New York blackout of 1965, and unable to see anything, she tumbles from her penthouse balcony to her death. She was at first horrified to discover that *Eyes* was to be directed by a twenty-one-year-old novice called Steven Spielberg, but once she realized he would treat her with respect and give her the control that she deserved as a star, she was able to relax into her performance.

Trog was released in the beginning of 1970, marking a new decade for Crawford where she felt that she was becoming a relic of the past. Despite her turn in horror movies, she was highly critical of the new movies coming out of Hollywood, particularly graphic horrors like *The Exorcist*. She was also beginning to feel old. She was profoundly affected by paparazzi shots splashed in the papers the next day, after appearing at a book launch party for John Springer, where she and Rosalind Russell were co-hosts. Despite throwing on the glitz, with a red chiffon gown, diamonds and a brunette wig, she was horrified by her appearance in the photographs, and canceled all other public appearances.

"My life as I had enjoyed living it was largely over because my life as Joan Crawford was over," she told author Charlotte Chandler. "I had to retire Joan Crawford from public view. What was left of me could only destroy that image. I couldn't bear people saying, 'Oh, look, she used to be Joan Crawford!' I would rather stay in my home and answer my fan mail."

PHOTOS

Bette Davis and Joan Crawford signing their contracts for Baby Jane -
The Academy of Motion Pictures, Arts and Sciences

Bette Davis and Joan Crawford with Jack Warner

Bette Davis as The Nanny - Hammer Horror Steve Chibnall Archive

Bette Davis in Jezebel - The Academy of Motion Pictures, Arts and Sciences

Bette Davis in The Anniversary -Hammer Horror Steve Chibnall Archive

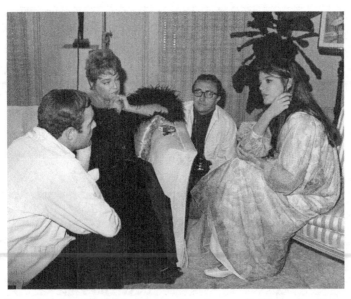

James Caan, Simone Signoret, Curtis Harrington & Katharine Ross during
the making of Games - The Academy of Motion Pictures, Arts and Sciences

Curtis Harrington in his eccclectic home in
the Hollywood Hills - credit Dennis Bartok

Curtis Harrington with Shelley Winters, while making Auntie Roo -
The Academy of Motion Pictures, Arts and Sciences

Cecil B DeMille and Gloria Swanson in Sunset Boulevard

Gloria Swanson on the set of Sunset Boulevard -
The Academy of Motion Pictures, Arts and Sciences

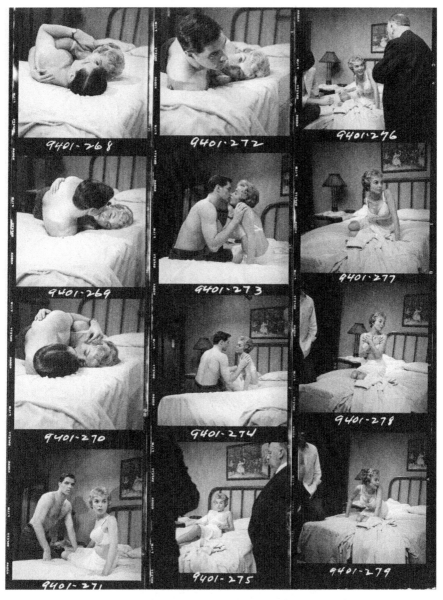

Janet Leigh as Marion Crane in Psycho, who later pays for her sins -
The Academy of Motion Pictures, Arts and Sciences

Joan Crawford and Bette Davis while making Baby Jane -
The Academy of Motion Pictures, Arts and Sciences

Joan Crawford in Humoresque

Joan Crawford in the sixties - Billy Rose Theatre Division,
The New York Public Library. Joan Crawford
The New York Public Library Digital Collections.

Olivia de Havilland resting between takes during the making of Lady in a Cage - The Academy of Motion Pictures, Arts and Sciences

Olivia de Havilland, Bette Davis & Robert Aldrich with a bottle of coke, during the making of Hush, Hush Sweet Charlotte - The Academy of Motion Pictures, Arts and Sciences

Paul Henreid and Bette Davis, Dead Ringer
The Academy of Motion Pictures, Arts and Sciences

Poster for Die! Die! My Darling! - Hammer Horror Steve Chibnall Archive

Shelley Winters and Debbie Reynolds Whats the Matter with Helen -
The Academy of Motion Pictures, Arts and Sciences

Tallulah Bankhead arriving in London to begin filming Die! Die!
My Darling! - Hammer Horror Steve Chibnall Archive

Tallulah Bankhead in Die! Die! My Darling! - Hammer Horror Steve Chibnall Archive

The photos on the wall at Curtis Harrington's home - credit Dennis Bartok

William Castle and Barbara Stanwyck during the making of The Night
Walker The Academy of Motion Pictures, Arts and Sciences

13. "Trailing clouds of faded glamour…"

After Robert Aldrich, one of the leading creators of the "Hag Horror" genre was Curtis Harrington, although he would have rejected that term as a description for the movies he enjoyed making. He considered them more of a tribute to the stories of Edgar Alan Poe, the films of James Whale and Val Lewton, and to the golden era of filmmaking, with his hiring of the older actors who he most admired.

As a film aficionado, he enjoyed casting some of the almost-forgotten names of cinema from the 1930s and 1940s, and purposely sought out actresses like Gale Sondergaard and Ann Sothern to bring them back to the screen. Harrington adored Hollywood and the movie industry, and a feature of his films was the Los Angeles of his childhood, in all its weird glory, of the people and the places, and the darkness that lay under the glitter.

Harrington first developed a taste for horror as a child, growing up in West Hollywood and then Beaumont, a desert town on the way to Palm Springs in the 1930s. "My earliest movie memory is begging, begging my mother to take me to *Bride of Frankenstein*," he wrote in his memoirs. "She wouldn't take me, because it was a horror film and I was probably only four or five years old. I finally coaxed and cajoled her to take me to see *The Raven*, and she took me out of the theatre after the first 20 minutes or so, at the moment when Karloff begins shooting the mirrors. She said I crawled under the seat!"

With singular determination, a teenage Harrington filled out an application to work for Paramount studios, and when they offered him the lowest rung position as messenger boy, he insisted on something better and was given a job in the publicity department. Working at Paramount in the late forties was a dream for a movie buff, as it was home to stars like Veronica Lake, Alan Ladd, Ray Milland, Olivia de Havilland and his ultimate idol, Marlene Dietrich, and he took every opportunity he could to visit the sets and see the magic take place.

He attempted to access the set to see Marlene Dietrich as she filmed *Golden Earrings* (1947) but most of his glimpses of her were in the commissary, when she was having lunch in her full stage makeup. Sometimes he was allowed into the projection booth, and one day he found executives watching 1934's *The Scarlet Empress*. "This was how I discovered that behind the magic of Dietrich there was a Master Magician pulling the strings. Josef von Sternberg was to become my teacher, my mentor, my idol." Harrington was so captivated by his work, that he wrote the first monograph on the films of Sternberg after graduating from UCLA with a film studies degree.

After gaining further experience at Columbia Pictures and 20th Century-Fox in the mid-fifties, and having first made his own experimental films as a teenager, he began working on his own project as director, writing a screenplay based on a short story inspired by Edgar Allan Poe. The title, *Night Tide*, was taken from Poe's poem *Annabel Lee*, and told the story of a young American sailor's encounter with a sideshow mermaid, who might or might not be the real thing. It was inspired by Val Lewton's *Cat People* in its depiction of a woman who transforms into a dangerous creature who can devour the man she's sexually attracted to.

Cast in the role of the sailor was Dennis Hopper, an actor who had taken an interest in Harrington's earlier avant-garde films. To play the fortuneteller, he hired Marjorie Eaton, a painter and character actress who would later play the uncredited Emperor Palpatine in *The Empire Strikes Back* (1980), and who would be the first of Harrington's respectful castings of the older actors he admired.

"She was a friend and had been a pupil of the great Michael Chekhov," he said. "Her own eccentricity as a person came across beautifully on film, especially in the scene with Dennis in which she gives him a highly ambiguous tarot reading."

Night Tide was released through American International Pictures in 1963, shown at the Venice Film Festival and was placed on a double-bill with Roger Corman's adaptation of Poe's *The Raven*.

Harrington followed *Night Tide* with two science fiction films for Roger Corman, *Voyage to the Prehistoric Planet* (1965) and *Queen of Blood* (1965) which both incorporated real Russian space footage that Corman had acquired. In *Queen of Blood* (1966), credited as an influence on Ridley Scott's *Alien*, he cast 46-year-old Florence Marly, star of 1951's *Tokyo File 22*, as the alien queen. It was one of the first of his counter-castings, where he chose an older actress, despite the studio's preference for a younger star.

"Having met her socially, I decided that she would be the perfect choice to play the exotic and beautiful alien queen from outer space. I had to convince a reluctant Roger Corman of my choice. With his exploitation-movie mentality, I am sure he would have preferred a sexy young floozy in the part, and it would have become just another run-of-the-mill sci-fi exploitation film," he said.

When Ned Tanen, a producer at Universal Pictures, came across *Queen of Blood*, he invited Harrington and his producing partner George Edwards to the studio's executive space, known as the "Black Tower," for a meeting and signed them up to a contract. Harrington admired Marlene Dietrich over any other star, and held out hope of working with her one day. Now that he was a director with the power of a Universal Pictures contract, he took the opportunity to devise a script especially for her.

Games was about an older European woman, "trailing clouds of faded glamour," who enters the lives of a rich and fashionable young couple, but she's not all she seems. Harrington described it as "a most unusual suspense shocker, with a contemporary New York setting, and deals with an element of the chic pop art crowd. It is going to be great fun to do."

After writing a two-page outline for *Games*, Harrington and Edwards submitted it to Ned Tanen and Lew Wasserman, head of Universal, who were both enthusiastic, and Gene Kearney, a young screenwriter under contract, was chosen to write the script. Harrington based the frivolous characters of the young couple, Paul and Jennifer Montgomery, who live in an expensive New York townhouse filled with art and arcade games, on Dennis Hopper and Brooke Hayward, who Harrington described as "easily the trendiest newlyweds in Hollywood." As well as acting, Hopper was also a poet, painter and photographer, and a keen connoisseur of modern art. He represented the new Hollywood, while Brooke Hayward, the daughter of actress Margaret Sullivan and talent agent Leland Hayward, was entrenched in old Hollywood. Their house demonstrated the contrast in tastes of Dennis's hippie side and Brooke's more classic taste, with pop art and art nouveau pieces.

Similarly, the hip, young Montgomerys, with their home full of arcade games, optical illusions and masks, offer a contrast with the frayed beauty of Signort. She plays Lisa, the mysterious cosmetics sales woman with psychic abilities, who arrives in their lives, and persuades them to play dangerous games for their idle amusement. One of these includes setting up a pretend affair between Jennifer and the boorish delivery man, and when Paul shoots at him with a gun supposedly loaded with blanks, they are shocked when he receives a bullet in the eye and falls to the ground dead. The more fragile Jennifer is tormented by her fear after having to cover up the murder, and believes she is being haunted. It's later revealed that she is the victim of a plan between Paul and Lisa to frame her for murder, so that Paul can inherit her fortune.

Unhappy with Kearney's work, Harrington gave the script to screenwriter Meade Roberts, who had collaborated with Tennessee Williams on *The Fugitive Kind* (1960). While the relationship between the couple is shown to be transgressive, with Paul kissing Jennifer while she wears a moustache, Harrington thought that there should be a hint of a lesbian relationship between the older and young woman. He suggested, in a production note, that "Jennifer's pull towards Lisa might have sexual undertones; suggest by implication, that Lisa (like the Dietrich image) is of a dual sexual nature...The sexual by-play should be no more overt than it is in *Turn of the Screw*; in fact, the subtler and craftier it is, the more sinister it will be and more propos for your story."

Marlene Dietrich hadn't been given a leading role in a film since *Judgment at Nuremberg* in 1961, and her last screen appearance was as a cameo in Audrey Hepburn's *Paris When it Sizzles* (1964). She was entertaining audiences with her hugely successful cabaret shows that showcased her eternal sex appeal, but she had been unwell, having recently been treated for cervical cancer. Despite her living legend status, Lew Wasserman was unimpressed with the idea of casting Dietrich, and despite Harrington's protestations that she was currently in a successful commercial for Boac airlines, Wasserman told him, "No one would be interested in seeing her," and insisted on casting Jeanne Moreau instead.

When Moreau passed on the script, they turned to Simone Signoret, the star of *Les Diaboliques*. With Simone Signoret having won the Academy Award for Best Actress for *Room at the Top* (1959) and her recent nomination for *Ship of Fools* (1965), Harrington felt that her name would bring prestige to the film, and held out hope throughout the production that she might be in the running for another nomination for *Games*. In her memoirs, Signoret wrote: "On paper it was a good story of theft and murder. The film was made at 'Universal speed' – that is, very, very fast, and I was absolutely *not* nominated."

"Her very presence meant world-weary French glamour," said Harrington. "From my point of view, she was an ideal second choice, preferable even to Jeanne Moreau."

Signoret was acting on stage at London's Royal Court Theatre playing Lady Macbeth opposite Alec Guinness when she was sent the script. She found it intriguing but wanted to find out more about the unfamiliar director. Curtis used his friend, a French ballet dancer and archivist of the Cinémathèque Française, to help persuade her to accept the part. Signoret wrote to Harrington from her dressing room at the theater in October 1966: "I so look forward to working with you on *Games*. With admiration and best wishes."

She later spoke to Harrington over the phone ahead of her arrival in Los Angeles to begin filming. "I warn you, Mr. Harrington, I am very fat!" she told him, and when Harrington and George Edwards met her at LAX airport, they found that "the great face, albeit a bit puffy, was intact, as was the warmth of her personality."

Simone Signoret's Lisa is depicted as a typical grande dame of horror, with touches of the grotesque to accentuate her age and undesirability. She slurps her wine, adds too much sugar in her tea, puffs on cigarettes and carries extra weight. She immediately seems to be a threat to the younger Katharine Ross, much like the theme of *Die! Die! My Darling!*

Katharine Ross was under contract with Universal when she was assigned to the film as her first leading role, and it proved to be fortuitous to her career. Signoret was so impressed with acting opposite Ross that she recommended her to Mike Nichols, who was in the process of casting *The Graduate*. When he asked to see Harrington's dailies for *Games*, it was enough to convince him to select Ross for what would be her critical breakthrough.

For the role of Paul, Harrington suggested James Caan, who had made his debut in an earlier "Hag Horror," *Lady in a Cage*, with Olivia de Havilland. "We couldn't afford a star name but we needed someone who, in my estimation, had the potential of becoming a leading man," said Harrington. "Like most young actors at the time, he was influenced by Marlon Brando. His wardrobe consisted of jeans and T-shirts. Since he was portraying a young man married to a rich woman living in a fashionable Manhattan townhouse, we had to dress him up."

When Harrington despaired at the initial set designer's lack of taste and style, he brought in costume designer Morton Haack to complete the film without credit. Morton Haack, with a background in New York theater, was a friend of George Edwards, and could be quite scathing to the actors he dressed. Because of the difference in shape between Simone and Katharine Ross, Haack commented, "I have to dress an elephant and a mouse." Florence Marly, who appeared as one of the guests in the opening party scene, informed Harrington that Signoret had a congested liver, not helped by her love of Scotch, which had made her face appear puffy.

As Signoret mentioned in her memoirs, Universal expected the film to be made to a tight schedule of seventeen days. After working ten hours on her first day, Signoret announced that she didn't work after 6pm and walked off set. Instead, the weight fell on Katharine Ross, who had to stay on for close-ups without anyone to deliver lines to her. Signoret told Harrington that if he couldn't make the day's schedule, he should blame it on her for being difficult, as she would be allowed more leeway as the star of the picture.

"It was an extremely kind and gracious gesture, and I have felt eternally grateful to her ever since. She was much more than an actress and a star; she was a great human being," he said. "The greatest part of my experience on *Games* was getting to know Simone Signoret."

Once *Games* was completed Harrington and Edwards went on a publicity tour to New York, with parties attended by Gloria Vanderbilt and Andy Warhol, and Mick Jagger and the Rolling Stones. "The film received good, if not great, reviews, and the Signoret fans turned out in force," said Harrington.

Vincent Canby in *The New York Times* described it as a "richly decorated little exercise in the macabre." He wrote that "Harrington's story might have been made to order for a 30-minute Alfred Hitchcock television show. In stretching it out to 98, commercial-free minutes, the director has been forced to pad, but the padding, which includes a strong, enigmatically humorous performance by Simone Signoret, is of top quality…Although she is not called upon to do much except appear enigmatic, Miss Signoret gives authority to the eerie make-believe, even when photographed through a distractingly fuzzy filter in the close-ups."

Time's review in September 1967 was flattering to Signoret, but more scathing to her young co-stars. "Old Pro Signoret walks handsomely through her part. Youngsters James Caan and Katharine Ross walk woodenly through theirs…. About the only fun in *Games* is the eye-beguiling set and what must be the most blood-drenched elevator between Fifth and Madison."

Hedy Lamarr went to see *Games* at a showing in Philadelphia with the writer Barnard L Sackett, who wrote to Harrington to say how much they both enjoyed it. "The film is damn well edited and we both loved the soft tones. I think you should be commended for your first effort at Universal and look forward to seeing even more exciting films in the future," he said.

Harrington wrote to author Charles Higham in May 1967 that it was "a marvelous experience working with La Signoret." He still had Dietrich on his mind, and asked Higham's opinions on the actress. "Did you get to interview Marlene when she was in Australia? And how was she and her act? Don't you think there'd be a world audience interested to see her in another film? I want so much to do something with her, but the studio executives think she's too old. What do you think?"

After the warm reception for *Games*, Harrington and Edwards aimed to take advantage of the momentum by coming up quickly with a new concept. They created an original scenario called *The Guests*, about a retired theater producer who holds a weekend house party on his country estate, where he gives the guests guns to hunt him down and kill him. They all have a secret, and they may be willing to kill to keep it from being exposed.

They asked their acquaintance, Joseph Stefano, the scriptwriter for *Psycho*, to work on the screenplay. But after clashing with Stefano, they ended up replacing him with Irene Kamp, who would go on to co-write the script for 1971's *The Beguiled*.

As well as having ambitions for Sir Lawrence Olivier to produce it, *The Guests* was to feature an older male star, and Universal agreed to finance the film if he could secure Kirk Douglas. "And thus I had my first experience of the old Hollywood catch-22: 'We'll finance your film if you get a certain star.' But without a "firm offer," you can't get the script to the star in the first place," he wrote. While Harrington was able to eventually get the script to Douglas through his people, the response was that he "felt it was not for him."

Harrington was thrilled when he heard word that Tony Curtis would be willing to take on the role, as he was suffering a career dip. But Curtis was vetoed by one of Universal's executives, who dismissed him as a has-been. "That bum. We wouldn't have him in a picture here in a million years. He's finished. Washed up. Forget it."

It wasn't just older women who had problems with staying relevant; many actors who'd been the big thing at one time, struggled to find work later in life. "One day Tony Curtis was a big star, and then overnight, for no apparent reason, he was consigned to the trash heap. My dreams for a quick launch of the picture were shattered," Harrington said.

Despite interest from NBC that it could be a television movie, ultimately the violence in the script was too much for television at that point, and *The Guests* was never made. Instead, Harrington turned his attention to a number of films that followed the formula set out by *Baby Jane*; casting older actresses in films that were marked by their bloodiness or Grand Guignol elements, although he preferred to consider them beyond the realm of the genre.

"I have yet to make a horror film," he said in 1977. "I would like to make one. Horror films are usually of a more fantastic genre, in the tradition of Frankenstein and Dracula. Those, to me, are true horror films. What I have made are really psychological mystery stories. Certainly I'm not unaware of the debt that *Games* owes to *Diabolique*. There are elements of horror in those films; I just wouldn't call them horror films."

14. "It's going to be a very special party. You have to be under sixty to get in..."

As audiences were becoming increasingly tired of infamous gimmicks, William Castle knew he needed a miracle to boost his flagging film output. That miracle would be Roman Polanski's *Rosemary's Baby*, one of the seminal films of the sixties; a horror that spoke to the counterculture generation, inspired a wave of burgeoning filmmakers, and ensured that the seemingly harmless older woman was depicted as a threat to new world order.

Ira Levin's novel *Rosemary's Baby*, published to great acclaim in 1967, depicted a young woman, Rosemary, who is sacrificed to the devil for her fertility, symbolizing the confusion women felt over their traditional roles in marriage and as housewives. Pregnancy is already something out of a horror film – a woman is taken over by a parasite, leaving her without control of the changes it makes to her body and her emotional state in the lead-up to the painful and bloody birth.

In *Rosemary's Baby*, the horror of pregnancy was pushed even further, as Rosemary's ripe body is used by a coven of witches as a vessel for carrying the devil's child. They are seemingly harmless old women who bake cakes and cultivate herbs, are dressed in garish shirts and slacks, blighted by their own sagging bodies and infertility. The concept of the witch is one of the oldest tropes in how women of a certain age are considered. They are dismissed for no longer being in possession of youthful beauty and the equipment to be able carry out one of women's primary functions, to procreate. As women get older they begin to feel invisible, and it's this invisibility from society that gives the witch their power to operate in plain sight.

"The film derives much of its strength from its portrayal of witches, for the witches are not bizarrely mystical creatures, but merely the kind of slightly strange people that we all encounter in our everyday lives," wrote film critic Charles Derry in *Dark Dreams*. "Polanski's witches are all fussy and friendly; it is precisely this ingratiating quality that makes them so horrific."

The story also seemed to be a parable of the real-life suspicions young people felt about the older generation at the time of the film's release, reinforced by the huge number of drafted young men who were being killed in the Vietnam War. In 1967, there was a sense that the world was on fire as students burnt their draft cards as a protest against war, and strikes erupted in cities like Paris and New York. The concept of God had been rejected in favor of political agendas or cultish ideals. Set at the time of the impending visit to New York of Pope Paul VI, the first papal visit to the United States, the novel and film also reflected the cynicism towards religion, reflected by the copy of *Time* magazine in Doctor Saperstein's Park Avenue waiting room, with the provocative headline 'Is God Dead?'

The horror of Satanism and witches was a tradition dating back to the Puritans of east coast America. It was a staple of American literature, such as Nathanial Hawthorne's *House of Seven Gables*, Washington Irving's *The Legend of Sleepy Hollow*, and the stories of Edgar Allen Poe, like *The Raven*, and Henry James' *Turn of the Screw*.

In the late fifties there was a resurgence of the occult and an interest in witchcraft as it offered an explanation to rising social and political problems. The threat of witches was representative of male anxieties around feminism and women's increasing demand for equal rights and control over their own bodies. The witches in *Rosemary's Baby* are geriatric, their bodies are decaying – they aren't the youthful romantic idea of the good witch, with her beauty, such as Kim Novak in *Bell, Book and Candle* (1958). In the television series *Bewitched*, first airing on television in 1964, Samantha is a beautiful housewife who uses her witch powers for good, while her mother, played by Agnes Moorehead, is the older, traditional witch, who uses her powers for mischief.

Rosemary's Baby depicted the darkness that lay under the gleaming surface of 1960s modernism, where witches were more terrifying because of their very ordinariness, and that a hip young couple could easily fall victim to them. Levin's novel first appears to be a typical New York domestic drama; it took turn after turn to reach its disturbing, nightmarish ending.

"Before Ira Levin, horror always happened somewhere else. Regular ordinary people were forced to pack their luggage and kennel their dogs and had to leave their homes and schlep seemingly forever to Transylvania, to Manderlay, to the House of Usher, or Hill House, or the Bates Motel," wrote Chuck Palanhiuk in his introduction to the 2011 reprint of the novel. "Such a stroke of genius: to haul all of the creaking, clanking monster movie clichés into the midst of sophisticated smart-alecky New Yorkers."

Before the book had even been released, the film rights were in discussion. When William Castle was sent the galley proofs ahead of publication, he initially dismissed the idea to option it, as he felt "the bottom has fallen out of the horror films." But as soon as he finished reading it, he was desperate to snap it up, particularly after hearing that Alfred Hitchcock had also been shown an early copy. Castle didn't have the $2 million requested for the rights, but he offered a counter deal of £100,000 in cash, an additional £50,000 if the book became a bestseller and 5 percent of the net profits.

It was exactly the type of material that Paramount Pictures' dynamic new studio head, Robert Evans, was after. He'd been brought in by industrialist Charles Bluhdorn, whose company Gulf and Western had recently acquired Paramount, to help the studio tap into the youth market. During his tenure he had already produced two hits for the studio, *Barefoot in the Park* (1967) and *The Odd Couple* (1968), but was looking for a special property to make his name.

"Bill Castle was a producer of B-films, and a very good one, but the quality of his films was not the quality I wanted to make," said Evans in an interview on the making of *Rosemary's Baby*. "At the time of the film I'd become head of the studio, and half his age. So he resented me a bit to begin with, and I don't blame him. I read his submission of *Rosemary's Baby*, and I loved it.... it wasn't a horror film, but it was. It was too good for Bill Castle."

When Evans suggested to Castle that he still produce it, but that they bring in Roman Polanski as director, Castle was reluctant to accept the offer. He had bought the rights because he wanted to direct, but begrudgingly agreed to a meeting. Polanski's vision and passion for the story, promising he wouldn't change anything in the book, impressed Castle and he agreed with Evans that the hot young director in the "Carnaby Street fashion of the time" was the only one who should direct it.

While Ira Levin described Rosemary as having a milk-fed, red-haired look, when it came to casting, Polanski envisioned blonde, innocent-looking Tuesday Weld, but Castle was convinced the part was written for Mia Farrow.

Like Polanski, Mia Farrow represented new Hollywood, and was very much a child of the hippie counterculture, with her interest in spiritualism and bohemianism. Her marriage to the much older Frank Sinatra reflected the film's theme of youth versus age; he was a father-figure to her, still stuck very much in the traditions of the previous generation.

The elderly witches' coven, led by Minnie and Roman Castevet, was a vital thread to the story, and just as "Hag Horror" had cast older, established stars, the film-makers sought names that would bring with them breadth of experience. Polanski suggested the famous theater duo Lynn Fontanne and Alfred Lunt to play the couple, but ultimately veteran actor Sidney Blackmer, known for his multiple portrayals of Theodore Roosevelt, was cast as Roman, and Ruth Gordon as Minnie Castevet.

As well as acting on stage and as a supporting actress on screen, Ruth Gordon and husband Garson Kanin were a successful writing team who scripted the Katharine Hepburn and Spencer Tracy films *Adam's Rib* and *Pat and Mike*. The 1953 film *The Actress*, starring Jean Simmons, was based on Gordon's autobiographical play about a girl growing up in Massachusetts in the 1910s, who persuades her father to let her go to New York to make it as an actress.

Gordon was too slight for Levin's description of Minnie as "a big woman" yet she played the role as a typically birdlike New Yorker of a certain age. While Gordon was often considered eccentric, she was not the sweet old lady that was expected of her.

She could be acerbic and difficult. It was this contrast between appearance and personality that suited the character, as Minnie plays the older witch who preys on younger women by disarming them with her seemingly harmless chatter.

Minnie Castevet looks comical in her garish clothing, but in the shadows she's very much a monster. Rosemary and Guy hear her before they meet her; her voice as she berates her husband echoes through the walls of the Bramton building. Older women are harpies; they stick their noses into the business of young women, and like Tallulah Bankhead in *Die! Die! My Darling!*, they trap them and enable their exploitation.

As Michael Newton wrote in his study of *Rosemary's Baby*: "Around this time feminists were busy reinventing the sexist image of the crone and hag, returning her to grandmotherly wisdom. Again, the film hardly touches on that: Minnie is a powerful and indomitable figure, but here women follow, men lead, husbands barter and women are raped."

In the novel, Minnie is described as "wrapped in light blue, with snow-white dabs of gloves, purse, shoes, and hat. Nurse-like she supported her husband's forearm. He was dazzling, in an every-colour seersucker jacket, red slacks, a pink bow tie, and a grey fedora with a pink band. He was seventy-five or older; she was sixty-eight or nine. They came closer with expressions of young alertness, with friendly quizzical smiles."

Costume designer Anthea Sylbert followed the novel by creating eccentric costumes for the Castevets as a way of disarming young women like Rosemary, and her predecessor, Terry, who falls to her death from the apartment block. The costumes help reinforce the generation gap, with Rosemary's Vidal Sassoon haircut and her mini-dresses and Mary-Jane shoes representing hip youthfulness, in contrast to Minnie's garish outfits giving her the appearance of a gossipy but wise grandmother. In the final scenes, when Rosemary drops her knife onto the Castevets' floor, after confronting the coven who have taken her baby, Minnie picks up the knife and polishes the mark it's left. It's a moment similar to Bette Davis's in *The Nanny* when she picks up the shoes as Pamela is dying; house-proud and fussy, yet uncaring about the plight of young women.

At Roman and Minnie's New Year's party, Rosemary and Guy are the only young faces amongst the group of elderly eccentrics. Tired of being surrounded by the old, Rosemary hosts a party where "you have to be under sixty to get in." Despite imposing their authority on the young, the witches are also subversive, dishing out their hallucinogens, which fits with the youth appeal of the LSD experience, all the rage in the mid-sixties.

Minnie is called "the old bat" by Guy, and Levin offered a description of Rosemary's delirious state, where she sees the naked women of the coven, "elderly, the women grotesque and slack-breasted." Minnie and her coven are attracted to unpleasant tastes and smells, they are wrinkled and repellent when naked (with Ruth Gordon and Patsy Kelly in body-suits to give the impression of nudity). Rather than showing the glow of an expectant mother, Rosemary withers when pregnant, as if she is slowly being destroyed by what's been put inside her by the elderly witches.

There is a pervading theme of celebrity within *Rosemary's Baby*, in the suggestion it has replaced God as the entity of worship, made clear as Guy is willing to sacrifice his wife to the devil because he's been promised great success as an actor. Rosemary boasts that Guy has been "in *Luther* and *Nobody Loves an Alba-*

tross and a lot of television plays and television commercials," and he's told by the concierge that the Bramford is "very popular with actors."

In the novel, when Rosemary chats with 'the girl before her', Terry Gionoffrio, in the building's basement laundry, Terry tells Rosemary she looks like the actress Piper Laurie, who Guy supposedly dated before he and Rosemary married. Rosemary's "It's alive" comment at the end of her party with her friends references James Whale's *Frankenstein* (1931). In another detail that crosses into real life, New York's Dakota building stood in for the fictional Bramford. The desirably gothic Dakota had strong links to classic Hollywood - Boris Karloff grew orchids on its rooftop, Lauren Bacall and Jason Robards lived in one of the apartments, and it was later where John Lennon would be shot to death by an obsessed fan.

Polanski's perfectionism and uncompromising vision led to delays to the shooting schedule, causing concern for Castle and Evans. It was not only costing money, but jeopardizing Mia's position in the film. Mia was due to begin work on Sinatra's next film *The Detectives*, and with the delays, he gave her an ultimatum – that either she quit *Rosemary's Baby* immediately, or their relationship was over. When she refused to quit, Sinatra couriered divorce papers to the Los Angeles set. The emotional distress she felt was used to effect when filming the final scenes, when Rosemary sees her devil baby for the first time and confronts the elderly coven with a knife.

Rosemary's Baby was a sensation on its release, becoming a box-office smash in the summer of 1968 at a time when America was reeling from the assassinations of Martin Luther King Junior and Senator Robert Kennedy. It delivered the message that evil is lurking in society, in some of the most mundane spaces – the doctor's office, or in an apartment belonging to a seemingly safe elderly couple.

The film provoked such a strong reaction from the public that William Castle was sent masses of hate mail and death threats, calling him a Satan worshiper and a "Purveyor of Evil." Shortly after the film was released he was hospitalized with serious uremic poisoning. There was further tragedy when the film's composer, Krzysztof Komeda, fell into a coma and died from a hematoma of the brain following a freak accident. Castle was convinced that real-life witches had cast their spell, after all the rituals and chants that had taken place during filming. Sidney Blackmer even commented: "No good will come of all this 'Hail Satan' business." Tragic events culminated with the murder of Polanski's pregnant wife Sharon Tate and three friends by the Manson Family in the summer of 1969. Whether or not this narrative from Castle was initially purely speculative to bring some publicity to the film, it was the first in a line of supposedly "cursed" horror films.

While 1967's *Bonnie and Clyde* is considered the start of a new wave of films that appealed to hip young audiences with its anti-authoritarian stance, *Rosemary's Baby* was a further symbolic shift away from censorship and from the traditional classic Hollywood narrative. The film's huge success tied in with a trend at the time for occult films. As well as Joan Fontaine's *The Witches*, *The Eye of the Devil* (1966) starred Deborah Kerr as a wealthy woman in danger from a mysterious and beautiful witch, played by Sharon Tate in her first role.

Rosemary's Baby was also reflective of the next generation of directors (Steven Spielberg, Brian de Palma, Martin Scorsese, Francis Ford Coppola and William Friedkin) who revisited popular genres such as the horror, the western and the gangster flick, and shook up their traditions by pushing the boundaries of violence and sex.

On its release in 1973, William Friedkin's *The Exorcist* would further terrify audiences as it depicted the threat of Satan in society, as a response to the urban decay, poverty and celebrity worship of modern life. *The Exorcist* tells the story of Regan Mac-Neil, a girl on the cusp of adolescence, whose body is possessed by a demon, Pazuzu, but on a further level, it can be seen as a representation of menstruation and the changes in girls as they approach womanhood. This theme is also explored in Brian de Palma's *Carrie* (1976), where a teenage girl's first period at the start of the film corresponds with her burgeoning telekinetic abilities and the unleashing of her monstrous nature.

After Regan's possession, the sweet young girl becomes a grotesque figure, spewing green vomit, rotating her head full circle, masturbating with a crucifix, and cursing with the voice of a vengeful older woman. Not only is it an allegory to the transformation of a girl approaching womanhood, and the dangers of her growing sexuality, but further reinforces the common belief that women at certain times of the month are truly possessed.

Women who are menstruating have long been seen as dangerous, with Pliny the Elder, in his writings, claiming that a woman on her period would destroy entire fields of crops, cause bees to leave their hives and insects to drop to the ground. Further, with the transformative nature of menstruation, and its connection to the lunar cycle, the myth of the werewolf could be considered symbolic of a woman on her period, in all her ferocious, dangerous, monstrous glory.

As she transitions into a teenager, Regan becomes a terrifying entity – something that many parents can attest to, and who would likely sympathize with Chris's cry of despair that the "thing upstairs is not my daughter!" As William Blatty described in his novel on which the film is based, Regan shows a sudden behavioral change. "Insomnia. Quarrelsome. Fits of temper. Kicked things. Threw things. Screamed. Wouldn't eat. In addition, her energy seemed abnormal. She was constantly moving, touching, turning; tapping; running and jumping about. Doing poorly with schoolwork...Eccentric attention-getting tactics."

Female sexual maturity has been considered so sinful, that there is a belief the devil can take hold within her once her period arrives. "In a culture where we're trained to protect children and loathe women, the border zone between the two states is the subject of intense superstition and terror," writes Jude Doyle in *Dead Blondes and Bad Mothers*. "Every woman is a girl who fell from grace, a monster who once was human." It's the mark of her fertility and of her sexuality, unleashed on her first period, after which the girl can now become a mother, and then, a monster.

The theme of *The Exorcist* could also be read as a statement on the mental deterioration of girls and women who come from a broken home, where they lack the influence of a stable man in their life, again allowing the devil to take root. Twelve-year-old Regan (Linda Blair) is the daughter of a single mother and well-known movie star, Chris MacNeil (Ellen Burstyn), who is shown lambasting her ex-husband over the telephone. From *Psycho* to *Strait-Jacket* and *Carrie*, the single mother is monstrous for refusing to take her proper place in patriarchal society, and prioritizing career, or rejecting the stability of having a man in her life. In the novel, the demon taunts Chris with the words "it is you who have done it! Yes, you with your career before anything, your career before your husband, before her..."

Older women also appear throughout *The Exorcist*. In the opening scenes set in northern Iraq, Father Merrin (Max von Sydow) is supervising an archeological dig, when he is struck by the appearance of haunting older women dressed in black. These post-menopausal women, wrinkled and toothless, are like the stereotypical witch figures and create a sense of foreboding. In Washington DC, Father Damien, played by Jason Miller, is tormented by his elderly mother who he reluctantly places in an asylum, populated by decaying old women, suffering at various stages of Alzheimer's. When his mother dies, he dreams that he sees her by a subway station, but he can't reach her across the busy road. The devil's face flashes on the screen; the face of evil.

While it's often thought that the demon in Regan is male, the voice is that of an older woman, Mercedes McCambridge, an Academy Award-winning actress for *All the King's Men* (1949), a nominee for *Giant*, and memorably, Joan Crawford's villainous foe in the camp western *Johnny Guitar*. William Friedkin envisioned the voice of the devil to be a neutral voice that was both male and female, and the person who came to his mind was Mercedes McCambridge. Her distinctive voice led Orson Welles to name her as "the world's greatest living radio actress."

In a BBC documentary, *The Fear of God: Years of the Exorcist*, McCambridge described how she used her voice to terrifying effect. "It wasn't hard for me to imagine the rage...You utilize everything. Don't analyze, utilize. And I utilized the thickness, all of that stuff, for the voice of Lucifer."

To create the wheezing, guttural sounds, she swallowed raw eggs, smoked cigarettes constantly, and, as Friedkin recounted, she told him he needed to "give me some booze which is going to make me nuts and I'm getting off the wagon to do this, so I want my priest around to counsel me."

Just as *Rosemary's Baby* played with the cult of celebrity, *The Exorcist* was infused with notions of fame; a horror theme that had been played with since *Sunset Boulevard* and *What Ever Happened to Baby Jane?* Regan's mother, Chris, is a red-haired superstar actress based on Shirley MacLaine, who has worked on a film with Edward G. Robinson, and has traveled around the world making movies. In the novel she's referred to as America's Sweetheart; invited to the White House, and in demand from "cabdrivers; poets; professors; kings. What was it they liked about her? Life?" She's divorced from her husband Howard, because he couldn't handle being second to his famous wife. She'd had a son, Jamie, when she was a chorus girl on Broadway, but he died at the age of three, leaving her with a deep sense of loss.

The film Chris is making, as recounted in the novel, is a musical comedy remake of *Mr. Smith Goes to Washington*, with a subplot dealing with a campus insurrection, and it's while filming the student protests on campus that Chris first meets Father Karris. The student protest scene reflects the sense of social disorder, and of young people rising up against the older generations, but it's a scene that Chris thinks is "dumb." Chris plays a psychology teacher who sides with the rebels, a scene which doesn't make sense to Chris. "But how come? she now wondered. Generation gap? That's a crock; I'm thirty-two. It's just stupid, that's all…!"

When Chris holds a party at her Georgetown home with her friends who come from the entertainment world, Regan interrupts the gathering by urinating on the carpet and telling one of the guests that he'll die. In the novel, the detective wishes to go to the cinema with Karras as he often gets free tickets, and in the final moments, after Karras's death, he asks Father Dyer to go with him instead, telling him he's reminded of the ending of *Casablanca* – "I think this is the beginning of a beautiful friendship."

The Exorcist was the top-grossing horror movie from 1973 to 2017. It proved to be so influential that the Catholic Church noted a boom in requests for exorcisms to be performed on loved ones who were showing signs of demonic possession. As Stephen King wrote in *Danse Macabre,* the film was about "explosive social change, a finely honed focusing point for that entire youth explosion that took place in the late sixties and early seventies. It was a movie for all those parents who felt, in a kind of agony and terror, that they were losing their children and could not understand why or how it was happening."

Rosemary's Baby and *The Exorcist* both used themes of the occult to explain the evil that was pervading society, reflected in a sense of unrest. In *The Exorcist* the threat was not only the devil, but was womanhood itself, and the dangers presented by working mothers who neglect their home. In *Rosemary's Baby,* the seemingly innocuous older woman, eccentric and beyond sexuality, poses a threat to a generation of young people, who they fail to understand. They also both delved into the cult of celebrity, in a much darker, twisted way than had ever been seen before.

15. "Imagine – too old at 30."

At a press conference at the St. Regis Hotel, New York, in March 1967, Judy Garland appeared alongside author Jacqueline Susann to announce her involvement in 20th Century-Fox's screen adaptation of Susann's smash-hit novel *Valley of the Dolls*.

For three weeks' work, Judy was to receive $75,000 to play aging Broadway star Helen Lawson, whom Susann described as "sad and beautiful and wonderful. Her loneliness that she has is very real. She doesn't realize she brought her loneliness on herself. She doesn't realize that no man could relate to her as a woman anymore because the power of a Helen Lawson is frightening to a man."

As Garland told the press: "Let's face it: the role calls for an old pro over 40. That's for me. It's for sure I am no longer Dorothy in *The Wizard of Oz.*"

Valley of the Dolls may not be a horror film, yet it has elements that align it with the trend for "Hagsploitation." Helen Lawson is the grande dame who commands every stage she's on. Off-stage, she knocks back the booze, is desperate for a man in her life, and punishes young starlets when their talent threatens to usurp her. She is also ridiculed and humiliated in a showdown between a younger woman, which exposes her insecurities around her looks. In one of the most famously camp moments in the film, Neely confronts Helen in the bathroom of a nightclub, and after their conversations descends into a full-blown argument, she grabs hold of Helen's wig to reveal her grey, thinning hair, and attempts to flush the wig down the toilet.

Helen may be foul-mouthed and coarse, but the greatest monster of the story is Neely, a hapless vaudeville hoofer who is elevated to Hollywood star, and the effects of fame turn her into a pill-popping harridan. As she destroys her career and pushes everyone close to her away, she ends up rattling around her mansion, blaming others for her failures. Like Faye Dunaway's turn as a monstrous version of Joan Crawford in *Mommie Dearest*, *Valley of the Dolls* pushed the boundaries of trashy camp in its attempt to show the dark side of Hollywood.

Alongside *Rosemary's Baby*, Susann's *Valley of the Dolls* was one of the most sensational novels of the sixties. Both of these best-sellers provoked controversy and dripped with celebrity, and from their different perspectives, explored the different lengths people would go to for fame. Susann's story told of three women working in show business in New York and Hollywood, and the dangerous pill addictions they succumbed to as a way of coping with the disappointments and struggles in reaching the top.

When it was published in February 1966, *Valley of the Dolls* scandalized its way to number one on *The New York Times* Best Seller list, where it stayed for twenty-eight weeks. Sales were driven by its addictive and juicy storylines of adultery, pre-marital sex, lesbian affairs, pill-popping, and abortion, and the promotion of it as a roman à clef. Rumors swirled as to who the characters were based on. Anne, with her New England pedigree, was thought to be Grace Kelly, the voluptuous, tragic Jennifer was assumed to be Marilyn Monroe, and Helen Lawson was Ethel Merman, the big-voiced stage star who was once Susann's friend, before they had a falling out. "We didn't speak before the book came out. Let's just say that now we're not speaking louder," said Susann.

Neely O' Hara, with her background in vaudeville, her huge voice that takes her to Hollywood, and her time spent recovering from addiction in a sanatorium, was clearly Judy Garland. When one reporter at the press conference asked Garland about pill addiction in Hollywood, pertaining to her own well-documented struggles with pharmaceuticals, she snapped back, to much laughter: "I find it prevalent among newspaper people." She also pointed out on an episode of *What's My Line?* that her character was "the only one in the book who doesn't take pills!"

The novel explored the perils of aging, the constant worries that when a woman sees those first wrinkles and slight changes to her body, she'll soon be over the hill. Young ingénue Neely watches in awe as Helen Lawson takes to the stage with her "bright and merry" smile, yet her figure "was beginning to show signs of middle age - the thickness through the waist, the slight spread in the hips."

Anne similarly observes of Helen that she was "gazing at the cruel distortion of a monument. Age settled with more grace on ordinary people, but for celebrities - women stars in particular - age became a hatchet that vandalized a work of art. Helen's figure had always been her biggest asset."

Jennifer, having found success in risqué European films, is told she must have a facelift to succeed in Hollywood. "But I'm still not exactly a hag. I look pretty good for thirty-seven," she argues. But it's pointed out to her that she has the slackness under the jaw "that tells the difference between the twenties and the thirties." When Anne reunites with Jennifer, she's amazed to find that she's forty, because to her, forty equates to old age. "She recalled how she had thought Helen Lawson old at forty, and her own mother - dried out at forty-two. But

Jennifer still had the incredible figure and the firm skin. She looked twenty-five."

By the 1970s Susann's novel had been registered in *The Guinness Book of World Records* as the best-selling novel of all time, with 30 million copies sold. Susann declared that on the back of its success, she'd be remembered as "the voice of the 60s" alongside Andy Warhol and the Beatles. With the book's monumental success, Hollywood came calling, and 20th Century-Fox snapped up the rights to adapt it for the screen. When it hit cinemas in 1968, it was ridiculed for the over-the-top performances and high-camp drama, but it earned a reputation for being enjoyably bad, and soon became a cult classic.

Born in Philadelphia in 1918, from a young age Jacqueline Susann was obsessed with the concept of stardom and the glamor of movie stars and pin-ups. At the age of seventeen she entered a beauty contest and won a Warner Brothers screen test in New York. The test didn't go as well as expected, and she moved into Kenmore Hall, a female boarding house in New York, where she met a vaudeville actress, Elfie, believed to have been the template for Neely. She married press agent Irving Mansfield in 1939, hoping that the marriage would help bring her stardom. As he rose up the ranks, from promoting CBS's Rudy Vallee show and into television, Susann won a part in the 1945 Carole Landis film *A Lady Says Yes*, but further success eluded her.

After having received a breast cancer diagnosis in 1962, and coupled with an autistic son being placed in a mental hospital, she vowed she was going to write a blockbuster novel, which would be her lasting legacy. *Valley of the Dolls* was the follow up to her first novel, *Every Night, Josephine!*, about her pet poodle, and which had been a modest success on its publication in 1963.

Despite the guessing games as to who the characters really were, Anne Welles was based on her friend and one time writing partner Bea Cole, and she was inspired by tragic former co-star Carole Landis in shaping Jennifer. Landis was a forties pin-up nicknamed "the blonde bomber" and "the chest," who committed suicide in 1948 from a Seconal overdose, reportedly over her heartbreak from a break-up with Rex Harrison.

When 20th Century-Fox bought the film rights, Susann was asked for her wish-list of actors to fill the roles. She thought of Raquel Welsh or Tina Louise for Jennifer, but was told Louise was too old. "Imagine, too old at 30," said Susann. She envisioned Grace Kelly as Anne, "if she'd lose 10 to 15 pounds," Tuesday Weld or Barbra Streisand as Neely, and Bette Davis as Helen Lawson.

Before being reduced to a nagging voice over the telephone, the role of Jennifer's overbearing mother had initially been a larger part, with a list of stars including Joan Blondell, Agnes Moorehead, Maureen O'Sullivan, Shelley Winters, Ann Sothern and Ruth Roman all considered as potentials.

Ann Sothern had also written to producer David Weisbart to put herself forward for Helen. "Would you possibly consider my doing a test for the musical comedy star in *Valley of the Dolls*? I like that bitch dame and I did start in musical comedy."

Sheilah Graham in November 1966 reported that Bette Davis was up for the role of Helen, and it was a part she very much coveted as a means of escaping the horrors she felt she was being typecast in. She admired Helen Lawson's toughness, and despite her fondness for booze, she was the consummate professional, like Davis herself. To help her win the role, she courted Susann, and they posed for photos at Bette's rented Malibu beach house as if they were old friends. There were also rumors in December of that year that the part had been offered to Rita Hayworth, and then Lucille Ball, who had stipulated the role be padded out to give it more importance.

With the casting decisions turning into an epic battle, Davis lost out, and instead traveled to the UK for *The Anniversary*. Stars like Debbie Reynolds and Shirley MacLaine were all considered for Neely at one point, but ultimately Patty Duke was cast, with *Peyton Place*'s refined Barbara Parkins as Anne, up-and-coming star Sharon Tate as Jennifer, and Lee Grant as Tony Polar's controlling older sister. Grant had been blacklisted by Hollywood in the 1950s by the House Un-American Activities Committee, just after winning a Best Supporting Actress nomination for her film debut, *Detective Story*, in 1951. She had been making steady progress in the sixties in her return to film and television, beginning with the TV series *Peyton Place*, and admitted she took the part in *Dolls* for the money.

In her autobiography Grant wrote that at forty-two she was aware that in the eyes of Hollywood, she was "no longer young enough or pretty enough for my next job, I was hungry to act, hungry to work, as hungry as a rabid dog….By Hollywood standards, I was already over the hill."

To play the first lady of Broadway, Helen Lawson, producers signed up Judy Garland, considered a scoop in terms of publicity. With Neely as a thinly-disguised younger version of the *A Star is Born* actress, she would ultimately be playing against herself.

Patty Duke, a Best Supporting Actress Oscar-winner at fifteen for *The Miracle Worker* (1962), would have had a sense of affinity with Judy. Coming from a troubled home, she had been exploited by her guardians John and Ethel Ross as they managed her career as a child star. They forced her name to be changed from Anna

Marie, kept her isolated from other children, strictly regulated her weight and placed her on diet pills and alcohol from a young age. To top it off, she then discovered those guardians had taken $1 million of her earnings. She also suffered extreme anxiety, mood swings, and suicide attempts, which was diagnosed years later as bipolar disorder.

Judy Garland was born Frances Gumm to a vaudeville family, making her stage debut at the age of two, when she toddled onto the stage to perform with her two older sisters. She was an awkward child and teenager, feeling lonely and hungry for affection. Judy and her two sisters were signed with the Meglin Kiddies, a Los Angeles agency that booked child acts. She was called "Baby" by her family, and, like Baby Jane Hudson, was expected to act the precocious child on stage.

"I was always lonesome," she later said. "The only time I felt accepted or wanted was when I was onstage performing. I guess the stage was my only friend, the only place where I could feel comfortable. It was the one place where I felt equal and safe."

After changing their name to the Garland sisters, and Judy changing hers to get rid of the nickname "Baby," she was spotted performing at Lake Tahoe at the Cal-Neva Lodge by Hollywood agent Al Rosen. He showcased the girl with the powerful voice to the major studios, and while they were impressed by her singing, they didn't know what they could do with a chubby and awkward twelve-year-old.

When Louis B Mayer met with her, he thought she seemed like the girl next door, the kid sister who would appeal to the American family, and signed her to a contract at MGM. Mayer held a huge influence over her life, including making her feel like she wasn't quite good enough the way she was. He referred to her as "my little hunchback," and placed her on a never-ending diet of chicken soup to keep down her weight, which deprived her of enjoying the teenage staples of burgers and malted milkshakes. She was also fed a constant supply of uppers to suppress her appetite and keep her alert while performing, and downers to allow her to sleep. For the seventeen years she was signed to MGM her life was controlled by the studio, from when she slept and ate, to who she could date.

Her first film part was in *Broadway Melody of 1938*, and she formed a successful team with her friend Mickey Rooney, where their on-screen chemistry in *Babes in Arms, Strike Up the Band, Babes on Broadway*, and *Girl Crazy* rocketed them to stardom as teen idols. When Fox refused to lend Shirley Temple to MGM for *The Wizard of Oz*, Judy was given the role, and she was instructed to slim down to play the dustbowl heroine who finds wonder in the Emerald City. Her teeth were capped, her hair dyed, and she was cinched into a girdle to make her image fit the envisioned role. She married Vincente Minnelli, her director on the hit musical *Meet Me in St. Louis*, in 1945, and her daughter, Liza, was born in March 1946, but as the marriage fell apart, she amped up her pill taking, and at the age of twenty-five she suffered a nervous breakdown and was sent to a private sanatorium to recover.

With hospital bills and back taxes to pay, she returned to work before she was ready, but she was sacked from *The Barkleys of Broadway*, opposite Fred Astaire, because of her unreliability in arriving on set, and instead was replaced by Ginger Rogers. She was also fired from *Annie Get Your Gun* and *Royal Wedding* for similar erratic behavior. In June 1950, despite having made millions for the studio in her sixteen years there, she was let go from MGM without compensation. The studio also made it public knowledge that she was so devastated that she tried to kill herself by cutting her throat with a drinking glass.

Her next husband Sidney Luft also served as her manager, helping her navigate the next chapter of her career. She went to London to perform her hits at the Palladium in April 1951, where memories of Judy helping the nation find happiness during the Blitz were seared into public consciousness. She brought the show to the Palace Theatre in New York City for nineteen weeks of performances that broke all previous records at the venue. The packed audience lapped up her songs and her stories which conveyed her vulnerability, her determination, her cheerfulness in the face of adversity, and that strong voice that quivered with emotion.

To help manage her debt, Luft encouraged Judy to return to Hollywood for a remake of *A Star is Born*. As the young singer who becomes a Hollywood sensation, the role seemed almost autobiographical. They shared the same humble beginnings, the clumsy-sounding birth names, with her character Esther Blodgett renamed Vicki Lester by the studio, and were both sculpted and shaped, and pushed and pulled, into becoming a huge star. She also felt a connection to Norman Maine, the star who suffers a fall from grace as he struggles with alcoholism. Judy couldn't shake her addiction to pills, washed down with drink, and, like Norman, it caused her Hollywood career to implode.

Her last film for MGM, *Summer Stock*, had been a hit, but she hadn't performed on stage for two years, and was firmly considered washed up. As *A Star is Born* reached the crescendo when Norman struggles to find his way back from the depth of his addiction, Vicki Lester's impassioned words must have seemed as if she was talking about herself. "You don't know what it's like to watch somebody you love just crumble away bit by bit and day by day in front of your eyes and stand there helpless. Love isn't enough."

In a report on production in *Time*, they wrote of Garland as "a thirty-two-year-old has-been as infamous for temperament as she is famous for talent…but after Judy had done her worst in the dressing room, she did her best in front of the camera, with the result that she gives what is just about the greatest one-woman show in modern movie history."

Her performance was hailed as a "stunning comeback," and she was nominated for an Oscar for best actress at the 1955 Academy Awards. She had just given birth to her son Joey, but such was the strength of belief that she'd win, a television crew gathered at the hospital to film her reaction. When Grace Kelly was announced as the winner for *The Country Girl*, the camera crew packed up their equipment and Garland's promised comeback fizzled out.

She didn't make a return to Hollywood until seven years later in *Judgment in Nuremberg* in 1961, for which was nominated for a Best Supporting Actress Oscar, and followed it with two other films, *A Child Is Waiting* and *I Could Go On Singing*, where she played a character very close to the bone. Jenny Bowman is an aging, boozy singer who is unhappy at having chosen her career over her family, and it was advertised with the slogan: "It's Judy! Lighting up the Lonely Stage."

After separating from Luft, she became effectively homeless, flitting between friends' houses and hotel rooms. She had problems with her liver and kidneys, a colon obstruction, and lack of coordination due to the pills, which made her unsteady, but still, she pushed on with a hugely demanding schedule. Garland had a loyal following of devoted fans who felt an affinity in how she rose above her troubles, from the addictions, the divorces, suicide attempts and money problems.

In an interview in the *New York World Journal Tribune* by journalist John Gruen, Garland lamented about how she'd just lost her Beverly Hills mansion due to bankruptcy, but she put on a brace face. "I never really liked it. It looks like a Swanson reject." She also revealed the loneliness she felt. "If I'm such a legend then why am I so lonely? If I'm such a legend, then why do I sit at home for hours staring at the damned telephone, hoping it's out of order, even calling the operator asking her if she's sure it's not out of order?"

She was given her own short-lived talk show, *The Judy Garland Show*, which premiered in September 1963, and after its cancellation, she was booked onto a tour of Australia and the Far East. Every step of her career was hailed as a comeback, including a spectacular London charity event, *Night of a Thousand Stars*, where she came on stage after the Beatles and received a standing ovation after singing *Over the Rainbow*.

"During the bad days I'm sure I would have perished without those wonderful audiences. Without that and a sense of humor, I would have died," she once said. "I think there's something peculiar about me that I haven't died. It doesn't make sense but I refuse to die."

In the spring of 1967, Judy arrived in New York and stayed at the St. Regis, where the press conference was held to announce her participation in *Valley of the Dolls*. She had doubts about the part from the beginning, particularly as she found the script objectionable in places, and she was also reeling from the collapse of her fourth marriage to promoter Mark Herron.

Her first day on production was March 27, 1967, when she took part in wardrobe tests for the costumes designed by Travilla, and where she seemed frail and unsteady. She also recorded her musical number for the film, *I'll Plant My Own Tree*, which she was not enamored with. Filming began in mid-March, and Judy's first scene was the moment when Anne, played by Parkins, delivers contracts to Helen Lawson's dressing room. Parkins was a television actress, used to getting the lines right in the first take due to the schedule, whereas Judy had been raised in film, which had a reputation for being more forgiving in allowing for multiple takes. Over the next few weeks, Garland was kept waiting in her dressing room for hours at a time, before the director, Mark Robson would call for her. She began to feel more and more insecure about her performance, and as she continually flubbed her lines, production fell behind schedule.

On April 27, the studio boss, Richard Zanuck, came to her dressing room to tell her that she was fired, because "her acting ability had faded and she just wasn't getting it." Ten days had only resulted in a minute of usable footage of Garland, but she was so distraught, that according to Patty Duke, she destroyed her dressing room, including the pool table and cues. In the press, it was used as another example of her unreliability and train wreck life.

That same day the studio announced she had resigned due to personal reasons, but rumors swirled that either she was fired, or she had quit in moral objection to some of the bad language she was expected to utter. An *Associated Press* article claimed that "Judy Garland and 20th Century-Fox are unable to agree over the circumstances of her abrupt departure from the movie *Valley of the Dolls*." A spokesman said she withdrew "for personal reasons."

While Garland countered: "I have not withdrawn. How dare they say I've withdrawn? I was up at six this morning to go to work. I've done my work. It's a shocking thing. Why? That's what I want to know, why?"

As compensation, she received $37,500 for the work she had put into production, and Travilla gave her the costumes as a gift, including the shimmering paisley-pattern suit which would become a favorite for her stage shows. Garland later told the *Ladies' Home Journal* that it was "a terrible part. I played a dirty old lady…I didn't like the role. I thought I could do it, but I couldn't – I couldn't force myself to use that kind of language."

It would be the last film she would work on. In a tough spot, and unable to pay her New York hotel bills following disputes with Sidney Luft, she was offered a show at London's glittering nightspot *The Talk of The Town*. As depicted in the film *Judy*, while she received a rapturous reception for the opening and closing nights, she struggled with her health and her extreme pill addiction which prevented her from sleeping. She died just a few months later, at the age of forty-seven, on June 22, 1969, from an accidental barbiturate overdose, having been discovered in the bathroom of her London home by fourth husband Mickey Deans.

On the back of Garland's firing, Abe Greenburg of Hollywood *Citizen-News* reported in his *Voice of Hollywood* column that the request to find a new Helen Lawson "could result in as dramatic a bit of casting as movieland has seen since Bette Davis virtually came out of retirement to make the offbeat *Whatever Happened to Baby Jane?*"

Valley of the Dolls was a different entity to *Baby Jane*, yet during its publicity, it was a film that came up again and again as a comparison, in its depiction of the dark side of fame. As one Hollywood columnist noted: "After *Valley of the Dolls*, Patty Duke will become the next Bette Davis and Barbara Parkins the new Joan Crawford."

Bette Davis was approached once more, but she had scheduling conflicts with *The Anniversary*, and when Ginger Rogers was offered the role, she quickly turned them down. "I simply couldn't stand having my ears hear that kind of language coming out of my mouth and I don't think anyone else could either."

Two weeks later, red-haired Susan Hayward was brought in to replace Garland. Director Mark Robson personally called her to offer her the part, having worked together decades earlier on *My Foolish Heart*. Hayward was icy, competitive, bold, and ten years before, had been the star at 20th Century-Fox, ruling the studio with her earning power. She was known for her meaty, dramatic parts, and like Helen, she learnt she had to be tough to get to the top in such a competitive industry. "I had to slug my way up in a town called Hollywood, where people love to trample you to death."

Born Edythe Marrener in 1917 in Brooklyn, red-haired Hayward's modeling photos were spotted by David O Selznick, who was carrying out a wide search to cast Scarlett O'Hara in *Gone with the Wind*. After a short stint at Warner Brothers, she was signed to Paramount in 1939, but it wasn't until 1946 when producer Walter Wanger signed her to a seven-year contract that she really thrived. During this period she took on challenging roles that earned her Academy Award nominations, including as an alcoholic nightclub singer in *Smash-Up: The Story of a Woman* (1947), *My Foolish Heart* (1949), *With a Song in My Heart* (1952) and *I'll Cry Tomorrow* (1955). Despite these successes, she suffered from depression and anxiety, having gone through two divorces, and in 1955, it was reported that she attempted suicide with an overdose of sleeping pills. She took a break from the movie business, marrying attorney Floyd Eaton Chalkley in 1957 and moving to Florida, where she enjoyed being a country club wife. On her return to acting, she once again received plaudits, and finally an Academy Award win, by playing a death row inmate in *I Want to Live!* (1958). Despite the critical and commercial success, Hayward was by now in her forties, and her career began to wane. Her husband died in 1965 after falling ill in Rome, which was one reason why she decided to return to Hollywood for *Valley of the Dolls*. Hayward told the *Hollywood Reporter* on her first day on set: "It's great to be back at my home studio – as long as I know I can go home again."

Hayward had recently taken on another lusty older woman role in *Where Love Has Gone* (1964), which was similarly based on a hugely successful roman à clef, by Harold Robbins. The story was startlingly close to the real life case where Lana Turner's daughter, Cheryl, stabbed to death her mother's abusive boyfriend, the shady gangster Johnny Stompanato.

The film also starred Bette Davis as the family matriarch. Davis, who was in reality only nine years old than Hayward, was made to look like a society matron in a white wig, and no love was lost between Davis and her co-star, who were said to have come to bitter blows during filming.

It may have been laced with camp, over-the-top dialogue, but *Where Love Has Gone* had all the elements of a horror; a daughter with murderous impulses who wishes to destroy her own mother, and a harridan older woman who controls the family. Mothers in turn are so damaging that they cause the family unit to collapse and children to go off the rails. Hayward's character, Valerie Hayden, is a wealthy socialite and artist whose sexual appetite is blamed for the collapse of her marriage and the troubled behavior of her teenage daughter, Danielle.

Her alcoholic ex-husband tells her, "you're not a woman, you're a disease," and even when he tries to rape her and then effectively accuses her of being a slut, it is her behavior which is condemned. When Danielle is in juvenile detention for having stabbed to death her mother's lover, Valerie is told by Danielle's caseworker that she has no legal rights to her daughter. "You lost them the day you brought a man into your house in front of your daughter without the benefit of marriage." In turn, Valerie's promiscuous behavior and the problems in her marriage are blamed on Bette Davis, the domineering and emotionally-void mother who haunts Valerie's apartment with her regal portrait. Valerie rips and tears at it as if she's murdering her own mother, just as it's revealed her daughter wanted to do the same to her.

"You have your day and then it's somebody else's day," Susan Hayward replied, in answer to a question as to whether she was jealous of younger actresses, as Helen Lawson was. "Why try to hang on? I'm not trying to hang on. I thought this part might be interesting, something different." Like Garland, she was also uncomfortable with some of the obscenities and tough language that she uttered in *Valley of the Dolls*. "It's the way crummy people talk," she said. "Personally I like to see a nice picture. But, then, I'm old fashioned."

For their big-budget publicity campaign for *Valley of the Dolls*, Fox held a month-long premiere on the luxury liner MV Princess Italia, with press screenings at different ports, beginning with Venice. It was the first time Susann had seen the finished film and was horrified at the happy ending, the excessive hair styling, and the weak male leads, and decided the film had ruined her book.

Despite being declared trash, it broke box office records when it opened in New York on December 15, 1967. Stephen Rebello said, in his book on the making of the film, that it turned out to be "clumsy, tone-deaf, unhip, quaint, unintentionally hilarious, and strangely unsexy."

Lee Grant later called the film "an unbelievable, laugh-out-loud disaster," but compared to her turn in *The Swarm*, Irving Allen's 1978 disaster movie, it was a "genius."

16. "Bob Aldrich loves evil things, horrendous things, vile things..."

In 1962 the question had been asked, *What Ever Happened to Baby Jane?* and by 1969, it was Aunt Alice whose whereabouts were being queried. In *What Ever Happened to Aunt Alice?* Geraldine Page put in a wickedly conniving performance as a widow who steals from her elderly housekeepers, then kills them and buries them, all the while laughing at her evil deeds. Jane Hudson may have murdered one maid, Elvira, and then had to dispose of the body, but for Claire Marrable, there are multiple bodies buried in her Arizona garden. To her nephew she's harmless Aunt Claire, who is supposedly dripping in wealth, but in reality she has been left with nothing following the death of her husband. When Aunt Alice, played by Ruth Gordon, comes to work for Claire as a housekeeper while investigating the disappearance of a friend, she soon discovers that Claire is a very dangerous foe.

The film, adapted from the novel *The Forbidden Garden* by Ursula Curtiss, was produced by *Baby Jane*'s director Robert Aldrich, as part of a four-picture ABC deal, and which served as the third in a trilogy of films about deliciously devilish spinsters and widows. The change in title was a blatant cash-in on the success of *Baby Jane?* and *Charlotte*, with a script that reversed the dynamics of the original film, with Claire, the murderer who is supposedly helpless in her wheelchair, and her maid, who becomes her victim.

In October 1967, while making a film called *The Legend of Lylah Clare* for MGM, Aldrich signed the deal with ABC, which as well as *What Ever Happened to Aunt Alice?*, also included *The Killing of Sister George, The Greatest Mother of 'em All* and *Too Late the Hero*. This series of films, with the exception of *Too Late the Hero*, expanded on the conventions formed with *Baby Jane* and further developed in *Hush, Hush Sweet Charlotte*. The first rule was to cast recognizable older movie stars to play an increasingly isolated, mentally-unstable woman who is often in a fraught relationship with another woman. These dynamics included Jane and Blanche Hudson in *Baby Jane*, cousins Miriam and Charlotte in *Hush, Hush Sweet Charlotte*, Lylah Clare and her double, Elsa Brinkman, Sister George and her girlfriend Childie, and in *What Ever Happened to Aunt Alice*, murderous employer Claire Marrable and her maid, Alice. The titles of the films, harking back to *Baby Jane*, also stirred up a sense of intrigue around these troubled women, questioning their safety and their stability. "Bob Aldrich loves evil things, horrendous things, vile things," Joan Crawford said in 1973. "It can take an awful lot out of you if you have to face those things every day."

"If *Whatever Happened to Aunt Alice?* sounds familiar it should, because it comes from the same man who produced and directed *Whatever Happened to Baby Jane?*, which pitted Bette Davis against Joan Crawford," said the *Los Angeles Times* in August 1969. "For all its early film did possess a genuine *Sunset Boulevard* note of tragedy as Miss Davis and Miss Crawford fought it out as a pair of aging, forgotten movie stars. *Aunt Alice* on the other hand, is pretty much out-and-out black comedy, and in it another pair of celebrated ladies, Geraldine Page and Ruth Gordon, go to it with delicious glee."

At 43 years old, Geraldine Page was significantly younger than her character, Claire Marrable, and wore a gray wig to make her look older than her years. The cultured but greedy older widow, who lives in a folk-art filled house on the outskirts of Tucson, hires lonely, elderly spinsters as housekeepers after finding out they have savings she can extract from them, and then uses them as fertilizer for her desert garden. Sharp-tongued and abusive of those who work for her, she wipes the side of her mouth with her fingers as she relishes her wicked doings.

Ruth Gordon plays sweet but shrewd Alice, who must pretend to be subservient to Mrs. Marrable as she investigates her friend and former housekeeper's disappearance. "It's a wonderful part and a wonderful script. There are two great parts, with Miss Geraldine Page and me," said Gordon.

After winning her Oscar for *Rosemary's Baby* at the age of seventy-one, Ruth Gordon was named the *Los Angeles Times'* Woman of the Year for 1969. "What an incredible year," she said. "It's all too astonishing to believe. But I believe it, believe me."

"It was my first starring role in a picture. Isn't that something after 54 years in this business?" Gordon said in December 1969 of playing Alice. "I know it sounds like just another one of those horror potboilers. But it had a real Ibsenesque quality to it. I play someone Geraldine Page is going to murder. In one scene, she trips and I have the chance to kill her and save myself. But such is the power of good over evil that I just couldn't and she ends up killing me just as she planned."

Geraldine Page, born in 1924 in Missouri, was a student at Lee Strasberg's The Actor's Studio, in the fifties, studying method acting alongside James Dean. Despite an Academy Award nomination for Best Supporting Actress for 1953's *Hondo*, she was blacklisted from Hollywood for eight years as a result of the McCarthy witch-hunts. She continued working on Broadway, winning a Tony award for Tennessee Williams' *Sweet Bird of Youth*, where she played the aging actress Alexandra Del Lago, despite only being in her mid-thirties. Page carried the role into the 1962 film adaptation, for which she was nominated for an Academy Award for Best Actress.

At the time of being cast in *Aunt Alice* her career wasn't suffering a decline, rather she was on a career high with the accolades she was receiving, with an Academy Award nomination for *You're a Big Boy Now* (1966) and Emmy awards for Best Actress in two Truman Capote adaptations for television, *The Christmas Memory* (1966) and *The Thanksgiving Visitor* (1967). As the *Calgary Herald* wrote in a profile of Page in July 1970, during the production of her follow-up movie *The Beguiled*, where she is an older spinster who runs a school for girls, she was known for playing "an aging movie queen or a slatternly spinster…quite a few unmarried ladies, a number of them southerners in *Summer and Smoke, Toys in The Attic* and *A Christmas Memory*." Of her preference for playing complex characters, she told the reporter: "Everyone in the beginning of my career would say to me 'what dreadful people you play'. I'd ask 'What kind of people do you want to see on the stage' and they'd say 'Nice, normal people like we know.' Well, it sure would deplete dramatic literature if we only played nice normal people. But the point is we wouldn't want to know the people we go to see on the stage. How would you like to have Medea for dinner? Or MacBeth slurping your soup?"

The filming of *Aunt Alice* began on October 23, 1968 in Tucson, Arizona, with interiors shot at Aldrich Studios in Los Angeles. It was initially directed by Bernard Girard, but he was replaced by Lee H. Katzin during production due to "differences in interpretation."

Ruth Gordon recounted how she had worn a pink silk scarf in the scene where Claire plunges her car, and Alice's body, into the lake, and she would later wear this scarf in *Harold and Maude* (1971). Bernard Girard had liked her suggestion that the pink scarf float on the waters of the lake, but after he was replaced, the shot was cut. "Alice stood for good against evil and the glimpse of pink would show that good survives. What survived was the old pink silk scarf around my neck for the first day of *Harold and Maude*," she said.

Gordon relished the reaction of the audience when she went to a special preview of the film in Boston. "When the film reached the scene where I have the chance to do Gerry in, the audience starts howlin', 'Give it to her, Ruth! Give it to her, Ruth! Isn't that great? They didn't yell 'Alice,' which was my name in the picture, they yelled Ruth!"

Aunt Alice premiered in New York in July 1969, grossing $540,000 in its first week, and placed at number one at the United State box office.

Gordon turned 73 years old October 30, 1969, but she didn't slow down. While she'd been in the business as a writer and actor for many years, *Rosemary's Baby* and *Aunt Alice* both gave her the chance for a complete revival, reaching younger, trendy audiences. "Gettin' the Oscar is the cherry in the sundae," she told the paper. "I don't need prizes. Long ago I developed a built-in confidence. You got to please something within yourself. That's the important thing. I'm really lucky. A long career is very remarkable…For a director like Roman Polanski to let me be in his picture and not say, 'Oh my God!' For me and Mia [Farrow] to be such great friends. She thinks I'm smashing and I think she's the top...And I can say that I'm at the top of my career in *Aunt Alice*."

As well as a punishing schedule of interviews and personal appearances, she collaborated on a screenplay with her husband called *Diamonds are Hilarious*, completed an adaptation of Thornton Wilder's *Heaven is My Destination*, she was working on her autobiography and penning articles for *Vogue* on the secrets of staying youthful.

Gordon followed *Aunt Alice* with Carl Reiner's black comedy *Where's Poppa?* (1970), playing George Segal's senile mother, which she called "the best part I've ever had on screen." She told the *Los Angeles Times*, "What's so marvelous is that nobody's comin' after me for Lady Macbeth or some antique thing. This is like *Easy Rider*, as far as out as you can get. It's so of today, but told with a Hellzapoppin screaming humor so that people can't sit in their seats."

Ruth Gordon was dining at Grenouille in New York, when sitting at the opposite table was Bob Evans and Ali MacGraw. "I've got a sensational script for you, Ruth," he told her. That script turned out to be Hal Ashby's *Harold and Maude*, a film that received an apathetic reception at the time but went on to become a slow-burning cult classic. She found that in her third act, she had transformed into a favorite amongst young audiences by playing a range of interesting roles that didn't shy away from exploring old age. Throughout her seventies and eighties she continued acting on stage and in films, such as a small role in Clint Eastwood's *Every Which Way but Loose* and its sequel *Any Which Way You Can*, and appearing on television, including playing a guest murderess on *Columbo* and hosting *Saturday Night Live* in 1977 at the age of eighty. She passed away in August

1985 after suffering a stroke. Husband Garson Kanin recounted that even on the day of her death she was still busy, working on a play and organizing talks and appearances.

While some of director Robert Aldrich's greatest successes were for his series of testosterone-fueled ensemble films like *The Dirty Dozen* (1967), he was also a director who could tap into the female psyche, as he had shown with his "What Ever Happened to" trilogy. His exploration of uncomfortably obsessive behavior was a theme he first delved into with villainess Lily Carver in *Kiss Me Deadly*, and Joan Crawford's sexually-repressed Millie in *Autumn Leaves*, and one which he would develop further in a series of twisted female-centric films in the late sixties.

Despite his hit Westerns like *Apache* and *Vera Cruz*, and the runaway cult success of *What Ever Happened to Baby Jane?* he also experienced disappointments. It was during the making of one of these disappointments, *The Flight of the Phoenix* (1965), that Aldrich was approached by Kenneth Hyman of Seven Arts Productions to direct a film based on the novel *The Dirty Dozen*, a Second World War drama about the US Army's worst prisoners who are recruited for a dangerous mission in France. On its release in 1967, *The Dirty Dozen* proved to be Aldrich's greatest success, and was influential on a new genre of male survival films. *The Dirty Dozen* tapped into the social upheaval of the time in the same way as *Rosemary's Baby* and *Bonnie and Clyde* did. It was an anti-authoritarian stance that reflected the Civil Rights movement and protests against the Vietnam War, and its amped-up masculinity offered a counterpoint to the burgeoning feminist movement.

The film's success brought Aldrich greater freedom, and allowed for him to work on independent projects through his own production company, Associates and Aldrich. He also financed his own studio in East Hollywood by selling the rights to *The Dirty Dozen*, with the hopes that it would provide some stability to his productions.

While *Aunt Alice* had been a follow-up of sorts to *Baby Jane*, it didn't deal with the exploration of the dark side of Hollywood; a theme which Aldrich took great interest in, and which would be at the heart of *The Legend of Lylah Clare*. Based on a 1963 tele-play starring Tuesday Weld, Aldrich envisioned *Lylah Clare* to be as successful as *Baby Jane* in its exploration of female identity in Hollywood. He had pitched the idea to MGM at the same time as *Hush, Hush Sweet Charlotte* in 1963 as part of the Associates and Aldrich production program, but on its release, its critical and financial failings would prove to be a great disappointment for Aldrich and the film's star, Kim Novak. Peter Finch plays a movie director, Lewis Zarkan, whose greatest actress, Lylah Clare, mysteriously falls to her death just a few hours after marrying him. He discovers a young American actress, Elsa, who looks uncannily like Lylah, and tries to transform her into the dead actress.

Aldrich had initially hoped to cast Jeanne Moreau in the dual role of the late European actress Lylah Clare, and Elsa, a mousy trapeze artist who has an uncanny resemblance to, and maybe possessed by, Lylah Clare. Instead, he cast Kim Novak in a role that seemed to owe a debt to one of her most famous films, Alfred Hitchcock's *Vertigo* (1958), where her dual characters, Madeleine and Judy, have the same fates as Lylah and Elsa, in ultimately plummeting to their deaths.

Thirty-five years old on the film's release, Novak had been absent from the screen for a couple of years, since 1965's *The Amorous Adventures of Moll Flanders*. She'd been replaced by

Deborah Kerr in *Eye of the Devil,* after Novak injured herself during a horse-riding stunt, and had hoped that *Lylah Clare,* for which she was paid $250,000, would be a dazzling comeback. Novak had been the number one box office star a decade earlier when she was signed to Columbia Pictures and marketed as a voluptuous, icy blonde. But she always felt pushed and pulled into being the ideal woman on screen, which didn't fit with her more introspective personality, preferring country living and painting to Hollywood parties and premieres.

Aldrich was initially thrilled with her casting, telling the *Washington Post* in October 1967 that "There are only a handful of actresses who can immediately establish the image of a movie star," he said. "Kim is one." Later, he would blame Novak for the film's failure, but before filming began, he had been hopeful of her potential. "I admit Kim Novak is a gamble," said Aldrich. "If I can get Novak to trust me I think she has the talent to pull it off. If she doesn't, it's a dodgy bet."

Lylah Clare is both a Pygmalion story and a tale of reincarnation, and it's never made clear as to whether Elsa is deluded or possessed. It was a self-conscious Hollywood film, raking the past in its styling and dialogue, and with Lylah Clare as a composite of European actresses of the 1930s like Marlene Dietrich and Greta Garbo. "You're borrowing a little heavily from *Sunset Boulevard* aren't you, Lewis?" says gossip columnist Molly Luther (Coral Browne); a moment in the film that was, for Aldrich, also a self-referential dig. On the film's release it was savaged by critics. Pauline Kael described it as "Heavy-handed camp about Hollywood - an attempt to fuse *Sunset Boulevard, Vertigo, The Barefoot Contessa* and *Whatever Happened to Baby Jane?...*Maybe an amusing macabre pastiche could have been made of it if the director, Robert Aldrich, hadn't been so clumsy; it's a static piece of filmmaking."

Novak was reluctant to put on a fake German accent for the role, but was shocked to find that Aldrich had dubbed some of her scenes with a German actress, without telling her he would do so. She was so marred by the critical mauling that, after *The Great Bank Robbery* in 1969, she took a break from the screen for several years.

Aldrich tied in a number of themes in *Lylah Clare* that would connect to other films. In both *Baby Jane* and *Lylah Clare* there is a scene where a dog food commercial is shown on television, and voiced by the same actor, Michael Fox. In *Baby Jane*, the showing of Blanche's film on television is interrupted by the advert, and in *Lylah Clare*, at the close of the film, we see a close-up of a can being opened. It was Aldrich's statement on the dog-eat-dog society that he's depicting in these films; a theme common in films of the sixties which depicted a rotten underbelly, including in *Lady in a Cage*, with its snarling dogs that was symbolic of increasing disaffection and violence in the city. Aldrich also obliquely referenced lesbian relationships in *Lylah Clare*, with Novak's character being hit on by older, exotically-European women. This theme of celebrity and lesbianism would be even more confrontational in another film which was part of the ABC deal: *The Killing of Sister George*, a shocking drama that tells the story of the fall from grace of a fading British television star.

The film was based on the 1964 play by Frank Marcus, with Beryl Reid winning a Tony Award for her performance as George in 1967. It had all the potential of offering a challenging, provocative role for an older actress, and after buying the rights, Aldrich considered casting Bette Davis or Angela Lansbury in the lead as they were more recognizable names. Lansbury thought the lesbian theme too risky for her career, and she told Aldrich, "I think not. I have my fans and my reputation to think of."

In 1976, Lansbury clarified her position to Keith Howes in *Gay News*. She said that "I didn't want to play a lesbian at that time. I wasn't mad about the play either – I'd only read it, not seen it – but not very many women played immediately recognizable lesbian roles in 1968. They do today but they didn't then and I suppose that had a bearing on my decision, and I was doing something else at the time."

As for Bette Davis, at that point she and Aldrich were on cool terms with one another following clashes during *Hush, Hush Sweet Charlotte*. "I called on Bette recently because naturally I thought of her for *The Killing of Sister George*," he said in July 1967. "We were supposed to be discussing the part, but I was really trying to decide if we could work together again. The outcome: doubtful."

Beryl Reid was one of Britain's great comedic actresses, known for the twinkling smile and her work in music hall, theater, radio and television, and who later earned plaudits for her role in the 1982 BBC adaptation of *Smiley's People*, alongside Alec Guinness. In her obituary in *The Times*, following her death at the age of seventy-six, it was pointed out that she "devoted her life to her trade, choosing not to have children and seeing both her marriages fail through the demands of her job." As a woman who devoted herself to her career, she was often judged for going against societal norms, such as opting to have a hysterectomy to make herself infertile, and in a similar way, one of her most famous roles was as a woman who similarly rebels.

When she was approached by Michael Cordon to star in Frank Marcus's controversial play, Reid was aware of the danger that she would be thought a disagreeable lesbian in real life, at a time when homosexuality was a taboo. She was also conscious that it would be a dramatic shift from the much-loved characters she had created on the BBC, including the schoolgirl Monica and housewife Marlene. She was insistent that George's sexuality wasn't all that defined her. "She was a lady who happened to be a lesbian," she said. "There's more to her than all that business."

The Killing of Sister George began as a touring production around England, and it didn't receive the warm response that had been expected. It had been written as a comedy, but audiences found few laughs in it and quickly abandoned it. As punishment for her depiction of a confrontationally gay character Reid was refused service in shops in the North of England. However, when it arrived in London, it was met with resounding success.

"The first night in London was different because Michael Cordon decided to hand-pick the audience and it was mostly comprised of gay men," remembered Eileen Atkins, who played Childie on stage. From its poor reception in its initial run, it quickly became the must-see show in London, and transferred to Broadway. Rumors of her sexuality continued in the United States. She recalled climbing into a Yellow cab after a matinee performance, when the driver asked if he could kiss her because "I've never kissed a lesbian before." Beryl replied: "Well of course you can, if you like, but you still haven't you know!"

Bette Davis, who had been interested in taking on the role for the film, visited Beryl backstage to praise her on her performance, and told her that "Nobody must do the movie but you! You're the only person to do it!"

After her spectacular Tony Award win in 1969, Reid became the toast of Hollywood, and Aldrich ultimately chose to cast her in his film adaptation, but she was concerned about his plans to play up to the lesbian themes in a more obvious way. "I'm terribly sorry but I can't do that," Beryl explained. "I have no intention of making a sex film." She insisted on a clause in the film where she wouldn't kiss Childie passionately or appear naked. "If he'd have said to me, 'I want you to fall off a cliff,' I would have done it in one take,' she later said. "I was devoted to him."

Lukas Hellar's script changed the Applehurst radio program of the play to a black and white television soap opera, and created a greater sense of homoeroticism with an explicit scene towards the end of the film. Aldrich was groundbreaking in his depiction of gay relationships in everyday life, and the sequence at The Gateways Club on The King's Road was the first screen depiction of the inside of a lesbian club. It was this sense of realism, of using real members of London's lesbian subculture, that gave the film a gritty quality, which perhaps made it even more shocking to audiences and critics at the time.

The *Killing of Sister George* opens with Reid's June "George" Buckridge drinking at The Holly Bush public house. As an overweight, middle-aged woman she at first seems jovial and harmless, but after making a phone call she storms out of the pub, and we see that she is not the benign character we thought. While she has made a name for herself playing mild-mannered Sister George in a BBC soap opera, in real-life she's an alcoholic with an anger problem. George is in a relationship with Alice "Childie" McNaught, played by Susannah York, and they live together as "flatmates" because of the stigma of two women co-habiting as lovers. George wears tweed suits, sits with her legs splayed and puffs on cigars, while Childie, dressed in baby doll nightgowns and with an extensive doll collection that suggests her stunted mental growth, is the submissive, feminine partner, who must eat the ends of the cigars that George chomps as part of their power play.

Like Norma Desmond and Baby Jane, Sister George's stage persona crosses into her real life, and the promise of success is the one thing that holds her together. George's mental health begins to unravel when she discovers the BBC's plans to kill off Sister George, partly due to George's disagreeable off-camera persona. She may go by her androgynous, fictional name, but June's real, dark emotions are always bubbling under the surface. In one particularly shocking sequence, Aldrich cuts between a fictional scene of a kindly Sister George on a black and white television, to June molesting two nuns in the back of a taxi. As George's career hangs in the balance, BBC executive Mercy Croft comes to their flat for tea, and George switches between the gentle screen persona to the rough, angry, and swearing June when she detects that Mrs. Croft and Alice are flirting with one another.

George and Alice go to the lesbian bar dressed as Laurel and Hardy, surrounded by crowds of women also dressed in drag. Their performance is reminiscent of Gloria Swanson's Charlie Chaplin impression in *Sunset Boulevard*. In the film's final scene, as a twist on the ending of *Sunset Boulevard*, George breaks into the BBC sound stage, a place where she can find comfort, just as Baby Jane finds solace performing her childhood tunes. She sees the coffin that will be used for George's funeral, and resigned to her fate of doing voiceover work as a cartoon cow, she begins mooing desperately.

During production the United States introduced a Motion Picture Association of America (MPAA) rating system and *The*

Killing of Sister George was one of the first films to be given an X rating for its depiction of lesbian sex. Aldrich considered it damaging to the success of the film, and was determined to fight the MPAA and the media outlets like the *Los Angeles Times* that refused to run adverts, but despite his lawsuits, ABC only partially backed him. However the promise of risqué scenes only helped to lure audiences into theaters to see the film.

"A shrewdly commercial producer-director with a strong taste for the grotesque and the violent, Aldrich has never been accused of being an excessively discreet or exquisitely subtle film maker," wrote Richard Schickel for *Life* in his review of the film. "In *Sister George* he has outdone himself with the most explicit sequence of lesbian seduction and lovemaking this side of a stag smoker. It is there to lure people into the theatre with the promise of titillation, a promise he more than fulfils."

Beryl Reid would go on to star in two more films which owed a debt to Robert Aldrich. In *The Beast in the Cellar* (1970), produced by horror specialist Tigon British Film Productions, Beryl co-starred with Flora Robson as two seemingly kindly spinster sisters who live together in a small English military town, which is experiencing a number of brutal murders, thought to be linked to a wild cat. However, the two sisters are aware the murders are being committed by their brother, who they've kept locked in a basement for thirty years, and who they discover has dug a tunnel out of the house, so he can fulfil his blood lust. In a parallel with *Baby Jane*, Flora Robson plays the mostly bed-bound sister, leaving it to Beryl Reid to bury the bodies in order to cover up their brother's crime.

Beryl also signed up to the film *Psychomania* (1973), released in the States as *The Death Wheelers*, playing the mother of the leader of a biker gang, who brings her psychopath son back to life through her practice of black magic. The role had originally been offered to Maureen O'Sullivan, and when she turned it down, Beryl confessed that she agreed to do the film solely for the money. She found herself acting with George Sanders, well-known for his work in Alfred Hitchcock's *Rebecca* and *All About Eve*. Tragically Sanders had been suffering from depression for some time, and after being shown an early print for the film he returned to his Madrid hotel room, where he took a fatal overdose of Nembutal. In his suicide note he wrote: "Dear World, I am leaving because I am bored. I feel I have lived long enough. I am leaving you with your worries in this sweet cesspool. Good luck."

In 1969, after struggling to find financing for one of his ambitious Hollywood-themed projects, *The Greatest Mother of 'em All*, Aldrich was inspired to create a promotional film to try and drum up interest. The script was a loose retelling of the story of teenager Beverly Aadland's affair with Errol Flynn, encouraged by her overly-ambitious mother. Aldrich cast Ann Sothern as Dolly, a stage mother who is desperate to make her daughter a star; going so far as pushing her to work as a stripper and encouraging an older producer to seduce her underage daughter.

In the first draft of A.I. Bezzerides' script there were several scenes showing Dolly's deteriorating life after her daughter's death. In one scene, after taking her daughter's place as a promotions girl, she is forced to look in a mirror, where the fantasy image of herself fades into the reality of her own reflection. With the dynamics of an older woman pitted against her younger daughter, and with a faded movie star, Ann Sothern, in the plum role, Aldrich felt that "a year before that picture would have sold like hot cakes," but he failed to sell it to ABC or any other studio.

To break his series of flops, Aldrich hoped that the war film *Too Late the Hero* (1970) would be a success in the realms of *The Dirty Dozen*, with a budget of $6 million and an all-star cast including Michael Caine, Henry Fonda and Cliff Robertson. But on its release it was one of ABC's biggest loss makers.

In 1970 Aldrich worked on *The Grissom Gang* for ABC, a grimier deconstruction of the 1930s gangster film. Ma Grissom (Irene Dailey) is a machine-gun wielding matriarch of a crime family, and monster mother who has a twisted devotion to her mentally-disabled son Slim. It was another flop and he was forced to sell his studio to Video Cassette Industries.

Finally Aldrich's series of money-losers was broken with *The Longest Yard* (1974), his first big hit since *The Dirty Dozen*, and which led to a new production partnership with Burt Reynolds. They developed a project which would co-star Reynolds with Brigitte Bardot, about working-class men who pick up a French woman on route to Mexico. Instead, Reynolds was teamed with Catherine Deneuve in *Hustle* (1975) and which proved to be a further box office success. Movies were Aldrich's life, and while he may have had career highs and lows, on his death in December 1983, he left behind a unique, provocative catalog of work.

In October 1969 it had been announced that Aldrich planned to film *What Ever Happened to Dear Elva?* as the fourth in his "What Ever Happened To..." films. It was based on the novel *Goodbye Aunt Elva* by Elizabeth Fenwick. By 1971 there were reports that ABC-TV were also interested in making a deal with Aldrich for a "What Ever Happened to..." television series of Gothic melodramas, but because of the box office failures of his last films, the deal failed to materialize. It would be left to Curtis

Harrington to take over the concept, as he developed a résumé of female-centric horror films that borrowed from the campy titles that had asked what happened to Baby Jane, Cousin Charlotte and Aunt Alice.

17. "What's the matter with Shelley?"

"I've got this movie called *What Happened to Helen?* Or *Where's Aunt Helen?* Or something like that," Shelley Winters told *The New York Times* in 1971. "Anyway, it's about two women during the thirties who run a school to turn out Shirley Temples, and in my next scene I have to stab Debbie Reynolds to death. Poor Debbie – they better not give me a real knife."

What's the Matter with Helen? was Curtis Harrington's ode to the thirties, riding on the back of a wave of nostalgia for the Depression-era in the late sixties and early seventies. The screenplay was by Henry Farrell, the writer behind *What Ever Happened to Baby Jane?* and *Hush, Hush Sweet Charlotte*, and with its provocative title, the film also sought to cash in on the success of his two earlier hits.

Just as Joan Crawford and Bette Davis famously clashed in *Baby Jane*, Farrell's script paired two older, and single, women against one other – Debbie Reynolds as Adelle Bruckner, the platinum-haired beauty who attracts admirers, and Shelley Winters as Helen Hill, who is so repressed and closeted in her sexuality that she descends into madness. As Debbie Reynolds described it, with just a little dig at Shelley Winters, "the complex story examines the lives of these women, one an overweight psychopath and the other a dancing teacher."

In what would be a signature of Curtis Harrington's filmmaking, *What's the Matter with Helen?* was steeped in gentle thirties nostalgia, telling the story of two mothers who run away to Los Angeles after their sons are convicted of murder, where they open a dance studio for little Shirley Temples, who, in typical thirties parlance, are considered "The cat's meow." Initially there's a sense of optimism to their story, as Adelle teaches tap dancing while Helen hammers out the tune *Goody Goody* on the piano. Yet they're haunted by the terrible crime of their sons who teamed up to murder a middle-aged woman; an idea which was inspired by the real-life Leopold and Loeb case. Like Norman Bates in *Psycho*, the murder carried out by their two sons could be considered an act of revenge upon their own mothers for a perceived resentment. As Helen says of the murdered woman: "She was a working woman just like us. About the same age. So our sons really wanted to kill us. They hated us. That was the substitute revenge."

As well as the theme of bad mothers, the finished film would follow many of the conventions set out in the "Hag Horror" genre, such as the clash between two women who are stuck in the past, the murder of someone who threatens to compromise their relationship, and the disposal of a body.

The New York Times in 1971 described *Helen* as belonging to "that singular genre of screen horror literature" which was about "two women, beyond or just at middle age, abandoned by the men in their lives, find themselves isolated from the normally neurotic world and locked into a relationship of psychotic dependency."

After they failed to get their original script for *The Guests* off the ground, Curtis Harrington and George Edwards were back to square one in finding a new project for Universal. It was then they remembered a story outline from Farrell called *The Box Step*. It was a contemporary thriller about two women who run a ballroom dance school, who become involved in murder. They took that idea, but switched its setting from the modern day to the thirties, and from ballroom to a children's dance school based on the Depression-era Meglin Kiddies child agency, of which Judy Garland and Shirley Temple were notable members. This would allow the film to capitalize on the nostalgia for thirties fashions, following the success of *Bonnie and Clyde* (1967) and *They Shoot Horses, Don't They?* (1968).

By mid-1968 the project was approved by Universal, now retitled *The Best of Friends*, on the proviso that they could cast a big enough star in one of the leads. Harrington and Edwards created a wish list of actresses, and suggested that if they were casting younger, their ideal pairing would be Joanne Woodward and Kim Stanley, and if they went older, it would be Rita Hayworth and Olivia de Havilland.

Other names for the part of Adelle included Angela Lansbury, Anne Bancroft, Shirley MacLaine, Janet Leigh, Susan Hayward, Doris Day, and Judy Garland. For Helen, they considered Estelle Parsons, who had recently won the best Supporting Actress Oscar for *Bonnie and Clyde*, Julie Harris, Joan Fontaine and Patricia Neal. Interestingly, Shelley Winters had initially been listed for the more glamorous role of Adelle.

"We needed an aging actress who could dance, and my first thought was Joanne Woodward," said Harrington. "She was hardly noted for her singing and dancing, but I was sure that her immense talent would permit her to fake it. However, she turned us down. She claimed that she liked it, but Paul (Newman), whose approval was needed, didn't think it was right for her."

Next, they tried and failed to pass the script to Shirley MacLaine. They did however succeed in securing a meeting with Rita Hayworth at her Beverley Hills home. The red-haired star had been the number one pin-up during the Second World War. She sizzled on screen in *Gilda* (1946) and Fred Astaire even named her as his favorite dance partner, ahead of Ginger Rogers, after working together on two 1940s musicals, *You Were Never Lovelier* and *You'll Never Get Rich*. As Curtis noted, "Although she was past the prime of her stardom, her name still merited lights above the marquee throughout the world."

Rita greeted Curtis Harrington and George Edwards at the door of her home and led them out to the garden where they sat by the pool and discussed the role over drinks. After a successful meeting where they chatted away comfortably, and she told them how much she enjoyed the script, Harrington recalled that her personality changed as she showed them to the door. Her face fell into anguish as she was convinced that they were laughing at her. This moment hinted at the undiagnosed early-onset Alzheimer disease she was suffering from, and Curtis described how "the incident remained in my memory as a deeply disturbing experience… I felt such compassion and pity for this beautiful and famous woman who was now overcome by those demons of insecurity and fear."

Despite their efforts, Edwards and Harrington were unsuccessful in securing a big name, and when their contact with Universal came up for renewal, they were let go. Yet they were permitted to purchase back the rights to *The Best of Friends* for $50,000 and by early 1970 they were working hard to secure funding with other studios.

In a letter to Thomas Tannenbaum of Paramount Pictures, Harrington wrote that: "It has an early thirties background, which is very fascinating to the young people today (i.e. the current success of *They Shoot Horses* and the long-running *Dames at Sea*). Directorially, I know I can build terrific suspense with this script – more than is indicated. Every actress who has read it has been interested in doing it, so I know we'll have no trouble putting together an exciting combination of interesting types in the leading roles...despite the fact that this features two mature actresses, I think it would have tremendous youth appeal in its suspense 'camp' elements."

To try to move ahead with the making of the film, Harrington and Edwards turned to Bette Davis. If there was a name that would secure funding it was Davis, particularly if it was a story with similarities to her previous smash-hit horror roles which had been penned by Henry Farrell. Harrington sent the script to her Connecticut home in February 1970, with a note describing how there is "a touching and poignant quality in the portrayal of Helen's growing confusion and madness." To further convince her, he suggested that Broadway star Gwen Verdon could fill the role of Adelle, bringing an authenticity to the dance numbers.

Bette Davis replied a few days later with a handwritten note that included her customary smiley faces. "Alas, I wish I wanted to do *The Best of Friends* – it is so much like Davis parts of *Hush-Hush* plus I don't want to lug any more dead bodies around and throw them in ditches!! Tell Henry [Farrell] I'm sorry – tell him he's a damn good writer and I <u>wish</u> I wanted to do this script! Find another – easier said than done, that I know!!"

Harrington, writing back to convey his disappointment at her rejection, told her he would continue to look for a script that they could both work on together. "I did feel that the characterization of Helen would be something different for you to do," he wrote. "Certainly this plain, repressed, Bible-quoting mid-Western lady is a far cry from either Baby Jane or the Southern Belle of Hush. I also feel that the early 1930s background of the story will give it a freshness of atmosphere for a thriller that hasn't been attempted before."

Finally, in the summer of 1970, they approached Debbie Reynolds with the script, and she agreed for it to be produced as part of her NBC contract. "At that point in her career, she wanted to change her image, wanted a challenge. And this was a great challenge, because she was no longer playing Miss Goodie Two Shoes," said Harrington.

Debbie Reynolds understood the Depression-era setting only too well. Born in El Paso, Texas in 1932 as Mary Reynolds, she, her parents and brother lived with her grandparents in a small house without a shower. "We used the bathroom at the gas station next door," she remembered. "I shared a bed with my brother and three uncles, who were close to us in age. My brother and I slept with our heads at the top of the bed, my uncles with theirs at the foot. I woke up every morning with toes in my nose. I never slept alone until I got married."

The family moved to California in 1939, and at the age of sixteen Debbie won the Miss Burbank beauty pageant and came to the attention of Warner Brothers. It was Jack Warner who gave her the nickname "Debbie" as he thought "Debbie is a cute name for a little girl."

She switched to MGM two years later and was cast in her first major role in *Two Weeks with Love* in 1950. It was her duet in the film *Aba Daba Honeymoon* which impressed the studio and led her to being cast in *Singin' in the Rain* in 1952, which catapulted her to stardom. She was the perky triple threat who danced, sang and could do slapstick comedy with ease, and when she and Eddie Fisher announced their engagement in 1954 they replaced

Marilyn Monroe and Joe DiMaggio as the most famous couple in America. Later, she would be unwittingly part of an international scandal when Eddie Fisher left her for Elizabeth Taylor, finding herself in the role of guileless divorcee with two young children to raise. Her second marriage to shoe salesman Harry Karl lasted from 1960 to 1973, following the heartbreaking discovery that he was a swindler who had spent her fortune.

As a starlet, Debbie had always been referred to as "cute" and "wholesome," and as she got older she worried this image was detrimental to her transition to more grown-up parts. "I was still thought of by many people as 'cute,' or 'the kid,' which is hard to maintain after you hit thirty. Cute can be the kiss of death for a movie career."

When she won the lead role in *The Unsinkable Molly Brown* (1964) over Shirley MacLaine, Debbie hoped it would provide a route into more serious roles, particularly after being nominated for an Academy Award for Best Actress. Yet she found that it was still difficult to find decent scripts that suited her. She was cast as Jeanine Deckers in *The Singing Nun* in 1966, which she called "the stupidest mistake of my entire career." She observed how Greer Garson, who had won the Best Actress Oscar in 1942 for *Mrs. Miniver* at the age of thirty-eight, was willing to take on the small role of Mother Superior in the film because of the lack of roles available to her. "Television was taking over the entertainment business, and movie parts were becoming scarce for aging actors, even for Academy Award winners," Debbie said.

As the film roles became hard to find, Debbie transitioned to television, signing a contract with NBC in 1969 to do a weekly family sitcom called *The Debbie Reynolds Show*, which was designed to be a rival to Lucille Ball's hugely successful shows on

CBS. As part of her television contract, the studio agreed to produce two films of her choice, and she chose Harrington's script as one of the options.

The title of *The Best of Friends* was thought too similar to that of Otto Preminger's *Such Good Friends*, which was in production at the same time. Instead, the title was changed to capitalize on the *Baby Jane* connection, with the similar sounding *What's the Matter with Helen?* "I hated this," Debbie bluntly wrote in her memoirs.

Shelley Winters, who was 50 at the time of filming, had in recent years been playing parts that accentuated her weight gain and underplayed her attractiveness. In *Harper* (1966) she was a once-glamorous starlet who is now an overweight alcoholic. It was the type of role given to actresses who were considered to be past their prime. Yet she was self-assured, brash and funny in real life. In 1996 she described herself as "a senior-citizen sex bomb." She said: "I get 1,000 letters a month. I send people a postcard of myself in short hair and a checkered blouse that was taken 50 years ago."

Winters began her career as the blonde bombshell pin-up, sharing an apartment with Marilyn Monroe when they were both sexually liberated starlets making their way in Hollywood. "We were sort of advanced for our time," she recounted, describing how they made a list of men they wanted to sleep with.

As the *Los Angeles Times* wrote of her in 1995, "She was a liberated single career woman long before it became acceptable." She once described her life as a "rocky road out of the Brooklyn ghetto to one New York apartment, two Oscars, three California houses, four hit plays, five Impressionist paintings, six mink coats and 99 films."

Born Shirley Schrift in St Louis, Missouri in 1920, her family moved to Brooklyn when she was nine, and it was here that her street-smarts and toughness translated into a blowsy, sexy personality. "I saw Shelley Winters in *A Place in the Sun*," said Joan Crawford. "She gave a very moving performance, which surprised me, because Shelley is not a sensitive girl socially." In return, Shelley spoke warmly of Joan. "My idea of a movie star is Joan Crawford, who can chew up two directors and three producers before lunch," she said.

Winters first came to the attention of George Cukor in 1938 when she barged into his New York office to insist she should be cast as Scarlett O'Hara in *Gone with the Wind*. He advised her to go to acting school, and so she worked as a model to fund her way through the New Theater School and tried out for Broadway musicals. She was hired as a contract player at Columbia in 1944, under her new name, which spliced romantic writer Percy Shelley with her mother's maiden name. When she arrived in Hollywood she appeared as a chorus girl in *Cover Girl* and *Tonight and Every Night* with Rita Hayworth. "She was very nice to me. She was very sweet and she was always having me stand near her so I would get in the picture."

Still, she fought for good roles and it was George Cukor who again saw her potential by casting her in the modern twist on Othello, *A Double Life,* in 1947. According to Shelley, ten other actresses were in the running, including Lana Turner and Kim Stanley. "I rehearsed it and then I barely made the test. I had a one-day part at MGM and I was hoping to get two 'cause I needed the other $100. I was going back to New York on the bus and giving up Hollywood to work in the theater," she said.

On the back of its success, she was signed to a seven-year contract with Universal in 1948. She earned her first of four Oscar nominations in 1950's *A Place in the Sun*, having dyed her hair brown and auditioned without makeup to convince George Stevens she was right for the role of the downtrodden factory girl whose rejection by Montgomery Clift for rich-girl Elizabeth Taylor leads to devastating consequences.

Despite being encouraged to play nightclub singers and gangster molls, Winters continued to fight for better parts. "I would make such a pest of myself, but I had to force them into letting me do theater instead of those crappy pictures whenever I could," she said. After a stint in Europe, she returned to New York to perform on Broadway, and joined the Actors Studio where she focused on Method acting and would later teach. "You mustn't be afraid to stink," she advised actors. "Bette Davis said that. Unless you do that, you'll never learn."

She won the best Supporting Actress Oscar for Mrs. Van Daan in *The Diary of Anne Frank* in 1959, and then in 1965 for *A Patch of Blue* as the vulgar prostitute mother of a blind girl. When she hit her forties, she settled into being a character actress playing the sexually voracious older dame, with roles as a married woman who embarks on an affair with a younger man in *Young Savages* (1961), and as one of Michael Caine's lovers in *Alfie* (1966). Despite a lack of leads for women over forty, Shelley continued working in a range of mediums; on Broadway in *Minnie's Boys* in 1970, and playing villain Ma Parker on television show *Batman*.

While she continued to be in demand, particularly with the success of her role in *The Poseidon Adventure*, for which she was nominated for an Oscar, Shelley's later career was marked by a series of B-movies in the United States, Britain and Italy. These included Roger Corman's cult classic *Bloody Mama* (1970) where she played Ma Barker, a murderous and incestuous mother of gangsters, and the Italian-produced *Tentacles* (1977), which was a *Jaws* rip-off.

The Mad Room (1969), directed by Bernard Girard, would be her first "Hagsploitation" appearance. It dealt with the popular conflict between the older and younger generation, pitting Shelley's older widow against a beautiful young woman called Ellen, played by Stella Stevens. Ellen's younger siblings are believed to have hacked to death their parents and drawn flowers in their blood (much like the Manson Family), but she receives news they are being released from the institution, and brings them to stay with the older widow, Gladys, who has been kind to Ellen.

Ellen's blond hair and pastel-colored dresses suggests her innocence, but in contrast, Shelley Winters is depicted as possessing a wilted and aggressive sexuality. She's first shown with her back and cleavage exposed as she's given a massage, a device also used with Bette Davis in *Dead Ringer*, and later with Miriam Hopkins in *The Savage Intruder* (1970) and Ann Sothern in *The Killing Kind* (1973). It reinforces the idea that an older woman's sexuality is desperate and almost grotesque. One of her houseguests, Chris, played by Carole Cole, daughter of Nat King Cole and one of the few women of color in horrors of that time, plays rock music in her room while Gladys is being murdered. This not only serves to muffle her cries, but further contrasts the younger generation with the older generation.

Shelley was said to have been particularly difficult to work with during production of *The Mad Room*. She was disturbed by the recent assassination of Robert Kennedy, and had dealt with her emotions by drinking wine on set. Stella Stevens found her so difficult that she vowed never to work with Winters again, although they did team up a few years later on *The Poseidon Adventure.* Stevens recounted to an interviewer, Michael G Ankerich, of a meeting with Shelley in 1994, after having been relegated to the monstrous older woman role herself in the 1995 comedy horror *The Granny.* "Shelley saw me the other day and asked me how *The Granny*, the film in which I replaced her, turned out. I said it turned out great, that it was a wonderful part and that I had a lot of fun doing it. She told me she had been ill (with the shingles) and didn't think she would have had the strength to have done it. Then she says, 'Stella, give me your number. I get so many scripts that I can't do. I'll tell them to call you.'"

She may have been known for the strength and vivacity that she brought to her roles, but in *A Place in the Sun, The Night of the Hunter* and *Lolita* she played the tragic victims of violent men. She described *The Night of the Hunter* as "kind of a horror picture," and that "The kind of beautiful horror that Charles Laughton wanted in *Night of the Hunter*, a kind of strange, beautiful horror – there was a similar thing with Curtis on *What's the Matter with Helen?*, the kind of jazzy thing of the 30s. You know, the little kids tap dancing, and the house, and her clothes and fixing her hair – and this kind of retreat for Helen. Getting all these beautiful things and then suddenly it's gonna be taken away from her. And maybe love! Maybe it's the first time in her life she had anyone care about her, and the idea of losing it just snapped her."

Shelley and Debbie Reynolds were long-time friends from their days as burgeoning Hollywood stars in the early fifties, before being cast together in *Helen.* "I found out that Debbie was gonna do it and I knew her socially for a long, long time," Shelley said in 1993. "Years and years ago she lived in a little house with a huge swimming pool...we used to play water polo, I think it was when I first came out here."

In 1983, when Debbie launched her own aerobics video to rival those of Jane Fonda, she featured a special guest – Shelley – who clearly hated exercise and turned up with a t-shirt emblazoned with the words "I'm only doing this for Debbie." She gossips about sleeping with Howard Hughes and asks if "the bulges are supposed to hurt?" as she follows along with Debbie's routines.

Despite their strong friendship, they often clashed, particularly when Debbie was exasperated by Shelley's perplexing behavior. Debbie recounted in her memoirs of a time she went to a party in Malibu with Hugh O'Brian. "When we went into the living room, there was Shelley, with her full skirt spread out, covering two young men who were servicing her. Hugh and I left immediately, not wishing to spend time around Shelley's double-header."

"The movie with Debbie Reynolds could be quite interesting, I think. I hope Debbie can carry it off," said Shelley with relish to *The New York Times* in 1971. "She's not such a bad actress, do you think? I mean, she wasn't so bad in *Molly Brown*, was she? If she asks me to make any little suggestions, I think I may suggest that she change her name. No woman her age should be called Debbie."

Shelley's antics while playing Helen veered into irrationality, and in her interview with *The New York Times* she hinted at a rivalry with Debbie to match that of Bette Davis and Joan Crawford. Years later Debbie described the nightmare of working with Shelley, claiming that when she checked the prop knives for the climactic murder, a fake blade had been switched for a real one, and she immediately suspected Shelley. Debbie described how Shelley became the "murdering crazy woman" that she played. "Shirley terrorized the entire cast and crew. She thrived on all her craziness and made everyone's life miserable."

Shelley's role as the anguished, confused Helen Hill could be considered a study in the effects of having to hide one's sexuality. Helen stays true to the typical character arc of older women in horror as she falls into obsessive, murderous despair. In a scene that would be almost replicated in *Fatal Attraction* fifteen years later, Helen slaughters her beloved pet rabbits as a final act before stabbing her friend, who she is in love with, to death. As she manically hammers out *Goody Goody* on her piano, we see the body of Adelle, hauntingly strung up like a puppet on a string, in her favorite tap-dancing outfit.

Shelley Winters in 1993 said: "Now that I look back, I don't know whether I would have showed a lesbian as being so crazy. But maybe that's the only way they'd allow it! Same as in the film *Basic Instinct*. If you're gonna be a lesbian, you gotta be crazy."

As with transgender characters, lesbian characters on screen are often punished for straying from the traditional gender roles. One of the most overt depictions was the closeted Mrs. Danvers in Hitchcock's *Rebecca* (1940), whose obsessive love for the titular character leads to her death. Sister George and her relationship with Childie, as well as the seduction of Childie by Mercy Croft, offered such a sense of realism that it led to Aldrich's film being given an X certificate.

Harrington chose to purposely depict Helen's sexuality through subtle actions. "The unspoken lesbian feelings of Helen are very intentional. And Shelley played it that way," he said. "If you'll remember, for instance, the little thing that Shelley does when the phone rings and Debbie comes out of her room in her teddie – the way Shelley looks at her, because she's partially nude...it's subtle but it's very much there...even when she picks up Debbie's teddie from the bed and presses it to her face."

While it was Reynolds' first straight, dramatic role, it referenced her musical days, from her tap-dancing scenes to the rainy street outside her apartment like that of *Singin' in the Rain*. Debbie, mindful of her girl next door image, fought hard against filming the scene where they carry the body out into the rain and throw it into a construction pit. Harrington held firm, as it was vital to the action, where the two women are now linked together by a crime, just like their sons.

The murder of Adelle had initially been planned to be as shocking as the shower scene in *Psycho*, with Helen descending on Adelle with the knife raised above her head, but this climactic scene was cut down for a PG certificate. A scene when Shelley kissed Debbie on the lips, as a moment of bonding after they bury the body together was also cut for the same reason. On the final, climactic murder in Helen, Harrington said: "I wanted to do a Hitchcock with that. I readily admit it. I wanted to do something similar to the shower scene in *Psycho*, because I thought it would be good to have something sensational to make the film more talked about."

Reynolds suggested her good friend Agnes Moorehead be cast as Sister Alma, a fraud evangelist who gives her followers oil for "everlasting youth." She was based on Aimee Semple McPherson, a celebrity preacher in the thirties who attracted huge crowds to her megachurch in Los Angeles. "We had some of the biggest battles of my life," said Moorehead of her experience making the film. "I loved the picture and hated the work (thanks to Shelley)."

For the role of Linc, the Texas millionaire who woos Adelle, Cliff Robertson, Van Johnson, John Gavin and Peter Lawford were all considered, before they settled on Dennis Weaver. The actor was most recognizable for his Emmy-award winning role in the television series *Gunsmoke,* and had just completed *Duel,* the film debut of Steven Spielberg. Debbie described Dennis as a "total delight." She also recalled that "he was also a great kisser, even better than Frank Sinatra. Since my marriage to Harry Karl was breaking up and I wasn't getting any sex at home, I thoroughly enjoyed my love scenes with Dennis."

Harrington was meticulous about recreating the era, using the memories of his childhood growing up in Los Angeles. Period costumes were designed by Morton Haack, who was nominated for an Academy Award for his work on the film. Debbie had previously worked with him on *The Unsinkable Molly Brown,* and so he had experience of dressing her to her specifications. Thirty-eight at the time of filming, she looked beautiful with her platinum-blonde Jean Harlow hair, and it was a glamorous transformation that was dramatically different from her wholesome image on her television show. Yet, as typical of the contrasted pairing of two women in "Hag Horror" films, Helen's costumes and makeup were more reflective of her repression.

While Adelle attempts to transform Helen with a Marion Davies haircut, the gleam of the scissors triggers a flashback in Helen to the accidental or deliberate death of her husband under the blades of a plow on their Midwest farm. Helen looks in horror at herself in the mirror after the make-over, and this moment also reflected Shelley Winter's own self-esteem when standing next to the slender Debbie. Despite having approved Morton's costumes during the fittings, on the first day of filming Shelley exploded when presented with them in her dressing room. She tossed them out of her trailer and trampled them, upsetting Morton so much that he walked off the set.

Debbie recounted the incident in her memoirs. "Shelley screamed at Morton that he was trying to make her look fat while making me look thin - I was down to 104 pounds, which worked for my character," she wrote. "Morton reminded Shelley that she was fat, which Shelley in her saner moments admitted, usually when stating that she was going on a diet (which she never managed to do). Furious, Shelley ripped off all her clothes, stomped out of the fitting room stark naked, and left the set. She refused to wear anything that Morton designed for her after that. Shelley so soured Morton on working with actors that he quit the movie, returned to London, and never made another picture."

Eventually Shelley calmed down, and she was able to explain to Morton that there were two costumes in particular that she hated because their elaborate style made her look fat. If he would design something dark and simple, yet still in the period style, she would agree to begin work.

"Morton was forced to do it, but it took away all the unique character that he had designed into the costumes. It was really a pity," said Harrington. "The fact of the matter was that Shelley was heavy, and Debbie was slender. This made for a wonderful contrast in the characters on screen, but Shelley was jealous. The contrast was visible in every scene between them, and it upsets her. Her vanity was sorely wounded."

Shelley was also upset after watching the dailies when she noticed that the cinematographer, Lucien Ballard, had lit Debbie in a more favorable way, to emphasize the lightness of her character, while making Shelley appear darker and more foreboding.

Debbie recalled that "Shelley was irrational about every detail in the film. She wouldn't show up on time, so I offered to pick her up on my way to work. It was a tense few months of production, which almost caused me to have a breakdown. I hyperventilated at one point, but fortunately was fine the next day."

Harrington worked hard to appease both stars, often summoned to both their dressing rooms first thing each morning. But there was one particular crisis that led to Shelley threatening to quit. She was upset with Debbie who spent her time backstage making the crew laugh with her impressions to help ease any tensions. "I can't work when the crew is laughing," she said. "I can't concentrate. That's all she does - tell jokes and make them laugh."

Curtis went to find Debbie to have a word with her, and at that very moment, she had the crew in stitches with her jokes and impressions. He took her aside to explain what was wrong, and she agreed to ease up on her antics to appease Shelley. "We knew that if we didn't humor her, there would be hell to pay," recalled Curtis. "Shelley was still pouting with resentment when I returned to her dressing room. She kept repeating, 'I just can't work this way. I really ought to go home.'"

Another of Shelley's antics was to play selections from Puccini operas on her portable phonograph before each scene. She claimed that having had two Italian husbands, and having lived in Rome for many years, she had an emotional connection to the music and she couldn't act without it. Harrington noted that when he directed Shelley Winters in his next film *Who Ever Slew Auntie Roo?* the Italian opera music didn't seem to be needed.

Reynolds was an uncredited producer on *Helen* as part of her deal with NBC, and she had some clout when it came to any decisions around Winters. She claimed that "Shelley's behavior did nothing to endear her to me, and after three weeks I decided to fire her. But the cost of reshooting her scenes with another actress would have put us way over budget. So we had to keep her, even though Geraldine Page was ready to step in."

When filming was over, Debbie vowed to never speak to Shelley again, but they'd known each other so long that this promise didn't last long. At the film's wrap party, Debbie reminded Shelley of her difficult behavior. "She protested that she'd never ripped doors off their hinges, made hysterical scenes, or acted like a maniac; that I was making it all up. Only when the crew gleefully chimed in, 'Yeah, Shelley, you really did that,' did she acknowledge that just maybe she might have been a wee bit out of line," said Debbie.

Helen was released on 30 June 1971 to a mixed response, and the obvious connection to previous female-led horror films were noted. *The New York Times* in July 1971 described Reynolds as "looking like an ageless kewpie doll with platinum hair, and Miss Winters, wearing the expression of a reproachful pudding most of the time…If they seem to be following in the footsteps of Bette and Joan and Olivia and Geraldine and Ruth, it's because their screenplay was written by Henry Farrell, who also wrote 'Baby Jane' and 'Sweet Charlotte,' which inspired, in turn, 'Aunt Alice.' This new movie is so perfunctory, it's likely to give misogyny a bad name."

As a summer movie, it did well in drive-ins, as horrors tended to do, and was gaining momentum in theaters by word of mouth, but audience numbers were disappointing. It didn't help that the poster, featuring an image of Adelle's body strung up like a puppet, gave away the twist ending.

Harrington was extremely upset with the "hideous poster" and the ineffective advertising campaign. "When we took that still on the set, I told everyone, including the producers and the powers that be...it is not to be released. It is not to be put in the lobbies of theaters. It is not to be put in magazines. I don't want that photo out at all because the image is the surprise at the end of the film....The publicity department chose to reveal the ending of the film on the poster! I can't tell you how furious I was. This all happened when I was in Europe, making *Who Ever Slew Auntie Roo?* It was all beyond my control."

The film was distributed by United Artists, but rather than support the publicity for *Helen*, they chose to focus their publicity budget for the year on *Fiddler on the Roof* and the latest James Bond, *Diamonds are Forever*. Harrington was also disappointed the film didn't take advantage of the 1930s setting.

"*What's the Matter with Helen?* didn't do well at the box office, but I think it's one of my better performances," said Debbie. "I just hated making it. I hated working on a project that I believed in with a temperamental actress who made life miserable. Cuckoo and crazy - that's what was the matter with Shelley! Still, in spite of all the difficulties, I love the finished film."

Debbie wouldn't star in another movie until *Mother* in 1996, apart from voice work on Japanese animation *Kiki's Delivery Service* in 1989. "Movie musicals had long since gone away, and parts for middle-aged musical stars were nonexistent. Thankfully, I had my stage work to fall back on. Many actors my age just stopped working," she said.

Shelley acknowledged that for Debbie, "if it had been more successful in terms of publicity, I think she would have had a career as a dramatic actress." Shelley later referred to the film as "a camp classic," and that "it had great style – the clothes and the props and the splash of the characters. And there was something very scary about that dance school."

Straight after the completion of *Helen*, Shelley Winters teamed up with Curtis Harrington to play the "wicked witch" in another "Hag Horror," *Who Ever Slew Auntie Roo?* Harrington could only guess how she would behave on their second film together. Actress Cheryl Ladd once reflected of Shelley that "she's like the little girl with the curl in the middle of her forehead. When she's good, she's oh-so-good, and when she's bad, she's horrid."

18. "She's taking A STAB at Motherhood!"

In late 1969 Curtis Harrington and George Edwards met with Bette Davis for lunch in Los Angeles, in the hope that she would sign on to one of their ever evolving film projects. In a follow-up letter in December 1969, Harrington offered her the lead in an adaptation of the Hansel and Gretel fairytale, to be produced by American International Pictures, and written by Jimmy Sangster, of Hammer Films.

"The screenplay bears the dreadful title, *Christmas at Grandma's*," Harrington wrote to Davis. To persuade her of its merits, he told her he had plans to change it to "*The Gingerbread House*," and that it was a story which had "the kind of fascinating ambiguity of Henry James' *The Turn of the Screw*, in which the children may be perfectly angelic or little devils." He wrote of his plans to set the film in the early twentieth century, "which would provide much more visual interest and color to the Christmas setting."

Harrington also informed Davis that Henry Farrell had written an original story that "could be a smashing vehicle for you – a suspense story about a lady who is the manager of a hugely successful pair of rock singers like Sonny & Cher. We are hoping to get a deal set on this shortly, so that Henry can start on the screenplay."

The Sonny & Cher script never materialized, and Bette Davis ultimately passed on his projects, but Harrington continued to focus on the concept for *The Gingerbread House*. Harrington eventually signed Shelley Winters to the film, and soon after wrapping *What's the Matter with Helen?* they both traveled to the UK to film what could be considered as one of the more obscure cult Christmas movies. The festive title *The Gingerbread House* would later be changed to *Who Slew Auntie Roo?* and then to *Whoever Slew Auntie Roo?* to bring it into line with the series of *Baby Jane*-esque horror films. Harrington claimed the title was "the producers' idea of a commercial title. It is my opinion that it harmed the commercial chances of the film."

Jimmy Sangster had previously written *The Nanny,* starring Bette Davis, and in this original story he explored the concept of a child fighting, and then coming victorious, against a troubled older woman. After Robert Blees made some changes to the script, Harrington hired his friend Gavin Lambert to make further changes. The final version was an amalgamation of different drafts, leaving some continuity issues that had to be ironed out during production.

Winters plays Rosie Forrest, a wealthy widow who is known as "Auntie Roo" to the children from the nearby orphanage who she invites to her mansion every Christmas. Rosie is a former showgirl from America, a "Floradora Girl," who gave up her career when she married her late husband, Mr. Forrest, a wealthy magician who left her his mansion, filled with his menacing tricks and props. Despite its gingerbread house appearance, the mansion is truly a house of horrors, as it's revealed in the pre-credits that Roo is a female Norman Bates, keeping the mummified corpse of her deceased daughter in a cot in the nursery, following her accidental death.

When orphan siblings Katy and Christopher Coombs sneak into Auntie Roo's house to enjoy the Christmas celebrations, despite not having been invited to attend, Roo takes a shine to the angelic-looking Katy, believing she can replace her dead daughter. Christopher is immediately suspicious of Roo, and begins to connect her to the wicked witch in the Hansel and Gretel tale he's been reading to Katy. Roo is being manipulated by her servants into believing that she's communicating with the spirit of her dead daughter, as a means of extracting money from her. As she becomes more delusional, she slips into mental despair, and holds Katy and Christopher captive in the house. In a grim and shocking ending, the children lock Roo in the cellar and set fire to the house, burning Roo to death, despite her not being the wicked woman they think she is.

Shelley Winters was fifty-one years old during filming, and rather than being made to look older and more ravaged to suit a witch-like character, the audience can still see her beauty and the appeal her character would have had in her youth as a showgirl. There are some ambiguities as to whether she is the evil character the children think she is, such as the close-up of her face showing beads of sweat as she munches on an apple, as if she's the Wicked Queen in *Snow White*.

The film featured many of the common tropes of the camp horror genre, such as the nursery filled with waxy dolls with blank, haunting eyes, the creepy butler, Albert, decapitating a turkey with a meat cleaver, and the supposedly trick guillotine, which turns out to be real. Harrington switched the film's setting to the 1920s rather than the present day, to create a sense of nostalgia, and used a predominately red color palette, not just to symbolize blood, but for the Christmas theme. "I have a great fondness for all the imagery and quality of the traditional Victorian Christmas celebration. I tried to put as much as I could of that in the film," he said. "It was just a rather thin little fable. I found Shelley Winters' mad behavior vastly amusing."

Despite her tantrums on the set of *Helen*, Harrington was keen to work again with Shelley, but this time he chose to handle her with caution. "We seem to understand each other," Harrington said in 1977. "She is sometimes a difficult, headstrong actress, but she is also extremely talented. She makes wonderful 'choices' as an actress, and has an unerring sense of dramatic truth. The little displays of temperament are easy to cope with when you know you are getting something worthwhile on the screen."

On their arrival in London, they were greeted by a crowd of photographers and reporters, which was Harrington's first experience arriving at an airport in the company of an established star. Shelley initially stayed at the Hilton Hotel in London, and was driven by limousine to Shepperton Studios every morning for filming. Harrington and the rest of the American crew stayed at a small inn in Shepperton-on-Thames, where Elizabeth Taylor and Richard Burton had recently stayed while filming *Under Milk Wood* (1971). "The proprietress at the inn had been preparing special food for them, and so I became the lucky recipient of the same wonderful homemade meals they had been given," wrote Harrington. Shelley tried the inn for a few days, but realizing it wasn't the luxury she was after, she swiftly checked back into the Hilton.

Not imagining he would ever accept the role, Harrington was thrilled when Ralph Richardson agreed to play the role of the fake medium. Richardson traveled by motorbike to the studio every morning. "He was funny and charming and a total delight," wrote Harrington.

Mark Lester, who had become one of Britain's most well-known child actors after starring in the big screen musical *Oliver!* was cast as Christopher Coombs, with Chloe Franks playing little sister Katy. "I think I've only seen it twice," Mark Lester told me, in an interview over video-link, "but I remember the making of it well. My sister was actually in it, she was one of the children in the orphanage. There were a few kids I knew from the Corona stage school, where I used to go. So it was a really good atmosphere on set. I think my parents tried to keep me level-headed, so I was hopefully not too obnoxious. I can't remember being a brat, so hopefully I wasn't. I got on really well with Chloe Franks. She was really sweet. I think she went on to the Corona school, because funnily enough her mum was a teacher there."

Because they were on a tight budget, the rest of the cast were British character actors including Hugh Griffith as the meat delivery man, Rosalie Crutchley as the owner of the orphanage, Judy Cornwell as the maid, Michael Gothard as Albert the butler, and Lionel Jeffries as the police inspector. "I remember Lionel Jeffries being the lovely, cuddly granddad in *Chitty-Chitty Bang Bang*, but the swear words he used to come out with, it was really funny coming from someone who you wouldn't expect it," recollected Lester.

With Shelley having caused such problems with the costumes in Helen, Harrington was nervous as to what her reaction would be this time around. The budget was so limited that it couldn't stretch to a costume designer, and instead the wardrobe was sourced from stock by wardrobe mistress Bridget Sellers. Shelley was satisfied with the red, purple and maroon Edwardian-style gowns that had been sourced for her, and her behavior on set wasn't as erratic as it had been during *Helen*, no doubt because she was the solo star on the film.

"Shelley Winters was an amazing character force. She was really good with me," remembered Mark Lester. "Maybe not so good with some of the other people on the film. I seem to remember she had an assistant, one of the personal assistants there, probably in his early twenties, and he was her whipping boy. His name was Howard, and she would scream at him. 'Howard!' Get me a cup of tea, Howard!' And treated this poor lad like he was some sort of slave."

While he was very much aware that she was the star, and "that everybody else knew that too," Mark wasn't terrified of her at all, because she was good with the child actors, but with the adults it was a different story. "She was lovely with me. She was really kind. I seem to remember she would randomly give us presents. I think she gave Chloe Franks a teddy bear, and she gave me a toy car. Just little things, random things. So she was really sweet to the kids, just not so sweet to the rest of them. I think the poor director, he was walking on eggshells all the time, trying to get her performance out of her. As she had to play a deranged woman in it, and I think he was actually really frightened of her."

"She might have had a spat with Lionel Jeffries, but I'm not sure because I wasn't there, but I don't think he was that fond of her. She was always the last one to come on to do her bit, and swan in, even though we were filming, and I think Lionel Jeffries was a bit put out about the ways that she behaved."

During the rehearsal of the scene where she digs up the body of her daughter, Harrington recalled that Shelley suddenly stormed off set to her dressing room and refused to return to the lot. With her dressing room located some distance from where they were shooting, Harrington went to fetch her, so they wouldn't waste any more precious shooting time. He was dismayed to find her sitting at her dressing table, brushing out her hair, as this would take up another two hours to redo the style. When he asked her what was the matter, she said that it was too upsetting to do the scene, as she couldn't stop thinking of her own daughter, after wardrobe mistress Bridget had mentioned her name. "I had no strong, easy answer," said Harrington. "I just had to coax, cajole, and ease her back into doing the scene. It took a while, but I finally managed to get her to agree to come back on the set."

Released in March 1972, *Auntie Roo* was advertised with dramatic slogans like "She's taking A STAB at Motherhood!" and "The hand that rocks the cradle has no flesh on it!," which reinforced the trope of the crazed mother who descends into madness when her child is taken away. With its PG certificate, the film turned out to appeal more to children rather than adults, particularly with its theme of abandoned children overcoming devious adults. Overall, it received mixed reviews and failed to sizzle at the box office. "An Edwardian horror movie that opens up the full scope of Miss Winters's acting talent, which is insufficient reason for making a movie," wrote Roger Greenspun in *The New York Times* in 1972. Harrington later found a supporter in Quentin Tarantino, who made available a print of *Whoever Slew Auntie Roo?* to the American Cinematheque for a retrospective of Harrington's work in 1997.

Whoever Slew Auntie Roo? was Shelley's third turn at camp horror, following on from *The Mad Room* in 1969 *and What's the Matter with Helen?* Throughout the seventies she continued to be busy with a wide variety of output. She was Academy Award-nominated for the big-budget disaster movie *The Poseidon Adventure* (1972), but also took on low-budget B movies in the "Hag Horror" genre, including *Poor Pretty Edie* (1975), where she played an ex-burlesque star and owner of a rundown lodge in the Deep South, who terrorizes a young woman who comes to stay.

Despite her roles in seventies exploitation films, in an interview in the eighties she lamented the violence in modern film. "Right now I would like the censorship on violence. I really would. Cars crashing and Robocop and gratuitous violence."

She contrasted it with the more subtle depictions of violence in the film *An Average Little Man*, where she was directed by Mario Monicelli. She described the moment in the film where "my son is going with my husband to take a civil-service exam. He has yellow pencils in his pocket. As they walk, you hear a machine-gun – a bank is being robbed – and the camera goes to the ground, and all the yellow pencils are on the ground. And you know the kid's been hit. That's filmmaking. The other thing is just grisly."

19. "A study in misogyny..."

After completing *What's the Matter with Helen?* and *Whoever Slew Auntie Roo?* with Shelley Winters, both of which found success in drive-ins but failed to cross over into mainstream appeal, Curtis Harrington looked for his next project. Without any further movie offers on the table, he followed *Auntie Roo* with a television movie that offered a male equivalent of the Hag Horror genre.

Written by Henry Farrell, and produced by George Edwards for Aaron Spelling Productions, *How Awful About Allan* told the story of a man whose paranoia and fear leads to hysterical blindness. Cast in the role was Tony Perkins, who had struggled to find decent work since playing Norman Bates in *Psycho*. His performance had been so strong, and the character of Norman so unique, that he would be typecast in mentally-disturbed roles, despite having been a teen idol in the fifties.

Harrington and his producer partner George Edwards were also drawn to a film script by Tony Crechales, which was initially titled *Are You a Good Boy?* before being renamed *The Killing Kind*, and told the story of a psychopathic teenager whose violence is sparked by his hatred of women, both old and young. He wishes to rape the young girls who find him attractive, and abuse and murder the mother figures who he blames for his ills. The film tapped into the trend for exploitative horror movies following the abandoning of the American film censorship code in favor of a ratings system in 1968. Without the rigidity of the Production Code, films could now push boundaries by depicting increasingly graphic violence and sex on screen. The 1970s marked a revolution in horror films, which critic Robin Wood in his essay *The American Nightmare: Horror in the 70s*, described as "the period in which the evolution of the genre produced films more gruesome, more violent, more disgusting, and perhaps more confused, than ever before in its history."

The horror genre was reimagined by a new wave of directors like George Romero, John Carpenter, Wes Craven, Tobe Hooper, and Brian De Palma, tapping into overarching concerns of out-of-control violence in society, and the ongoing Vietnam War. Robin Wood noted how the "celebratory family film disappeared from the American cinema in the '50s. What happened was that its implicit content became displaced into the horror film." He described how family-themed films, once a staple of cinema, became *Psycho*, *Rosemary's Baby* and *Night of the Living Dead*. He drew particular attention to the "remarkable anticipation in *Meet Me in St. Louis* (1944) of the terrible child of the '70s horror film, especially in the two scenes (Halloween, and the destruction of the snow people) in which Margaret O'Brien symbolically kills parent figures. What is symbolic in 1944 becomes literal in *Night of the Living Dead*, where a little girl kills and devours her parents."

In Tobe Hooper's *The Texas Chainsaw Massacre* (1974), a group of healthy, liberal young Americans are slaughtered by a psychotic cannibal family. They are literally being consumed and devoured by a twisted family unit, as the traditions tied in with the gothic house of horrors crushes the hopes of young people.

Wes Craven's low-budget *Last House on the Left*, released in 1972, proved to be groundbreaking in the genre, with its disturbingly real depictions of rape and murder, cinematography which at times feels like found footage, and an unnervingly upbeat soundtrack. It also used the same tagline that William Castle had employed for *Strait-Jacket*: "To avoid fainting, keep repeating it's only a movie, it's only a movie, it's only a movie…" But rather than the camp horror moments featuring Joan Crawford that generated laughs, Craven's movie was terrifying and unnerving because it felt too real. In this new climate of horror movies, Harrington chose to move away from the Grand Guignol, to something more exploitative and confronting.

"*The Killing Kind* is my most realistic film; even though it deals with murder and obsessive personality, it really deals with the everyday," said Harrington in 1977. "There is no exoticism in it whatsoever. There, I was trying to make an overall comment on the whole thing, which is ultimately, in a way, a kind of nightmare. I wanted that slight removal from reality to put you in a more subjective world."

Crechales' script told the story of a Norman Bates-style serial killer, Terry (John Savage), whose good looks and love of chocolate milk hides his misogyny. Following his release from prison, where he served time for his role in a gang rape, Terry plans his revenge on the women who he blames for putting him there, including the rape victim, his female lawyer, and his own mother, whose transient relationships with men are deemed the cause of Terry's dysfunction. The film contains many unflinching scenes of violence against women, which at times seem excessively gratuitous. Richard Valley, editor of *Scarlet Street* magazine, called the script "a study in misogyny. Not only are its women, more often than not victims, they are also fools who, playing the mating game, all beg to be terminated."

Like many horror films in the 1970s, *The Killing Kind* is particularly troubling in its depiction of rape. "I wanted the opening rape scene to be as brutal as possible. That was very important," Harrington said. "It was a new-found freedom, but I feel I was totally justified in what I did with it."

The misogyny goes beyond the graphic violence in the rape scene. As Terry lies on his bed masturbating to pictures of vintage girls who are from the same era as when his mother was young, he phones up the girl he gang-raped years earlier. She's at home with a new boyfriend, but not recognizing the voice of Terry, she flirts with him and agrees to go on a date. The next night he follows her in his car as she's driving, runs her off the road and kills her.

She's ultimately blamed for her own fate, because she was seen to be flirting with young men despite the trauma inflicted on her by the rape, which is not how "real victims" are supposed to behave. Similarly, his spinster neighbor delivers a particularly problematic line to Terry, with whom she is infatuated. "It must be wonderful being raped. I wouldn't have told on you."

Women in *The Killing Kind* are depicted unflatteringly – they are middle-aged drunkards, grotesque elderly ladies, or flighty young women who flirt and tease men, such as the new guest at the boarding house, Leah, who immediately takes a liking to Terry and is graphically strangled to death in the bathroom. It's a blatant homage to *Psycho* that pushes the boundaries with its violence. In the dream sequence, Terry's father appears in drag. "That's just a little Harrington touch," the director said. "The Savage character is smothered by women, so that everyone becomes a female to him because he has so many sexual hang-ups."

It's the older women who are especially treated with disdain, particularly those who stay at the boarding house. Just as Harrington looked to the Los Angeles of his youth in *Helen*, he also added his own memories to *The Killing Kind*. He based the rooming house on the Hollywood lodge he stayed in when at college, run by a woman called Mabel Evans whose son was a "neurotic" who "played out his real-life frustrations on a broken-down piano in the living room."

He hired several elderly women from a nearby retirement home to play the lodgers, as well as bringing in two favorite actresses who had both appeared in *Night Tide*. Luana Anders was cast as the lonely spinster next door who is both suspicious and turned on by the activities of Terry and his mother, while Marjorie Eaton is an elderly lodger who Terry torments with a dead rat, in a direct reference to the infamous scene in *Baby Jane*.

Terry's mother, Thelma, played by Ann Sothern, is depicted as slatternly and feckless, and who is blamed for the murderous impulses of her son. As research, Harrington read books on the psychology of serial killers, whose horrific crimes, he said, were often triggered by a deep hatred of their mothers. As well as owning a boarding house for old, single women, Thelma is a photographer who enjoys taking pictures of her son, reflective of the horror film trope of mothers who are obsessed with their children. The final image Thelma takes is of him dying; an act of deliberate filicide as she poisons his glass of milk to stop him from killing her, and from harming others, after she makes the grim discovery of the body of Leah in her bathroom, and helps him cover up the murder.

Following her applauded role in *Lady in a Cage*, Ann Sothern found that her career was partly shaped by mother roles. She played a domineering stage mother in Robert Aldrich's teaser film *The Greatest Mother of Them All*, and in the bizarre TV series *My Mother the Car* (1965 - 1966) she was the voice of Jerry

Van Dyke's mother, who has been reincarnated as a 1928 Porter automobile.

She also made an appearance in a 1964 episode of *The Alfred Hitchcock Hour* called *Water's Edge*, adapted from a horror story by Robert Bloch about predator rats. In a direct reference to Ann's hugely successful TV show *Private Secretary*, her frumpy character was described as being like "that actress who plays the secretary on TV."

By the early 1970s, Ann was doing summer stock and the dinner theater circuit, and making the odd guest appearance on popular shows like *Alias Smith and Jones,* to pay the bills. Despite calling the 1970s "a time of ugliness," she embraced whatever opportunities came her way. After meeting Curtis Harrington and George Edwards to discuss their latest project, she accepted the role of Thelma, regardless of the unflattering depiction of a once beautiful, but now out of shape, former nightclub hostess with a number of failed relationships under her belt.

"It was a big departure," she said of the role. When asked if her career would be experiencing a similar revival to that of Olivia de Havilland, Bette Davis and Joan Crawford on the back of a horror film, she said, "In the first place each has her own audience. They got those audiences through the years. And you can't bury real talent. Talent gets better as it ages. All artists do."

Harrington soon discovered that Ann still displayed "the old star syndrome" and "was demanding and certainly no angel." He said that "she still had the pretty Ann Sothern face, but she had put on a great deal of weight over the years and was, like Shelley Winters, self-conscious about the additional weight to fit the role she was playing."

John Savage was a relative novice, having only appeared in one previous movie, the western *Bad Company*, but Ann was immediately aware of the impact he was making in his scenes. When he looked to the veteran actress for support and encouragement, she refused, and with a degree of jealousy, she tried to upstage him and disrupted his moments when doing the reverse angles.

With her self-consciousness around the weight she struggled to shake off, she found the insults about her appearance on screen to be particularly difficult. She took particular exception to the scene where Terry tells her that she's "like this big heavy pillow over my face, and you're suffocating me! Thelma and her bastard son! You fat whore! You're nothing but a fat whore!" She demanded that the word "fat" be removed from his speech. Harrington appeased her by appearing to agree to her request, because he already had the original version on tape, and which he sneakily reverted to in the editing room.

"There was some rivalry from her. I mean, she realized that he was very good, and I think she was a bit jealous of him," Harrington told *Scarlet Street* magazine in 1993. "She was sort of thinking, 'Oh God. Maybe he's stealing the scene from me' – particularly in the scene where he denounces her and calls her a fat whore. She got very difficult during that scene."

Harrington was heavily influenced by Hitchcock's films, and the shower murder was just one of the many references to Hitchcock in *The Killing Kind*. The film has a voyeuristic theme, of neighbors watching one another with lewd or murderous intent, sometimes through the lens of a camera, as with *Rear Window* (1954). The poisoned glass of milk owes a debt to the glass served up to Joan Fontaine by Cary Grant in *Suspicion* (1941). Terry whistles *The Merry Widow Waltz* from *Shadow of a Doubt* (1943) as he prepares to kill his lawyer Rhea, who is played by Ruth Roman, the heroine in Hitchcock's *Strangers on a Train* (1951). "I think it was just a matter of work," said Roman on agreeing to do *The Killing Kind*. "It was a very interesting role. It wasn't a big part; it was a small part, but it was very interesting." As Rhea, she is one of the older, single women that Terry takes his rage out on.

Born in Boston in 1922, Roman trained in acting at Bishop Lee Dramatic School, and moved to Hollywood after struggling to find work on Broadway. "I came to Hollywood during the war," Roman later reflected. "I was gonna conquer the world. I had about a hundred bucks on me. It took me 10 years to get successful." She was initially cast in a number of bit parts, including *Stage Door Canteen* (1943) and *Since You Went Way* (1944), and as the poster girl for the Marx Brothers' *A Night in Casablanca* (1946), despite her brief appearance having been cut out of the movie.

Roman's first major role was in RKO's thriller *The Window* (1949), followed by the film noir *Champion* with Kirk Douglas, the same year. She was signed to a long-term contract with Warner Brothers on the back of these parts, and was cast in *Beyond the Forest* (1949), Bette Davis's last film under contract at Warners. "We had a lot of fun together. We got along beautifully," she said of working with Davis. "She hated the part. She didn't want to do it, and there was a story around that if Bette walked, I would get the part – which would have been great! Bette was a big star – I mean, you just don't bother big stars – but she used to have me in her trailer for tea, and she was very friendly. She thought I should fight for better parts, and I think she was right."

Because she was their contract actress, Warner Brothers insisted Alfred Hitchcock cast Roman as the female lead in

Strangers on a Train (1951), despite his hesitancy that she wasn't right for the part. "Now, him I got along with beautifully!," she said. "He wanted some cool blonde, you know? I think Hitchcock told Truffaut that he didn't want me, but it wasn't because he thought I was a bad actress; he just didn't think I was right for it... It didn't matter, really, because we got along beautifully after we got to know each other."

Life magazine in May 1950 may have featured Roman on their cover, with the headline *The Rapid Rise of Ruth Roman*, but she never quite achieved star status. After leaving Warner Brothers, she worked with Universal on *The Far Country* (1955), and with United Artists for *Five Steps to Danger* (1957). With film offers becoming scarcer, she transitioned into television, where she worked regularly throughout the late fifties and early sixties with guest roles in popular shows like *Bonanza*, *Gunsmoke*, *The Untouchables*, *The FBI* and *The Mod Squad*.

By the early seventies, as veteran Hollywood actresses were being sought for low-budget horrors, she agreed to a role in the gross *The Baby* (1973). A particular low point in the horror movie genre, *The Baby* told the story of a grown man who is kept as an infant by his eccentric family. It was the first of four "Hag Horror" roles she would do after eight years off the screen. "Horrible thing! I'm sorry I made it," she reflected in 1993. "Oh, it was a terrible piece. It was very, very difficult. They had no money; they were on a string and nobody got along with anybody. I was surprised it came out at all, you know? Well it's sick!"

Roman's scenes in *The Killing Kind* were filmed in only a couple of days, and because it was made on such a low budget, she provided her own wardrobe. When it came to the scene where Terry holds her captive with a knife, slashes her, forces whisky down her throat, and then burns down her home, Harrington wanted her to be physically surrounded by fire. Roman steadfastly refused to do this stunt, and Harrington was forced to use a mannequin, dressed up in her own clothes.

"Curtis explained it to me, and I said, 'My dear, you have to get a dummy for that.' They wanted to put me in the middle; they said, 'Well, there's no danger!' But I'd been in the business a long time, and I just don't do my stunts. I said, 'No, I won't do it'...other than that I thought the scene was really a fine scene, directorially. It was so realistic that even I was a little shocked when I saw it – and I had performed it!"

In order to be able to finance *The Killing Kind*, Harrington secured private financing from a couple of Texas businessmen, but it would be a deal that turned out to be disastrous for the distribution of the film. These financiers, inexperienced in promoting a film, gave away the distributing rights, and it was limited to drive-in theaters in the south, and a brief showing in Los Angeles, where it quickly fizzled out.

Despite its failure to make an impact, Harrington considered *The Killing Kind* one of Ann Sothern's best performances, but because of its limited release, Ann didn't earn the accolades he thought she deserved. "I think it's one of my best films, and Ann Sothern is very proud of it," he said in 1993. "They had a special tribute to Ann Sothern at the Santa Barbara Film Festival three or four years ago, and she insisted that they show it. It was very well received at the Festival and Ann is very proud of it. She should be, because she's absolutely wonderful."

Ruth Roman followed *The Killing Kind* with further roles in low budget horror movies that were also tainted with misogyny. *Impulse* (1974), written by Tony Crechales, starred William

Shatner as a serial killer who targets widows, and *Knife for the Ladies* (1974) was a horror western about a serial killer targeting prostitutes. She jokingly described *Day of the Animals* (1977) as "Another winner! That was sort of fun. We were up in Sonora, and it's so gorgeous up there. It was worth the trip, believe me. That was sort of a tricky little piece, but it's not going to win any prizes."

In the eighties Roman took advantage of the popularity of soap operas by appearing in *Knot's Landing*, and she also had a recurring role in *Murder, She Wrote*, as a beautician. She enjoyed her semi-retirement at her home in Laguna Beach, California, where she died in 1999 at the age of seventy-six. She was level-headed about the lack of film roles that were coming her way as she got older. "I'm in the position that most actresses my age are in," she said when in her early seventies. "They're not writing those parts. It's nice if they would and, if something comes up, I certainly would love to take it – but I'm very content."

The Killing Kind shared similarities with another obscure serial killer horror, *Savage Intruder*, made in 1970, which also took advantage of the end of the Production Code to push extreme violence on its aging female star. Also known as *Hollywood Horror House*, it was a re-imagined version of *Sunset Boulevard*, starring Miriam Hopkins as a drunker, more delusional Norma Desmond, who invites a serial killer into her home.

Depicting a clash between the psychedelic counterculture of the late sixties, and the traditions of old Hollywood, Vic Valance, played by John David Garfield, is a hippie serial killer who targets older women in Hollywood. Like both Terry and Norman Bates, his fixation with his mother has led to a hatred of women. After killing a drunk middle-aged woman who he meets at the bar, Vic Valance turns up at the mansion of reclusive, faded star Katharine Packard, played by Hopkins, and pushes his way into a job as her personal nurse, where one of his tasks is to give her personal massages.

We first see her drunk and unsteady on her feet and under the delusion that she's still entertaining the glamorous guests in her home, until reality hits when she falls down the stairs. As the staff in Katharine's mansion become more suspicious of Vic, he kills them one by one, and like Joan Crawford in *Whatever Happened to Baby Jane?* or Olivia De Havilland in *Lady in a Cage*, she becomes a prisoner in her own home. Eventually he grows tired of Katharine and kills her too, replacing her with one of the mannequins she keeps in the home, reflecting his hatred of real women with real emotions, and his preference for a docile plastic object.

Katharine's mansion shares similarities with Norma Desmond's. It's white, to reflect a sense of the innocent past, but her pool is unkempt and dirty, symbolic of the tarnishing of Hollywood. Showing the difference between modern life and the Hollywood of the past, Vic takes Katharine for a night out on the Sunset Strip, where she ends up at a psychedelic youth party. Later, Katharine drinking in her home is intercut with images of Vic and her maid, Greta, at Sunset Strip bars, further reinforcing the clash between the young and older generations, a theme which was also depicted in *Lady in a Cage*, *Games* and *The Mad Room*. Katharine's housekeeper, Mildred, played by another veteran, Gale Sondergaard, even calls young people self-centered animals.

Filming took place at The Norma Talmadge estate, in the home that once belonged to the silent-era actress, and just as Norma Desmond screens her old movies for Joe Gillis, Katharine shows Vic one of hers – using a clip of Hopkins in *Wise Girl* (1937). The film opens with real-life publicity photos of Miriam Hopkins over footage over a premiere for *The Dancing Cavalier*, a film within 1952's *Singin' in the Rain*, at Grauman's Chinese Theatre. The glamor of Hollywood becomes more tawdry, with the dilapidation of the Hollywood sign as a symbol of the decrepitude of aging stars like Hopkins.

Hopkins' last lead role was more than twenty-five years before, when she starred with Bette Davis in *Old Acquaintance* (1943). "Miriam Hopkins was a wonderful actress," said Bette, "but a bitch. The most thoroughgoing bitch I've ever worked with."

Born in 1902 in Savannah, Georgia, Miriam Hopkins began her career in New York as a chorus girl before moving to Broadway. After being signed up by Paramount Pictures, she found success in the 1931 horror film *Dr. Jekyll and Mr. Hyde*, directed by Rouben Mamoulian. She was famed for her work with director Ernst Lubistch in *Trouble in Paradise* (1931) and *Design for Living* (1933) and had a notable place in Hollywood history for her lead role in the first three-strip Technicolor film, *Becky Sharp* (1935), for which she was nominated for an Academy Award. Known for her huge ego and her diva-like behavior, she could be incredibly difficult on set. "Like most actresses, she was in love with the sound of her own voice. Her ego was so gargantuan it frequently turned and fed on itself," recalled George Cukor.

She also had a voracious sexual appetite, and was known for her many lovers, both male and female. "When I can't sleep, I don't count sheep," Hopkins said, "I count lovers. And when I reach thirty-eight or thirty-nine I'm fast asleep."

Bette Davis feuded with Hopkins on numerous occasions. The two actresses had first worked together in 1928, when Hopkins was the star of George Cukor's theater company, and Bette was just starting out. Several years later Hopkins played *Jezebel* on Broadway and purchased the film rights, but when Jack Warner gave Bette Davis the film role, for which she won the Oscar for Best Actress, Hopkins never forgave her. The two actresses were lined up to co-star in *The Old Maid*, and on the first day of filming, Hopkins swept on to the set dressed in a duplicate of one of Bette's *Jezebel* costumes.

They were paired up again in *Old Acquaintance* (1943), about two friends who compete as novelists, and production became a battleground between the divas, driving the first director Edmund Goulding to a heart attack, and testing the nerves of his replacement Vincent Sherman. Production was so fraught with tension that Hopkins announced she was finished with Hollywood and moved to New York. She returned in supporting roles, but her next lead role wouldn't be until she was sixty-six years old, in *Savage Intruder*.

Savage Intruder was only given a limited release, despite the campaigning efforts of Miriam Hopkins and Gale Sondergaard, and its hippie serial killer Vic Valance failed to make the same impact as Terry in *The Killing Kind*. As film critic Richard Valley wrote:

"In the Movie Psycho Hall of Fame, the forgotten Terry Lambert deserves his place with the Immortals. Vastly superior to such robotic madmen as Jason Voorhees and Michael Meyers, humanly flawed in ways denied such otherworldly assassins as Freddy Kreuger, Terry stands side by side with Norman Bates, a boy only a mother could love."

20. "Oh yes; I was beautiful, once..."

In the 2017 movie *Film Stars Don't Die in Liverpool*, Annette Bening depicted Gloria Grahame in the final years of her life. The sultry star of 1950s film noirs had improbably ended up in the north of England doing regional theater and dating a younger actor from Liverpool, all the while struggling with a cancer diagnosis.

Gloria skulked onto screens in the late forties and early fifties, playing brooding femme fatales and wisecracking tarts with a heart. With the lazy, girlish voice, the pout, the eyes half closed, and the sheen on her face from nights spent in sleazy dives, her image and persona seemed so well suited to film noir that she struggled to move into lighter roles, despite her well-received performance as Ado Annie in *Oklahoma!*, where she sings "I'm Just a Girl Who Cain't Say No."

As Dan Callahan wrote in his 2017 article on Grahame in *Bright Lights Film*: "She generally makes her entrance on-screen accompanied by a wail of hot jazz, eating candy, applying lipstick to that puffy mouth, flipping her dirty hair and cheap hoop earrings, extending her toned legs so we can see her shapely feet tied up in ankle-strap high heels."

Between 1951 and 1955, Grahame acted in over a dozen movies, winning the Best Supporting Actress Oscar for *The Bad and the Beautiful* in 1953, but scandal and rumor damaged her career, most notably for her relationship to former stepson Tony Ray, the son of her ex-husband, director Nicholas Ray. All four of Gloria's marriages were tumultuous; her first to Stanley Clements in the forties was abusive, her second to Nicholas Ray was troubled by his heavy drinking, her third to writer Cy Howard was notorious for their blazing rows as they traveled around Europe, and at one point it was reported that she even pulled a gun on him. Her fourth marriage to Tony Ray in 1960 was tarnished by rumors she had seduced him when he was thirteen, and she disappeared from screens soon after, due to reputational damage as a result of the scandal. She spent the next decade raising her four children, while fighting various custody battles with her ex-husbands.

In one of her comeback roles in the seventies, Gloria played a faded actress, Carolyn Parker, in the NBC TV movie *The Girl on The Late, Late Show* (1974). Carolyn Parker has completely disappeared from public consciousness as she hides away in her dilapidated mansion in the Hollywood Hills following a career-ending scandal. The TV movie, modeled on both *Sunset Boulevard* and *Baby Jane*, used real clips of Gloria from her classics like *The Big Heat* (1953). Gloria doesn't appear in person until the last three minutes, when we see the aging actress sitting in darkness in her mansion, with tears streaming down her face as she watches her own performance in *In a Lonely Place* (1950). It was the ultimate meta moment, particularly when Don Murray's TV presenter asks the question "What Ever Happened to Carolyn Parker?" But what he and the audience were really asking was "What Ever Happened to Gloria Grahame?"

Born on November 28, 1923 in Los Angeles as Gloria Hallward, her Scottish mother was an actress and teacher who went by the stage name Jean Grahame, and she inspired Gloria to drop out of Hollywood High School to pursue acting. Gloria began her career performing on Broadway, as an understudy to Miriam Hopkins in Thornton Wilder's *The Skin of Our Teeth*, followed by

A Highland Fling, in April 1944, which brought her to the attention of Louis B. Mayer. Signed to an MGM contract, Mayer swiftly insisted on changing her name to Gloria Grahame, because Hallward was "too theatrical," and cast her in her first feature, *Blonde Fever* (1944). But no other roles were forthcoming, and she spent her time posing for glamor shots that marketed her as another sexy blonde.

Frank Capra, who was making *It's a Wonderful Life* at RKO, was struggling to cast the role of flirtatious Violet Brick. Unhappy with Ann Sothern being assigned to the role, when he came across tests for Gloria Grahame he recognized that she possessed the qualities that could make her a star.

Dancing the Charleston with older men at the town dance, Violet Bick is the opposite of George Bailey's wife, played by Donna Reid. Later, in a vision of what would happen if Bailey didn't exist, we see the older Violet as a drunken, immoral woman – a warning that this is what happens to town floozies. One of Gloria's lines in the film - "I only wear it when I don't care how I look" – became a classic movie quote, and her performance triggered MGM to finally pay attention to her.

She was cast in a musical, *It Happened in Brooklyn* (1946), and was splashed on the cover of *Life* magazine on October 21, 1946. Listed as being twenty, when she was really twenty-three, *Life* said she was "practically certain to be a movie star. Her talent and native sexiness, especially when dancing, caught the eyes of the most imposing of all movie magnates, Louis B. Mayer of MGM who now has made her career his personal concern."

Still unwilling to promote her as a star, MGM loaned her to RKO, which turned out to be a good move. Her performance as a bar girl in *Crossfire* (1947), the first Hollywood drama to deal with anti-Semitism, earned her an Academy Award nomination for Best Supporting Actress, and her performance led her to being signed to a contract with RKO in June 1947.

Gloria first met future husband Nicholas Ray when he directed her in the film noir *A Woman's Secret* (1949), her second film under contract for RKO. After a Las Vegas divorce from her first husband Stanley Clements, she married Nicholas Ray that same day, on June 1, 1948. Her son Timothy was born five and a half months after the wedding.

Mostly relegated to supporting roles, husband Nicholas Ray cast her in a rare leading role in *In a Lonely Place* (1950), opposite Humphrey Bogart, as a cool, wry blonde with a dark past, and who is once again a victim of domestic abuse. In one of the big disappointments in her career, RKO refused to loan her out for George Stevens' *A Place in the Sun*, with the role of Alice going to Shelley Winters, and instead she was cast in *Macao* (1952), a dated exotic drama directed by Josef von Sternberg. She cut ties with RKO in October 1950, and chose to work freelance for the rest of her career. Over the next five years she was featured in a series of prestige films, beginning with Cecil B. DeMille's *The Greatest Show on Earth* (1952) where she performed dangerous stunts as the "elephant girl." DeMille described her as having "the manner of a schoolgirl and the eyes of a sorceress."

When Gloria played the vampish younger rival to Joan Crawford in *Sudden Fear* (1952), she found the veteran actress to be unpleasant to her. It was partly down to jealousy – Gloria was said to be having an affair with Jack Palance behind the scenes, and this soured the feelings of Crawford, who preferred to be the one who was adored by her co-stars.

"What do you think of Gloria Graham?" Hedda Hopper asked Joan in a 1958 interview. "I never think of Gloria Grahame," she replied. "I know you're going to print that, so I'd better elaborate. I hate unprofessionalism in anybody. If you could find this girl – she'd wander on the set two hours late."

She was cast as the doomed wife of Dick Powell in Vincente Minnelli's *The Bad and the Beautiful* (1952), and this thirteen-minute supporting role won her an Academy Award. At the ceremony on March 19, 1953, twenty-nine-year-old Gloria was so nervous going up to the stage that she looked unsteady on her feet, and felt too self-conscious to do the typical post-win interviews. Her behavior was blamed on being too drunk, which damaged her reputation at a time when she should have been star-bound.

One of her most famous roles, as Debby in Fritz Lang's *The Big Heat*, was initially intended for Marilyn Monroe. Debby is a good time girl who cha-chas while mixing cocktails, and enjoys the "expensive fun" of a life with gangsters. It's a world where women are roughed up by men, and then given some money to buy "something nice." As she enjoys her own reflection in the mirror, carefully applying lipstick to her proud mouth, Lee Marvin throws boiling coffee in her face; an act of punishment for all vain women like Debby. But her ditziness covers up for her toughness, and after being horrifically scarred, she makes sure she has her revenge, and the final act of the film becomes her moment of vengeance.

In brutal film noir *Naked Alibi* (1954), a Ross Hunter production for Universal, she plays a sexy singer who has to be tough enough to survive both a sleazy club, and the turbulence of her life. Gloria's characters were so often the bad girl – the threat to family stability as she seduces married men, and whose behavior will never lead to a happy ending. "She was a hell of a dame. She called a stone a stone, and knew exactly what she wanted," said Ross Hunter.

Despite her successes in the early fifties, she suffered from crippling self-doubt and worries about her looks. Hedda Hopper pegged her "a shy little introvert so self-conscious it hurts," and she was particularly insecure about her lips, which she tried to fix with successive surgery. When one botched operation left her with paralysis in her top lip, she began stuffing it with tissue paper and cotton wool to make it look more pronounced, which her leading men discovered during their love scenes. By 1960 she had earned the unflattering nickname "The Girl with the Novocaine Lip" after Sidney Skolsky wrote in *Photoplay*: "Gloria Grahame has returned to the Hollywood scene. She is as sexy as ever, although she manages to speak as if her upper lip is novocained."

When he was casting for *Oklahoma!* Fred Zinnemann was convinced Gloria was his Ado Annie, despite her lack of musical experience. She was nervous about doing the role, but was persuaded by the $100,000 salary and the royalties from the soundtrack. The environment on the set was hostile, and she felt she was stumbling through her performance, having to sing one note at a time to create the recording. With rumors of her conduct on set, she found her career stalling and that she had become a pariah in Hollywood.

After her vampish supporting role in *Not as a Stranger*, and parts in *The Man Who Never Was* (1956) and *Ride out for Revenge* (1957), *Odds Against Tomorrow* (1959) would be her last performance in film for twelve years, as she became embroiled in personal problems around her controversial marriage to Tony

Ray. In an interview in 1979 with Arthur Bell, he asked: "There were reports that you were rude and uncooperative to a lot of people. Was that because you didn't play the Hollywood game?'" She replied, "'I don't know what that game is. I don't think I ever understood Hollywood.'"

Finally, after a long absence from the screen, she made a return to films, first with *The Todd Killings* (1971), where she played Richard Thomas's mother, and then in *Blood and Lace*, a low-budget slasher produced by American International Pictures in 1971, which did well on the B-movie drive-in circuit. Grahame plays the sadistic Dorothy Deere, a widow who runs a government-funded youth home, and returning to the screen after so many years away proved to be a shock for Grahame. "It isn't that you forget your craft - it's just that so many things today seem different," she said.

Directed by Philip S Gilbert, the film exploited the popular horror theme of a conflict between the generations, and while it reveals the dangers of older women, it also played up to the fears around out-of-control youth and the increasing levels of violence in society.

With no makeup, and her naturally curly hair worn lank and unkempt, Grahame is depicted as a vicious monster who laments the loss of her looks, and her bitterness drives her to treat the teenagers in her care with cruelty. Mrs. Deere may be charming on the surface, but in reality she's the wicked old crone of fairy tales like *Hansel and Gretel*. When her wards try to escape, she sends her handyman after them with a meat cleaver, and then hooks them up in the basement freezer, where she has also stashed the body of her beloved husband Jamieson, to preserve him. She laments that he was "the only thing in my life that mattered; no children, no friends." She also reveals that he left her when she became old – because for a woman aging can be a fate worse than death. "I suppose things are always different when you are beautiful," she says. "I can remember - oh yes; I was beautiful, once."

Teenager Ellie Masters (Melody Patterson) is sent to the home following the gruesome murder of her prostitute mother and her client. A middle-aged detective, Calvin Carruthers (Vic Taybeck), investigating her mother's death takes an inappropriate interest in Ellie, who soon discovers that Mrs. Deer runs the home like a workhouse. She sends the handyman to chase after and kill any of the children who escape. In the climactic twist, as Melody is revealed to have been the murderer of her own mother, Carruthers blackmails her into marrying him. However, he then reveals a close familial connection to her, and she finds herself in an unthinkable incestuous bind.

"There's a good deal of blood and a minimum of logic, or lace for that matter, in *Blood and Lace*," wrote AH Weiler in *The New York Times*. "Exposed also are Gloria Grahame and a clutch of decidedly lesser-known performers in a low-grade exercise in shadows, screams, traumas and slayings that are largely more laughable than shocking…The haggard Miss Grahame, who simply walks through her assignment and at one point says, somewhat wistfully, 'Oh, yes, I was young once,' also ends up in her own deadly freezer."

Grahame followed up *Blood and Lace* with a small part in CBS's horror western *Black Noon* with Ray Milland and Yvette Mimieux, and a bit part in *Chandler,* a TV movie starring Leslie Caron and Warren Oates, both released in 1971. She was also offered a small role in *The Loners* (1972), an *Easy Rider*-inspired film about hippie motorcyclists who come into conflict with local rednecks. Dressed in a cheap blonde wig, she played the waitress mother of a teenage girl who rebels and runs away with Dean Stockwell. Sutton Roley, the director, recalled that "She knew her shots, and was absolutely no trouble of any kind. The only demand she made was for a shoulder-length, straight blond wig, which I thought was not flattering but for some reason made her feel comfortable in the part."

In March 1974, Gloria filed for divorce from Tony Ray, in what would be a bitterly contested action involving custody of her two sons, as well as a protracted battle over finances. As a result of her divorce, Gloria pared down her living, and instead of a mansion in Beverly Hills, chose to live in a caravan near the Pacific Palisades, with views over the ocean. It was easy to clean, and affordable, at a time when she didn't know when her next payments would come in.

"It took me fourteen years to make money as an actress," she said in her deposition. "Since my marriage has kept me in the kitchen for approximately fourteen years, it has reduced my earning capacity to near zero, which is understandable, in that the experiences perfected in the kitchen are little in demand on stage, screen or TV."

During a heated argument just before she filed for divorce, Tony threw a can at her during an argument, and it hit her right breast, causing bruising. After a medical examination, she received a devastating breast cancer diagnosis, and with the singular determination to reduce the tumor, she followed the principles of Adele Davis by embarking on a program of healthy eating. Now that she was single once again, and having gone through a health crisis, she sought to continue with acting in this second stage of her life. Her small but important role in *The Girl on the Late, Late Show* was followed by a cheap exploitation movie, *Mama's Dirty Girls* (1974), where she played a brassy and blood-thirsty character called Mama Love, who trains her three daughters to seduce, marry and murder men for their money. It was produced by *Blood and Lace*'s Ed Carlin and Gil Lasky, and despite the film's low budget quality, Gloria was at least allowed to look glamorous with wavy blonde hair, sleek suits and heels.

With a need to keep working, Gloria took up offers for performing in the UK, where faded stars like Stan Laurel and Oliver Hardy had also had success doing tours. She arrived in England in spring 1978 to play Sadie Thompson in *Rain*, for a three-week run at the Watford Palace Theater. It was here that she met Liverpudlian actor Peter Turner, three decades her junior, who was staying in the same boarding house for actors in Primrose Hill. "She didn't dress up or look glamorous. It didn't feel like I was hanging out with a film star at all," he said.

As a Hollywood star acting in local theater, she found she was in high demand with reporters wanting interviews. Referred to as a "legendary floozie" in one feature, she received invitations to cocktail parties, film premieres and first nights at West End theaters. With all this attention in the UK, she found she was also receiving more offers in America, including a cameo role in the romantic comedy *Head Over Heels* (1979).

Gloria was paranoid about her aging and losing her looks and repeatedly lied about her age, knocking more and more years off. Turner recollected a time in New York, when walking through Greenwich Village, they were invited into a vintage shop, where the owner had a huge collection of photos and posters of classic films. He proudly showed her a still from when she appeared in *It's a Wonderful Life*. As Turner wrote: "Gloria looked horrified when she saw that the image had been captioned with the year it was released, 1946. "No, it wasn't," she told him. "That's a mistake. It should be 1956."

After her role in the controversial 1976 horror *Mansion of the Doomed*, she took on another low-budget horror, *The Nesting*, which would be her last feature film. It was directed by Armand Weston, best known for his soft porn flicks, and like *Mansion of the Doomed*, it would later be confiscated in the UK under section three of the Obscene Publications Act of 1959, as a reaction against video nasties in the early 1990s. She played the ghost of a brothel madam, Florinda Costello, who avenges the murders that took place in the house years before. With its release delayed until May 1982, it played only in grindhouse theaters.

Her cancer returned in spring 1980, and she made the decision not to go through chemotherapy, which could only prolong her life and not eradicate the cancer. She refused to tell friends and family of her suffering, as she didn't want her illness to impact on her career.

While rehearsing a local theater performance of *The Glass Menagerie* in Lancaster, she collapsed from an infection in her stomach and was taken to Peter Turner's family home in Liverpool in the hopes that she would agree to have treatment. She refused. She died at St. Vincent's Hospital in Manhattan three hours after being flown home from London to New York.

Gloria once reflected on the highs and lows that an actor will go through, from winning an Oscar to playing the "hag" in violent B-movie horrors. "You go through life in a series of peaks and valleys," she said. "Like you do a picture called *Crossfire* and you get an Academy Award nomination, and you do a picture called *The Bad and the Beautiful* and you win an Oscar and you find yourself in a situation where you get offered all kinds of interesting things that nobody would have dreamed of offering you before. You're the flavor of the month, you're news. Then it goes down a shade, and you do something else; then some slight thing happens, and you do a television series, now your life comes up to a peak again. It's all highs and lows. I feel there's so much I've got to learn. In a sense I think we are always moving toward something, never feeling that we've ever achieved it, and never feeling that we've done the best that we're able to do. And I think that's healthy."

21. "The untamed woman is always ready to strike..."

"She was one of the dreaded 'Cat People' – doomed to slink and prowl and court by night…fearing always that a lover's kiss might change her into a snarling, clawing KILLER!"

In RKO's horror classic *Cat People*, the French actress Simone Simon plays a cursed Serbian woman, Irena, who is worried that when she is sexually aroused she will turn into the mythical cat creature from her homeland, and kill her lover. The trigger that ultimately sparks the release of her true animal nature is jealousy.

Val Lewton, who produced some of the most significant horror films of the 1940s during his tenure at RKO, was inspired by his fear of cats in developing the script with director Jacques Tourneur and screenwriter DeWitt Bodeen. The film followed after the success of Universal's *The Wolf Man*, released in 1941, with Kim Newman, in his BFI study of *Cat People*, speculating that Lewton was tasked with coming up with an alternative shape-shifting film for RKO that fit the title *Cat People*. Val Lewton was also inspired by Paramount's *Island of Lost Souls*, and their much publicized "panther woman." Lewton said: "I'd like to have a girl with a little kitten-face like Simone Simon, cute and soft and cuddly and seemingly not at all dangerous."

The themes of the film tapped into society's fear of female sexuality as women gained new freedoms and independence as a result of the Second World War. As with the popularity of Film Noir at the time, it played into the paranoia of independent women taking the place of men. As Robin Wood noted, Val

Lewton's 40s horror films "strikingly anticipate, by at least two decades, some of the features of the modern horror film. *Cat People* is centered on the repression of female sexuality in a period where the monster is almost invariably male and phallic."

Cat People's legacy would continue to have an influence on supernatural and horror film makers, including Curtis Harrington when devising the script for his first feature, *Night Tide*, about a mermaid who fears she'll be unable to control her siren instincts when she falls in love with Dennis Hopper's sailor. Women are often associated with cats in films, from *Bringing up Baby* (1938) to *Alien* (1979), where Ripley's ginger cat, Jones, is juxtaposed with the alien, and is named after the office cat, John Paul Jones, in Tournier's film.

In the same realm as the vampire, the werewolf and Dr. Jekyll and Mr. Hyde, the woman who transforms into a fearsome creature, often after the sun goes down, is a threat to both men and women with her deadly female sexuality. She is sometimes depicted as a lesbian, a notion that is dangerous to the patriarchy as it places women outside the realms of male understanding. She's also beautiful on the surface, but it's twisted – there's a flaw to her, something that marks her out as being from another realm.

"She may appear pure and beautiful on the outside but evil may, nevertheless, reside within," wrote Barbara Creed in *The Monstrous-Feminine*. "It is this stereotype of feminine evil – beautiful on the outside/corrupt within – that is so popular within patriarchal discourses about woman's evil nature."

As the publicity poster for *Cat People* declared, "Like a jungle cat, the untamed woman is always ready to strike, to tear man apart with claw and fang." Centuries ago, in Irena's once devil-worshiping village in Serbia, King John kills with his sword some of the villagers, but the "wisest and most wicked" escaped to the mountains, where they could turn into cats. From her apartment Irena can hear the animals in the zoo, the roaring of lions and the panther. "It screams like a woman…I don't like that." Irena is fascinated by the caged panther, and throws a dead bird, which had died from fright, into its cage, as if offering up a sacrifice.

Irena pushes away her new husband, Oliver, refusing to have sex with him in case she mauls him to death. "Oliver, we should never quarrel, never let me feel jealousy or anger. Whatever it is that's in me is held in, is kept harmless, when I'm happy," she tells him. Beware the anger, rage and desire of women, as it's dangerous when uncontained.

As Irena becomes jealous of Oliver's coworker, Alice, her wild-side is unleashed, and tension is built with the much-replicated stalking scenes. Alice sets out to walk alone through the park at night to get home, when she hears footsteps behind her and panics that she's being stalked. As she starts to run, she reaches a bus stop, and when the bus pulls up, it makes a hissing noise at the same time as we expect to see a panther. The panther's footprints turn back into Irena's feet, and we see that animals in the zoo have been killed. Irena cries in the bathroom, aware of what she's become, but she also wants revenge on Alice. In another tense moment, Irena stalks Alice as she goes to her apartment's swimming pool changing rooms. There's the sense that Alice is being watched as she changes, and when she hears the growl of a panther, she jumps into the water, where she's trapped as Irena prowls in the shadows.

By the late sixties and early 1970s there was a rise in the number of B-movies that depicted female creatures and vampires which linked femininity with sex and death, and was connected with the emergence of the women's liberation movement. The films explored the concerns that women were becoming more aggressive as they demanded equal rights, and this call for more agency of their bodies was considered dangerous. Men feared that they would become maligned as a result of their shifting status in society. The female cat, vampire, or siren was a threat because she destroyed men and seduced her female victims, taking them away from their expected roles in society as a good wife and mother. There was also another version of the cat film. It depicts the older woman, unable or unwilling to have a fulfilling love life, who has a twisted love of cats, provoking the suspicions and hatred of the younger generation.

A film that combined the conventions set by *Cat People* with the tropes of the "Hag Horror" genre was 1969's *Eye of the Cat* (1969), penned by Joseph Stefano, the screenwriter for *Psycho*. Eleanor Parker plays Danielle, a wheelchair bound, elderly aunt who plans to leave her significant inheritance to the cats that flock to her. She becomes the victim of a plot by her beloved nephew, Wylie, and a mysterious younger woman, Kassia, to murder her for her money.

Arguably best known for her role as the icy baroness in *The Sound of Music* (1965), Parker had a fierce talent that was unappreciated and underused. She was nominated three times for the Best Actress Oscar for *Caged* (1950), *Detective Story* (1951) and *Interrupted Melody* (1955), and ambitiously took on a triple role in *Lizzie* (1957) as three separate personalities of one woman. By the mid-sixties she was mostly relegated to television guest appearances and supporting roles in films where her age was unflatteringly depicted. As an actor's agent in *The Oscar* (1966) she was referred to as an "old lady" and she was cast as a violent alcoholic in the crime drama *An American Dream* (1966). The poster even played up to the notion of the older female harridan, with a picture of a slatternly Parker and the tagline "This is Mrs. Rojack. Be glad you're not Mr. Rojack."

Parker was only forty-six years old at the time of filming *Eye of the Cat*, and looked beautiful, despite playing a supposedly elderly widow. While still glamorous, her character was often dressed in purple, to reflect the old-fashioned concept of wearing the color for half-mourning. The film also deals with the contrast between the older generation and the youthful counterculture. In a montage, Wylie and Kassia wander through the hip communities of San Francisco in their sleek, off-beat costumes, interacting with the hippies and students who discuss French filmmaking and coming out as gay to their mothers.

As well as requiring a wheelchair, Danielle is further incapacitated by her need to sleep under an oxygen tent after having two thirds of her lungs removed. Like Blanche Hudson in *Baby Jane* and Mrs. Hilyard in *Lady in a Cage*, she is more vulnerable due to her illness, particularly when a shock leaves her struggling for breath. In one thrilling scene, she is unable to stop her wheelchair from rolling back down a steep San Francisco street. The film also paid homage to the sound effects in *Cat People*, where the hiss of a cat turns out to be the sound of a bus pulling in. In *Eye of the Cat*, it's the brakes on Danielle's wheelchair that replicate the sounds; a moment similarly designed to make the audience jump.

Her nephew Wylie, who left Danielle and his brother Luke in favor of leading a bohemian lifestyle, has an irrational fear of cats following a repressed childhood memory. He asks her to get rid of the cats, and she does so, yet they always return to her. It's revealed through an uncomfortable exchange between Danielle and Wylie that she has always been sexually attracted to him, and while it appears incestuous, she was married to his deceased father, rather than being a direct aunt. She's the degenerate older woman with grotesque sexual desires that link her to the cats that surround her, and protect her. Wylie jokes with her that the reason she keeps her cats is because she holds orgies with them. "They're your link with the devil. You all get together and perform unimaginable acts of darkness." She tells them the cats just come, "I'm never sure from where."

Curtis Harrington also had a turn at exploring the mysterious cat woman, inspired by his appreciation of the works of Val Lewton. When Harrington was offered the script for an ABC Television Movie of the Week called *The Cat Creature*, he worried it was the start of a slippery slope into what he considered an inferior medium. "It is just like a feature film, only without the star power, without the budget, and most often with an inferior script that has not been tailored to bring out the best of its intrinsic merits, but rather to please TV executives whose mind-set is influenced by the demands of advertisers," he said.

The script by Robert Bloch was adapted from an old story he'd written for *Weird Tales*, a popular pulp horror magazine, about a girl who is the reincarnation of an ancient Egyptian cat goddess. ABC television executives were keen to cast Patty Duke in the lead, as she had recently won an Emmy for the TV movie *My Sweet Charlie* (1970). Harrington rejected her for not being sexy enough to play a "beautiful, dark, exotic, sexually alluring girl." Instead, the part went to blonde-haired Meredith Baxter, star of sitcom *Bridget Loves Bernie*, who wore a dark red wig, and green contact lenses. As a tribute to *Cat People*, Harrington cast Kent Smith, the actor who had played Oliver in the original film.

In Bloch's story, the mysterious owner of an occult shop, and purveyor of a cursed ancient Egyptian amulet, was a man, but Harrington asked him to rewrite the role for a woman, as he hoped he could place Gale Sondergaard in the role; an actress whom he fondly remembered from his cinephile childhood.

Born in 1899 to Danish immigrants in Minnesota, Gale Sondergaard was the first winner of the Best Supporting Actress Oscar category in 1936, for her film debut *Anthony Adverse*. She had never received the physical award, and during the making of *The Cat Creature* a press event was held for her to finally receive the statuette.

Sondergaard had been the original choice for the Wicked Witch of the West in *The Wizard of Oz*, with an interpretation of the character as strikingly beautiful, like the villainous queen in *Snow White and the Seven Dwarves*. When the decision was made for the witch to be made into an ugly crone, she felt that the makeup might typecast her, and the part was given to Margaret Hamilton instead.

Ultimately, she still found herself typecast, this time in sultry, exotic roles. She out-acted Bette Davis in *The Letter* as a vengeful Malaysian woman, in an example of Hollywood's problematic casting. "It was a big help that I hardly spoke! Otherwise the mystery and allure would have been gone, fast! I just did my best to be evil, to think evil, and hoped it wouldn't seem foolish. I think the picture was photographed beautifully," she later told the magazine *Scarlet Street*.

After supporting roles in *The Cat and the Canary* (1939), *The Mark of Zorro* (1940) and *The Black Cat* (1941), she became a cult favorite as the Spider Woman of the 1943 Sherlock Holmes film, which she later admitted "was something to help pay the bills. I knew it wasn't art. I certainly didn't think it would outlast all my pictures other than *The Letter*."

She said: "I had a certain range, and so they cast me in supporting roles. That can be a trap, because if you win for supporting, they decide you're a wonderful supporter to their stars, and you get those very good but smaller roles. Fortunately, I was never grandly ambitious, you know. I was not like my friend Bette."

As John J. O'Connor wrote in *The New York Times* in 1973, "In most of her screen roles, especially some of the Sherlock Holmes episodes, Miss Sondergaard made the perfect villain, her elegance somewhat sinister, her smile calculatingly dazzling, her eyes chillingly cool."

Sondergaard's career was cut short as a result of her left-wing political beliefs. Her husband Herbert Biberman was one of the Hollywood Ten, a group of writers and directors who refused to testify before the House Un-American Activities Committee in 1947. She and Biberman were exiled from Hollywood for many years, with most of their movie-colony friends deserting them. "I sort of lost the spirit to fight. You don't fight and fight without paying a price – and my background instilled in me that I could survive without a career. For a man, well, he's more defined by his work, or so he thinks he is."

By the late sixties those who had been shunned were slowly finding work again, and Sondergaard began to take up offers with trepidation, making a comeback in 1969 in an episode of *It Takes a Thief* called *The Scorpio Drop*, and in an off-Broadway show, *Woman*. In 1970 she played spinster editor Amanda in *The Best of Everything* TV series, a part played by Joan Crawford in the 1959 film, and she was given a small role in the low-budget horror *Savage Intruder*.

"I knew, for one thing, that I was old, which is not the Hollywood way," she said, of her career in the sixties. "I knew I'd never been a great star; I couldn't do what Bette or Joan were doing, and perhaps I was somewhat lazy about chasing opportunities. Believe me, I wasn't eating my heart out over not working!"

Harrington had wanted Sondergaard's mysterious character to be gay, to "lend a bit of spice to the show," but the network, nervous of any controversy, stated that there must be no suggestion of it in the script. But the casting of Sondergaard hinted at this, as the Spider Woman had a particular following amongst lesbians, and there had been plenty of rumors around her own sexuality. She said she had "never been very conventional. I was not traditionally pretty or girlish. Often, I portrayed strong, domineering characters. This can lead to rumors."

Lana Turner had her turn as the grande dame in a mysterious cat movie, *Persecution* (1974), which was given the alternative titles *Sheba*, *The Graveyard* and *The Terror of Sheba* – a clear indication it struggled to find an audience on release. It was written by Robert Hutton, an American actor who had starred in a number of Hollywood films in the 1940s and 1950s, including *Destination Tokyo* (1943), and claimed to have once had an affair with Lana Turner. Most recently he had co-starred with Joan Crawford in *Trog*.

The original title of the film, about a cat that destroys an entire family, was called *I Hate You, Cat*, which he thought was much stronger than *Persecution*. "Everyone who read the script thought it was good," said Hutton. "I sent it to Bette Davis, who complimented me on it, but she said that the lead character was *so* bad, *such* a horrible woman that she didn't dare play it, although she would like to."

The film was directed by *Trog* director Freddie Francis's son, Kevin Francis, who raised funds to make the film, which he hoped would break him into the industry. The script went through a number of changes, and with Hutton lamenting the rewrites. "What they did to it broke my heart," he said. "Why Kevin didn't hire his father to direct it, I'll never know. Freddie would have made a doggone good movie out of it, I guarantee you – he would have shot what I wrote. And Lana Turner wouldn't be ashamed of it."

Turner, who was fifty-two at the time of filming, hadn't had a leading role in a film since 1969's *The Big Cube* (1969), but had appeared on television. She was directed by Curtis Harrington for a couple of episodes of the television series *The Survivors*, first airing in fall 1969.

"Miss Turner was still petite and attractive, but she had had some sort of minor face-lift that had left her perfectly formed Turner mouth not quite the same. In agreeing to do the series, she had insisted that her contract specify that she would never be required to wear the same dress twice in one show," Harrington recalled. "The trappings and imperatives of MGM stardom were hard for her to relinquish…in her attitudes and prerogatives she was still very much the movie star."

She had recently married for the seventh time to Ronald Pellar, a Los Angeles hypnotist on the nighttime circuit, who she soon discovered to be a fraudster. He ran off with $100,000 worth of jewelry and spent a large chunk of her money.

Turner was considered one of the sexiest stars of the 1940s, bringing heat to films like *The Postman Always Rings Twice*

(1946). She was a woman who loved the luxuries and trappings of fame, the costumes and the jewels, and the evenings spent at nightclubs. She was also notorious for her tumultuous love life, which culminated in the 1958 murder of her gangster boyfriend, Johnny Stompanato, by Turner's fourteen-year-old daughter, Cheryl, who was defending her mother against his physical abuse. The scandal almost derailed her already lagging career, but she made a comeback in 1959 in Douglas Sirk's *Imitation of Life*, which mirrored Turner's mother-daughter relationship. The incident would be the basis of Harold Robbins' novel *Where Love Has Gone,* and the 1964 film adaptation, starring Susan Hayward and Bette Davis.

Turner, in her 1982 memoirs, recollected being unemployed again in spring 1971, just after having turned fifty. She called it "the toughest age for an actress. I was a bit too mature to play a bubbling ingénue but certainly too young to be a frumpy dowager. Scripts still flooded in, but I read nothing even remotely suitable. I was waiting for a role with dignity, but with a little spark too."

Despite her hopes, she failed to find that role with dignity in *Persecution,* later referring to it as a bomb. Turner plays Carrie Masters, a wealthy widow whose son David drowned her beloved cat Sheba when he was a boy, and she struggles to forgive him, even into adulthood. He continues to be suspicious of her new cat, which she's also named Sheba and which she dotes on and walks with a lead. Just as fellow cat lady Eleanor Parker is confined to a wheelchair, Turner walks with a cane, and similar to Olivia De Havilland in *Lady in a Cage,* she also proves to be a cold mother who has driven away her child. Like other older female characters in horror movies, she has her own portrait hanging in her living room, and keeps a box of mementoes so that she can delve into memories of the past, and relive the moments when she was young and beautiful. Turner refused to be anything but glamorous on screen, and ensured she was given a stylish wardrobe, including a leopard-print nightgown, which links her to felines, as Irena's fur coat does in *Cat People*.

Following the death of his son, and then his wife, which he blames on Sheba, David is unable to control his anger at his mother for replacing her affection for him with that of her cats. As he descends into madness, Carrie becomes his victim and he degrades her by forcing her to meow and drink milk from a bowl, like her beloved cat. The film was released in October 1975, with the tagline "Now it's David's turn to get even…and he has a very special treat for his mother."

22. "A bore never crosses over my threshold twice..."

In 1965, to publicize two television appearances on ABC's *Ben Casey* and *My Three Sons*, Gloria Swanson invited a reporter to her New York apartment and expressed her openness to acting on television. As she explained, "I've seen the Twenties, the Thirties, the Forties and the Fifties. What's left? Outer space? Besides, I know television."

By the early seventies television was the place for Hollywood's iconic stars to make guest appearances in popular TV shows, to regale talk show hosts, and their audiences, with tales from the Golden Age of Hollywood, or to star in made for TV movies, which often had a particular horror slant. As *The New York Times* wrote: "A week can't go by in prime-time without a made-for-TV Gothic, starring people like Bette Davis, Joan Crawford, Tallulah Bankhead, Gloria Swanson, returning from the graves of their careers, or their impersonators. The long watches of the night are filled with old horror movies and reruns of *Boris Karloff Presents*, *Twilight Zone, Outer Limits, Science Fiction Theater, One Step Beyond, Night Gallery* and *Evil Touch*."

It was only natural that Gloria Swanson would also embrace this phenomenon. As the first movie star to earn a million dollars, it was as if the word "glamor" was invented for her. The mention of her name conjured images of decadent parties in Beverly Hills mansions, extravagant costumes sprouting peacock feathers and studded with jewels, and extraordinary spending habits, such as the $10,000 she spent in a year on lingerie.

Even after her Hollywood career had faded in the thirties, Swanson continued to preside over Hollywood, where she carried on with the lifestyle she was accustomed to, and relished the legendary status she had had earned. This was further reinforced following the huge success of *Sunset Boulevard*. As she told *The New York Times* in 1965: "So many people identify you with the characters you play. Even the young Hollywood producers who've never met me – and I am something of a legend – think of me as Norma Desmond, with a dead man in the swimming pool."

After the huge success of *Sunset Boulevard*, the real Gloria Swanson and the fictional Norma Desmond were seen as one and the same, and for each eccentric old lady role she was offered, she steadfastly turned them down. She knew that if she accepted them she would become "some sort of creepy parody of myself, or rather, of Norma Desmond - a shadow of a shadow."

She did bring Norma Desmond back to life on *The Steve Allen Show* in 1957, and had hopes to develop *Sunset Boulevard* as a musical, but by 1957 the planned project had been rejected by Paramount. After seeing Carol Burnett's constant spoofs of Norma Desmond, Gloria wrote a fan letter saying how much she enjoyed it, leading to her own guest appearance on *The Carol Burnett Show* in September 1973, where her skin glowed with health and she looked trim in a sleek one-shoulder gown, as she poked fun at her Norma Desmond persona. She was aware that *Sunset Boulevard* was likely to be the only one of her extensive filmography that people under the age of forty had seen.

"I'm not a glamor puss, and I'm not an old shoe. I'm somewhere in between. I'm like a parrot...That's why the world's greatest impersonators have never been able to impersonate me. You can impersonate Norma Desmond – but not me," she told the *Los Angeles Times* in 1974.

In 1971 she returned to Broadway with much acclaim after a 21-year absence in *Butterflies are Free*. Backstage at the Booth Theater, Swanson booked appointments with shiatsu masseurs, and ensured there were pots of vegetable broth steaming in her dressing room. "The younger people who come backstage know more about me than the older ones. They know I'm a health food buff. I'm really with the younger people. Older people are so programmed you can't help them."

When the show closed in July 1972, it was reported she had performed it 666 times, and when asked for her secrets to maintaining her youthfulness, she gave an almost vampiric answer, that "a bore never crosses over my threshold twice. And nobody crosses my threshold unexpected or uninvited."

In 1974, after making occasional appearances on television shows, including playing herself in a 1966 episode of *The Beverly Hillbillies*, Swanson accepted a role in her first television movie for *Killer Bees*, an ABC Movie of the Week directed by Curtis Harrington. *Killer Bees* also starred *Charlie's Angels* actress Kate Jackson, and Craig Stevens, star of the detective series *Peter Gunn*. "Although I read the script with trepidation, I ended up thinking it was terrific and said yes," Swanson wrote in her memoirs.

The character she was to play, Madame Van Bohlen, is revealed to have a mystery power – she can control a swarm of killer bees with psychic abilities, and for Swanson, the film's concept "appealed to something primeval in me." In an interview in 1965, she revealed her interest in "extra-sensory perception." She said: "I've had some interesting experiences myself. Right now

I'm big on mind control – Indian philosophy – know yourself. There's something beyond what the eye sees, what the ear hears."

With increased concern around environmental issues, horror films began to represent a warning on man's manipulation of the natural world through mutated creatures. In *Them!* (1954), giant killer ants rise up and cause havoc in New Mexico before emigrating to Los Angeles, and *The Beginning of the End* (1957) featured large grasshoppers that have been mutated by radiation. These similar plots could be read as a parable of the dangers of both atomic experimentation and communist infiltration.

Alfred Hitchcock's *The Birds* (1963) further explored this phenomenon, with birds terrorizing a small coastal town en masse for an inexplicable reason beyond our knowledge or control. "Without God or the devil to take the rap, we have only ourselves to blame," said *The New York Times* in 1974, in an article on the ecological film phenomenon. "That burden is insupportable, and so we desperately look elsewhere - psychic energy within, deep space without, invisible demons, spooks, nameless evil."

This genre offered further opportunities for veteran actors who were open to the possibility of a hit, no matter how poor the concept. Oscar winner Ray Milland, who had found B-movie success in Roger Corman's *X: The Man with X-Ray Eyes* (1963), starred in 1972's *Frogs*. He played Jason Crockett, a disagreeable millionaire who lives on his own island in the Florida Everglades, and whose family comes under attack from a variety of mutated creatures. Like many of these ecological horror films, it owes a similarity to *The Birds* as the family fights off nature invading their own home. By the end they are rescued by a passing car whose son has a pet frog, much like the love birds brought to Bodega Bay by Tippi Hedren.

Vincent Canby in his *New York Times* review of the film wrote: "*Frogs*, which is not to be confused with *The Birds* for an instant, is an end-of-the-world junk movie, photographed rather prettily in Florida and acted by Milland as if he were sight-reading random passages from the dictionary."

This genre of killer creature films culminated in *Jaws*, the first summer blockbuster when released in 1975, but in the meantime Gloria Swanson made a valiant effort as she summoned a swarm of deadly bees.

If *Killer Bees* owed a similarity to *The Birds*, Kate Jackson was the equivalent of Tippi Hedren's character; the city girl who arrives in a small town and clashes with the older woman over her relationship with her son/grandson.

One of the strongest scenes in the film takes place in the chapel during the funeral for Swanson's matriarch, where the air is ominously filled with the buzzing of bees, as they angrily swarm around the flowers on her coffin. And just like in *The Birds*, the townsfolk are chased down by swarms of bees, unrelentingly buzzing around them. The climactic scene takes place in the attic of the house, which, along with the basement, is the place of terror in gothic horror. For some inexplicable reason, Kate Jackson, like Tippi Hedren, enters into the attic, where she discovers the space is the nerve-center of the swarm as it's filled with bees and their honeycombs.

"Back into your hives, all of you. It is time once again to deplore a trend," wrote *The New York Times* in 1974 on the release of *Killer Bees*. "I believe in rational explanations of complex phenomena, even Watergate. I do not believe in killer bees. Nor do I believe in killer turtles, killer iguanas, poisonous bats, defrosted monster mantises, deadly jellies, man-eating blue mists and homicidal rabbits. With the exception of the homicidal rabbit, you could have enjoyed all the aforesaid menaces on television during the past month."

Producers at ABC had originally hoped for Bette Davis to star as the matriarch, but after Curtis Harrington approached her with the offer, she quickly turned it down. She was allergic to bee stings, she told him, and if any of the stunts went wrong she could die of anaphylactic shock.

"Secretly, I was not unhappy that Bette had turned down the role," said Harrington. "Of course, I would have been thrilled and excited to work with the legendary actress, but she had been in a number of TV movies lately. The next name on our list was Gloria Swanson. Gloria had hardly been seen on screen since *Sunset Boulevard.*"

The entire film was shot on location in the Napa Valley, in a Victorian mansion that would be purchased by director Francis Ford Coppola. Joel Schumacher, later the director of films including *St Elmo's Fire, The Lost Boys* and *Batman Forever*, was hired as costume designer. "He managed to flatter Miss Swanson in his choice of clothes for her, but he put a hideous Mexican sweater on Kate that she wore virtually throughout the film," said Harrington.

To publicize *Killer Bees*, Swanson chose to be interviewed by the *Los Angeles Times* at the Beverly Hills salon of designer Werle. "In person, up close, Gloria Swanson does not disappoint," wrote the interviewer, Kevin Thomas. "Dressed in a smart beige sport outfit she is chic and contemporary without seeming as if she were trying to look like a young woman. The face that has been called one of the greatest of the silent screen still is: large, piercing eyes, gleaming teeth, that famous mole on the left side of her chin and those bold, sculptured features. Barely five feet tall, she is a tiny dynamo, a lady of wit and wisdom, full of passion for life."

Before beginning the shoot, Gloria Swanson informed the producers that she expected to be addressed by all crew, including the director, as Miss Swanson. While she could be an intimidating presence, she soon warmed to Harrington, particularly when he brought his juicer to the set so that she could have fresh smoothies each day. "Motion pictures are make-believe. It's OK for motion pictures to be make-believe, but I'll be damned if I want my food to be make-believe," she commented at a luncheon to celebrate her 80th birthday.

Harrington later recounted that after they finished shooting, he rang Gloria's hotel room to say goodbye and to thank her for working with him. When he addressed her as "Miss Swanson" she corrected him. "It's Gloria to you."

Swanson's character, Madame Van Bohlen, is the German-born matriarch of a Napa Valley wine-growing family. Strong-willed and overbearing, she makes her first appearance sitting regally upon a throne in a gothic reception room, wearing cinnamon-bun braiding on each side of her head, just a few years ahead of Carrie Fisher's Princess Leia.

"When I got to the Coast they said, 'We don't want a German accent after all," she recounted to Kevin Thomas. "I said, 'Of course, I'll do the accent.' I thought, How am I going to do her? She's German and I had a great-grandmother who was German. She always looked like she was sitting on a rod. I thought, 'That's it! I'll get a corset!' It shoved my breasts way up on my chest. And I walked with a cane. I was concerned about how I was going to wear my hair. Then I thought of how Lila Lee wore her hair braided in coils over her ears in a picture of mine (*Male and Female*, 1919). They looked like beehives."

For the crucial scenes where Gloria was to be completely covered in bees, an on-set bee wrangler was hired to ensure it was completely safe. Jim Dannaldson was the long-time supplier of insects for film and television, and was dubbed "The Bug Man of Burbank" by Johnny Carson. As the curator of reptiles at the University of Southern California, he had first been hired by George Stevens to work with the snakes on *Gunga Din* (1939). From there, he imported iguanas and reptiles for Hal Roach's *One Million Years, BC*, and cockroaches for Robert Aldrich's *The Choirboys*.

Dannaldson described *Killer Bees* as his most difficult assignment. Originally he had planned to use drones, as they didn't have stingers, but production took place out of season. Instead, the bee wrangler placed the bees in a box of dry ice, to send them to sleep. A group of beekeepers were then hired to take each bee, squeeze it gently to force out the stinger, and then cut them off, so as not to kill them.

"We hired ten girls for a solid week, ten hours a day," he said. "They put the cooled down bee in a shadow box and clipped off the end of the stinger with a sharp little knife. Then we took all 10,000 bees to the location and turned them loose in this room with Gloria Swanson and thank goodness not one strange bee got in from outside and no one was stung."

Working with the bees reminded Gloria of her time filming Cecil DeMille's *Male and Female*, where she fearlessly allowed a real lion to paw her back, all the while dressed in an elaborate white peacock feather headdress. And just as DeMille had saved that scene for last, so did Harrington. She took the scenes with the bees in her stride, placing cotton wool in her ears to protect them.

"Imagine me getting up by 5am on the first day of *Killer Bees* and 6am every day thereafter. Sometimes I didn't eat till 9 or midnight. That was the schedule of this old woman! For one sequence I had a thousand bees on me at one time. They put them in the Frigidaire box to make them sleepy. Then they put them on me. They were only partly de-stinged. Then they started buzzing – bzzz, bzzz, bzzz," she said.

The New York Times described *Killer Bees* as "a tedious, prolonged bore that makes Alfred Hitchcock's "Birds," a home screen perennial, seem better than ever," and that it moved "like molasses." To the reviewer, and no doubt most of ABC's viewership, Gloria Swanson was the main attraction for the film, with an audience tuning in because of their curiosity as to how she had fared since *Sunset Boulevard*. He described Gloria's grande dame as "no mere gargoyle but a fascinating, at times even likeably forthright woman with both dimensions of poignance and grandeur."

Veronica Lake had less success in dealing with mutated creatures, in the horror movie *Flesh Feast*, which is most notable as her final screen role. With a strange plot involving the disgusting premise of flesh-eating maggots, and very low production values, it was a blip on her legacy in film noirs such as *This Gun for Hire* and *The Glass Key*, both from 1942. She was just over 5ft tall but became larger than life on screen, as the sultry femme fatale with the peek-a-boo hair.

Believed to have been made in 1967, and released in 1970, *Flesh Feast* was Lake's last screen appearance before her untimely death at the age of fifty as a result of years of alcoholism. She played Dr. Elaine Frederick, a German scientist who experiments with the use of flesh-eating maggots for youth restoration, and discovers Adolf Hitler is alive and well, and planning to use the treatment to disguise his appearance. Lake also served as producer of the film and had used the proceeds of her autobiography to fund the venture. Perhaps she believed the film, directed by Brad F. Grinter, would be an easy moneymaker, made on the cheap and then profiting on the B-movie drive-in circuit.

Born in 1922 as Constance "Connie" Ockleman in Brooklyn, her father died when she was 10 years old, and her mother and stepfather moved to Montreal, and then Florida, where the teenage Connie took part in beauty pageants in her teens. She arrived in Hollywood in 1938 with her mother and stepfather, and it would be home until 1952. After beginning her career as a movie extra, she was spotted in spring of 1939 by Metro director, Freddie Wilcox, who was struck by her glacial looks. When producer Arthur Hornblow Jr. saw her screen test, he cast her as the nightclub singer Sally Vaughn in *I Wanted Wings*, a patriotic film about aviators, which also starred Ray Milland and William Holden. Hornblow Jr. didn't like her name, and selected Veronica, to suit her classic features, and Lake, for the cool blue eyes. Signed to Paramount, Lake, and her blonde hair, found instant stardom.

Much-lauded in magazine editorials and copied in hairdressing salons, her hair also became a popular joke. "I opened up my mop closet the other day and I thought Veronica Lake fell out," said Groucho Marx, while Bob Hope joked that "Veronica Lake wears her hair over one eye because it's a glass eye." Such was the peek-a-boo hair phenomenon, that the War Manpower Commission made a request that to protect workers from getting their hair caught in machinery, she should tie her hair back for the rest of the war.

She made *Sullivan's Travels* (1941) when she was six months pregnant and dressed in baggy clothing, with her hair under a cap, and was hailed for going against type. *This Gun for Hire* in 1942 was the first of a successful screen partnership with Alan Ladd, which was followed by *The Glass Key* that same year and *The Blue Dahlia* in 1946.

She earned a reputation for not playing the Hollywood game by being difficult on set and for disappearing on drinking benders, and by the late forties her career had waned. "No asking why I was no longer in favor with Hollywood," she wrote in her memoirs. "Just a long spiral down into a bottomless well, the only buoy a bottle - of Scotch. I realized I really didn't want to go back through the grind of playing sexy sirens in grade-B thrillers all for the silk purses of the studio management."

In the 1950s, after her third divorce and serious money problems which resulted in bankruptcy, she moved to New York, where she worked in television and on stage. She admitted she lacked in mothering skills as she sank into alcoholism. She is also believed to have been diagnosed with schizophrenia. In the 1960s, a journalist discovered Veronica Lake working as a cocktail waitress at the Martha Washington Hotel in New York, and it made headlines as a humiliating climb-down for a once-great star.

"When the *New York Post* broke the story, people felt very sorry for me," she wrote. "But you know, I really enjoyed that job. Sure, I needed the money. But I liked the people there, the merchant marine seamen, the occasional hookers, the broken-heart guys and the problem drinkers."

Living in Miami, Florida in the mid-sixties, and working as a waitress to fund a destructive lifestyle, she agreed to star in two low-budget horrors. As she wrote in her autobiography, they were "in vogue with today's trend of putting older stars in horror movies."

The first of these was the thriller *Footsteps in the Snow* (1966), for which she was paid $10,000 to film in Canada, and marked her return to screens after a sixteen-year absence. The second, *Flesh Feast*, was initially known as *Time Is Terror*. It was made by a Miami production house who had heard that Veronica Lake was working as a waitress locally, and asked if she would like to appear in it. Becoming involved in all aspects of the production, she helped with the raising of the money for this film.

"Making movies, even low-budget ones, is an expensive and demanding chore. You'd better know what you're doing or your low-budget job will blossom into a bankrupting one. That pretty much is what happened with *Time Is Terror*," she wrote in her memoirs.

Lake sounded optimistic in the last pages of her autobiography, describing her satisfaction in performing *The World of Carl Sandberg* in 1967. She also traveled to England, where she performed in local theaters. "Lately, I find more and more offers coming through to me. I seem to be coming around full circle to the point where Veronica Lake is almost in vogue again...I am working again, working good and worthwhile things, not horror films but good theatre, substantial shows, meaty scripts and warm audiences."

Yet she also hinted at the destructive nature of her lifestyle as an ex-star in Miami. In 1973, just after carrying out publicity for her autobiography, she was diagnosed with cirrhosis of the liver due to heavy drinking, and passed away as a result of hepatitis and kidney disease. She was just fifty years old.

Shortly after finishing *Killer Bees*, Curtis Harrington was offered another Robert Bloch story from *Weird Tales* to direct; this time about zombies. Like films dealing with nature going out of control, zombies were also symbolic of man's fears of atomic destruction, as well as a collapse of humanity. George Romero's *Night of the Living Dead* (1968) was released five months after Martin Luther King Jr.'s assassination, and its grim ending was reflective of the Civil Rights movement. It also stood as a comment on the Vietnam War, as every day Americans viewers were exposed to horrific battles unfolding on their television screens, and with news of young men being killed while fighting overseas.

Harrington chose a camper, more comedic approach to his zombie film than Romero, and set his film in the 1930s, a period that Harrington relished. Ray Milland was cast as the owner of the dance hall who turns out to be the zombie master, in one of the many low budget horror movies he made in the seventies. Milland refused to wear a wig in the film, as he believed he should be accepted for the way he looked, rather than pretending to be something he wasn't. As Harrington remembered, Milland "told me that he had been talking to his friend James Stewart, who expressed envy at the fact that Ray was working and he was not. James Stewart was still the bigger star, and I doubt if anyone would have had the temerity to offer him a part in an ordinary television show."

Popular 1930s actress Joan Blondell was cast as the shopkeeper, Levenia, and Harrington insisted she have her hair styled the same way as she did in *Dames* in 1934, a Busby Berkeley-choreographed musical where she played her staple wise-cracking chorus girl. Austrian character actor Reggie Nadler, often seen as a villain in Hitchcock and Fellini films, was cast as the sinister central zombie. Nadler would later achieve his greatest genre fame as the Nosferatu-inspired vampire Barlow in the 1979 TV adaptation of the Stephen King novel *Salem's Lot*.

The TV movie was met with poor reviews, with Robert Bloch writing in his autobiography: "*The Dead Don't Die*. Maybe they don't, but the show did. Despite Curtis's casting of accomplished character actors, their supporting roles couldn't prop up the lead. And Ray Milland…merely plodded through his part here like a zombie without a deadline."

23. "woman-weak, wicked, sinning souls..."

As a young up-and-coming director in the sixties, Brian De Palma was heavily inspired by the works of Hitchcock. His first thriller, 1972's *Sisters,* explored the supposed dangers of repressed female sexuality. He reinterpreted the elements of *Psycho*, combining it with references to *Rear Window* and a score by Berman Herrmann, and told the story of model Danielle (Margot Kidder), whose separated Siamese twin Dominique is thought to be a vicious murderer, slashing to death the men who are sexually interested in her sister. When a young journalist, Grace (Jennifer Salt), witnesses the murder of Danielle's date, Philip, she calls the police, but when they fail to find the body in Danielle's apartment, she chooses to investigate it herself.

Sisters shares a similar theme to Bette Davis's twin roles in *Dead Ringers* and *A Stolen Life*, with the idea of a good twin and bad twin, with one trying to steal the other's life. Robin Wood named it as "the most complete and rigorous analyses of the oppression of women under patriarchal culture in the whole of patriarchal cinema." Danielle's extensive scar, from where she was separated from Dominique, is symbolic of her repression. As sweet and compliant as Danielle is, her dark side hides in the shadows, ready to castrate and kill any man who arouses her. It's a twist on the themes of *Cat People*, demonstrating the dangers of female sexuality when unleashed.

Later, De Palma took elements of *Psycho* and *Vertigo* for his controversial erotic slasher film *Dressed to Kill* (1980), where actress Angie Dickinson plays the role of an older Marion Crane, who, in the first thirty minutes, is knifed to death by a figure dressed as a woman. The violence meted out to her is as punishment for her sexual deviance; an older woman who enjoys extra-marital sex, and who is only too willing to pick up a strange man in an art gallery.

It was the critical and commercial success of De Palma's film adaptation of *Carrie*, the first of Stephen King's novels to be adapted to the screen, that brought him to the forefront of "New Hollywood" when it was released in 1976. It became the indelible success he'd been looking for, making a lasting impact on pop culture (that jump scare with the hand shooting up through the ground), and in the representations of both teenagers and women in horror films.

Critic Barbara Creed described *Carrie* as "a particularly interesting representation of woman as witch and menstrual monster." The trauma placed on Carrie by her dysfunctional, religious zealot mother, combined with the sudden, unexpected arrival of her menstrual cycle, unleashes her telekinetic abilities.

The film offers a warning to the disintegration of family values, where a child is raised by a single mother. Not only does it damage the woman as she becomes more extreme without the stable influence of a man, but it traumatizes the child. Carrie struggles to resist her mother's zealous control, as she imparts on Carrie her belief that female sexuality is evil and corrupting. The house is the trap, the repressive womb, where the older woman punishes the younger for her perceived sins. Mrs. White tells Carrie they must pray for their "woman-weak, wicked, sinning souls."

As seen in *Psycho* and the "Hag Horror" movies that followed, such as in *Strait-Jacket*, *Blood and Lace*, or *The Killing Kind*, the mother and child relationship is twisted by the mother's (and surrogate mother's) desire to dominate the child, forcing the child to rebel and act out their darkest desires. Carrie wishes she could be a normal teenager, but not only is she repressed by her mother, but she grapples with crippling shyness while desiring only to be normal. Her powers of telekinesis, the discovery of which coincides with her first period, is the way that she can let out all her rage - the dark side of the female that is destructive when released.

Mrs. White is similar to Mrs. Bates in that due to her own repression, she instills in her child a fear of sexuality, with the belief that woman is essentially sinful. In the age of second-wave feminism, Margaret is the anti-feminist, speaking out for the patriarchy and condemning women for wishing to have agency over their own bodies. As Barbara Creed writes, "As in *Psycho*, the monstrous child is ultimately depicted as a creation of the psychotic, dominating mother."

Carrie's shower, like Marion Crane's, is an awakening of sorts, but they are both punished for their enjoyment of it. Carrie's moment is ruined by the sudden, unexpected flow of menstrual blood, while Marion's by the knife that slashes her over and over again. De Palma would later use the shower as a form of ritual cleansing, with Angie Dickinson in *Dressed to Kill*. She's a single mother and career woman who is fully in control of her own sexuality, pleasuring herself in the shower until she is suddenly grabbed and attacked by an unknown man. While this turns out to be her fantasy, ultimately her murder is punishment for that enjoyment.

After the utter destruction of her classmates and teachers at the gym hall, Carrie returns home, changing into her nightgown and seeking comfort in her mother's arms. Instead, Mrs. White assaults her with a knife to eradicate her sin. Carrie summons her powers to free herself from the trap set by the older woman, causing the repressive home, the metaphorical womb, to collapse around them.

Playing the demented mother in *Carrie* was Piper Laurie, who hadn't made a movie since her Oscar-nominated turn in *The Hustler* (1961). After a decade away from the screen, and having retired to Woodstock with her husband and daughter to make sculptures and bake bread, forty-five-year-old Piper Laurie was sent the script for *Carrie* – the first she had received for many years.

Piper Laurie began her career in the early fifties, as the red-haired and wholesome starlet at Universal studios, before leaving Hollywood to start a new career in live television and theater in New York. Born Rosetta Jacobs in Detroit, on January 22, 1932, she was nicknamed Sissy as a child. Her parents struggled to raise Sissy and her older sister during the Depression, and sent them to a children's institution in the San Fernando Valley for three years. "We were living in Detroit at the beginning of the Depression, my father had no work, my sister was sick with asthma, and I was almost six years. They sent us to this home in the mountains, and left us there for three years," she recalled in her memoirs.

Once her parents were financially able, they moved to Los Angeles for work and removed their daughters from the home. Piper remembered the family going to see 1940s Technicolor musicals together, or to see horror films like *Cat People* and *I Walked with a Zombie*. "I had so many crushes. I was in love with Paul Henreid, Warner Baxter, Betty Grable, John Garfield, Joan Leslie, and John Hodiak," she remembered.

As a shy child who found more confidence when acting on stage, her mother had ambitions for her pretty red-haired daughter to become a star, and after entering beauty contests, going for screen tests, and taking action lessons, she came to the attention of Universal-International, who were looking for teenagers to bring fresh blood to the studio. She was asked to audition with another up-and-coming star, Rock Hudson, and in 1949 they were both signed to seven-year contracts, with her name changed to Piper Laurie.

As publicity for her first film, *Louisa* (1950), Piper was launched as the girl who eats nothing but flowers to keep her complexion luminescent, inspired by one scene where Edmund Gwenn prepares a salad by throwing marigold petals into it. "I threw myself into it, playing my new part with gusto, nibbling on orchids, rose petals, and marigolds "Oh yes, they're really delicious!" Each day there was a feature story in one of the newspapers about my eating flowers."

Playing her father in the film was the much older Ronald Reagan, who began to take a real-life interest in her, ultimately leading to her losing her virginity with him some time after filming had been completed, and which she described in her memoirs as being an awkward, embarrassing experience.

She followed *Louisa* with *The Milkman* (1950) starring Donald O'Connor and Jimmy Durante, and was then paired with Tony Curtis, another hot new star at Universal, for the adventure movie *The Prince Who Was a Thief* (1951), and its follow-up *The Son of Ali Baba* (1952). It was her first big role in a Technicolor extravaganza, and they went on a cross-country publicity tour to promote it. As part of the movie factory, she was photographed in bathing suits and dresses, as Miss Firecracker for the Fourth of July, or Miss Thanksgiving. During this time she obsessively watched what she ate, and was prescribed amphetamines as diet pills, to ensure she kept her weight down. It was an addiction that she would struggle to shake off for years.

On a promotional tour for *The Mississippi Gambler* in 1953 she found herself frustrated with the questions from interviewers. "The questions were addressed to a fictitious creature that I had nothing to do with: Pretty Perky Piper Laurie, the girl who ate flowers. I felt pressure to take on the persona of that girl just to get through the interview. I despised the persona, but it helped me control my anxiety."

She found the material she was being offered at Universal frivolous and unchallenging, and chose to opt out of her contract, no matter the consequences. She hoped to try her luck with live television, a medium that was growing in popularity. "I wanted people to see it and perhaps think differently of me," she said. "Perhaps someone would even let me do a live television show. That was where all the exciting things were happening, with new actors, writers, and directors, some of whom would go on to have fifty-year careers," she said.

After moving to New York, the home of live television, she was thrilled to be cast in Playhouse 90's *Days of Wine and Roses* in 1958, about a young married couple's harrowing descent into rock-bottom alcoholism. Critically-applauded, it was one of the most celebrated live television shows of all time.

After being shown the script for *The Hustler*, she immediately knew she wanted to return to Hollywood to play complicated, tragic Sarah, the girlfriend of Paul Newman's pool shark, "Fast" Eddie Felson. After a four-year absence from Hollywood, the role was considered to be something of a comeback for 29-year-old Piper. To her surprise, it led to an Academy Award nomination for Best Actress, as well as nods for Paul Newman, George C Scott, and Jackie Gleason and to Bob Rossen for Best Picture, Best Director, and Best Screenplay.

"Sadly, the nomination meant so very little to me then. I'm sorry now that I wasn't at a place in my life where I could have enjoyed that sort of thing," she wrote in her memoirs. "I thought it was silly to measure performances in the first place. There were more important things going on in the world. It was the early 1960s, a time of turmoil. The civil rights movement had begun. U.S. military advisers were beginning to participate in Vietnam. The fuss over a movie seemed all wrong."

She found that despite the critical acclaim for her performance, the only other roles being offered were for tragic characters similar to Sarah. After playing Laura in a production of *The Glass Menagerie*, she made the decision to withdraw from acting. Instead, she enrolled in art school in New York, moved to a farmhouse in Woodstock with reporter husband Joe Morgenstern and later adopted a daughter.

"I had a lovely life for fifteen years and never imagined I would work again as an actress. Then one day I got a phone call from the woman who had once represented me as an agent, and she said, 'Piper, I'm going to send you a script. This is not an offer, but would you read the script and tell me what you think about it.'"

She wasn't impressed when she first read the script for *Carrie*, thinking it was "awful," but when her husband Joe suggested that sometimes Brian De Palma had a comedic approach to his work, she began to consider it as a satire. She agreed to meet De Palma in New York to discuss the role, arriving for the interview wearing a black velvet coat and her long red hair down.

By the time she got back to Woodstock she had a message that she'd won the role of Margaret White, and for three weeks of shooting she would be paid $10,000. Her agent advised her that it was the best she could expect after being absent from the screen for so long. "I heard later on that the producers were thinking of Joan Fontaine for Mrs. White," she added. By winning this role, she found she was entering into a successful third act, and she flew to LA to begin rehearsals.

In Stephen King's novel, Margaret White was described as wearing her hair in a tight bun, but after seeing Piper with her hair flowing around her shoulders, De Palma agreed that her wild red hair suited a character who preaches fire and brimstones. "I had personally not been happy to wear it in a bun; it seemed cliché, though I would have done it if Brian had insisted," she said.

Piper was still convinced the film had comedy elements, and in the scene when Margaret tries to prevent Carrie from going to the Prom, instead of tearing at her dress as was noted in the script, she began dragging herself around the room by her hair to show her character in complete torment. "I figured it would look absurd and funny. When I was about to do it a second time, Brian suddenly stopped me. He said, 'Piper, you can't do that. You're going to get a laugh!' Oh boy, how could I have gone so wrong? I was embarrassed. He meant the movie to be serious. It was too late to back out, and I was just plain enjoying myself," she said. "I decided to just move the line of reality slightly…I toned things down just a little, to a place of possible believability. I pulled my hair, but with deeper inner emotional pain, and threw out any attempt at visual comedy."

For Margaret's violent death, where she is impaled and crucified against the wall by the kitchen implements that have been propelled by Carrie's telekinesis, Piper chose to act the scene as if she is dying in ecstasy at the thought of finally meeting God.

"I think I was funny in it," she says, looking back on it in 2021. "I couldn't think of her as a crazy woman. She had great passions and deep feelings, and commitments to what was right and wrong in life. And it just had to be full and important to her."

After fifteen years of being absent from a movie set, it felt good to be back. "They had the old-fashioned dressing rooms with wheels like they did when I first started at Universal," Laurie remembered. "It was a very sweet and sentimental time for me. I felt so welcomed by the crew, a few of whom I had known before."

After completing *Carrie*, she was asked to star in another horror movie, *Ruby*, to be directed by Curtis Harrington. This time she was offered a much larger salary, and despite her hesitancy around the quality of the script, she accepted the role. "It was a strange script, with a couple of genuinely original scenes, in which I would play a woman who runs a drive-in theater and always dresses in red, but it was not what I wanted to be doing. It would, however, pay a lot of bills."

After *Killer Bees* and *The Dead Don't Die*, Curtis Harrington had reluctantly moved into directing for television, which he called his "descent into the hell of episodic television," including an episode of the detective series *Baretta*, starring Robert Blake, *Tales of the Unexpected* and *Charlie's Angels* in 1978.

His former producing partner George Edwards temporarily rescued him from television with the script for *Ruby*, which was written by Steve Krantz, and owed a debt to the trend for satanic stories following *The Exorcist*, with its storyline about a female drive-in owner who is possessed by the spirit of her dead father.

The producers had hoped to cast Tina Louise, the red-haired bombshell on the hit 1960s TV show *Gilligan's Island* in the lead, but Harrington fought for Piper Laurie, even though *Carrie* hadn't been released at that point. "Many people have suggested that we cast Piper because of her role in *Carrie*, but the script that became *Ruby* had been written long before that film's release," he stated in his memoirs. He had admired her as the 1950s Universal starlet, and for her role in *The Hustler*, and was interested in bringing her out of retirement.

"Curtis Harrington was a very dear person, what a nice, nice person," remembered Laurie in 2021. "And I enjoyed every moment of it, and we were still friends afterwards. I would come to his big house up in the hills, his spooky looking house, and he'd show me other films and things. One of the best things I know about Curtis Harrington is the story he told me…he'd come back from the Berlin film festival, and when he arrived there was a message from him to please call Leni Riefenstahl [Hitler's propaganda filmmaker], because *Ruby* was her favorite movie."

While Piper found the film "kind of fun," the final version proved to be Harrington's greatest disappointment. While the film was steeped in classic film lore, with its drive-in setting, and scenes shot at the Old Studio Club in Hollywood, which was designed by Julia Morgan, the architect for Hearst Castle at San Simeon, it didn't turn out as he'd imagined. Harrington later described it as "the most nightmarish experience of my career" because Steve Krantz "did everything possible to destroy the film."

When it was edited for television, Krantz hired a new director and filmed a new subplot to slot into the film. Harrington was so appalled by the new edit that he went to the Directors

Guild and insisted they replace his name with the generic Alan Smithee. "The theatrical version, however compromised, showed in Europe and at drive-ins across the U.S. to receptive audiences. It became one of the highest-grossing independent films before *Halloween*," he said.

While filming *Ruby*, Piper saw a midnight preview of *Carrie* at a Halloween showing in Westwood, with a packed lobby that offered a hint at the success the film might become. She was shocked to hear she had been nominated for the Academy Award for Best Supporting Actress for *Carrie*. "I was proud of my work in the movie because I had been brave, but it surprised me that the Academy members would even go to see a horror movie."

Despite the huge success of *Carrie*, and the moderate drive-in success for *Ruby*, Laurie wasn't being offered the scripts she hoped for. A few years later, she was sent a treatment for *Tim*, based on the Colleen McCullough novel about an older woman who is attracted to her handsome gardener who has an intellectual disability. Director Michael Pate had considered other older, established actresses to bring gravitas to the part, including Jean Simmons and Deborah Kerr, but ultimately turned to Laurie, who was forty-seven years old at the time. She flew to Australia for filming in August 1978, where she took up a regime of running and swimming to appear in her bathing suit opposite Mel Gibson, in his first role. She recounted in her memoirs that she was instantly attracted to him, and revealed that they had a brief affair at the end of filming.

As she approached fifty, she felt rejuvenation in her life and career, with parts in the 1983 *The Thorn Birds* television series, for which she was nominated for an Emmy for Best Supporting Actress. She received her third Oscar nomination for her role in the movie version of the play *Children of a Lesser God* (1986) and won the Best Supporting Actress Emmy for Hallmark's *Promise* in 1986.

"Though I never pursued projects that would become cult favorites, as it turned out, they found me," she said. "Fifteen years after *Carrie* jump-started my career and assured me immortality among followers of horror films, I was offered a part in a quirky gothic melodrama named *Twin Peaks*."

David Lynch's television pilot proved to be hugely successful, and she was committed to working on the series. While filming *Twin Peaks*, she starred opposite Gregory Peck in *Other People's Money*, directed by Norman Jewison. Other roles included a supporting part in Robert Rodriguez's horror film *The Faculty* in 1998, and as George Clooney's mother in *ER*.

"I had been fortunate in getting so much work when many actresses my age didn't," she wrote in her memoirs. "I had been working steadily for a very long time, far longer than I had had the right to expect since returning to the third career of my life with *Carrie*. They were often fine parts, good enough to get me Academy Award nominations. With the exception of what I did in the theater, however, I was no longer being offered leading roles. I had stopped expecting them."

After *Ruby*, Curtis Harrington directed soft-porn actress Sylvia Kristel in *Mata Hari*, and was given the opportunity to work as a director of *Dynasty* and its spin-off, *The Colbys*, where he was thrilled to work with veteran actress Barbara Stanwyck, who was taking advantage of the new opportunities for grande dames in soap operas. "At this point in her career, she was in her seventies, about the same age as Gloria Swanson had been in *Killer Bees*. She had been a chain smoker and had emphysema, which required her to keep an oxygen tank at all times. I often saw her trundling the tank about on its little cart, but this did not interfere with her performance or her presence on the set," he remembered.

While he tried to develop new films, including directing his own short film version of *The House of Usher*, Harrington never had another hit. His love of movies was evident in his Hollywood home, filled with his menagerie of bizarre paintings and sculptures, collected over many years, and which had featured in his films, including *Games*. The guests at his regular salons always enjoyed his hospitality, and as they examined his eclectic furnishings, they would have been drawn to the photographs on the walls, of the classic screen actresses who he had brought back to cinema in his horror tales – Gale Sondergaard, Shelley Winters, Simone Signoret, and Debbie Reynolds.

24. "No screams – except for my silent ones."

During one of Bette Davis's live appearances in the seventies, she was asked by an audience member if she was disappointed not to have been considered one of the glamor girl movie stars. She responded, to much laughter: "Wouldn't it be a rather meager ambition if that was all one strived for?"

Davis was proud to be considered a character actress, and in her later career she had proved that she was willing to throw herself into some of the more devastating and uncompromising roles, unafraid to look haggard or grotesque on screen. She was a regular guest on popular television talk shows throughout the seventies, hosted by Johnny Carson, Mike Douglas, Merv Griffin, Dick Cavett, and in the UK, Michael Parkinson, where she relished delivering her line from 1932's *Cabin in the Cotton*: "I'd like to kiss you, but I just washed my hair." Despite her popularity as a guest, where she was always guaranteed to provide a witty one-liner or to do self-aware impressions of herself, the quality roles were still not forthcoming.

She followed *The Anniversary* with the British drama *Connecting Rooms* in 1970 and *Bunny O'Hare* in 1971, in which she co-starred with Ernest Borgnine as elderly bank robbers who disguise themselves as hippies. It would be another five years until her next film role, in *Burnt Offerings*, released in August 1976, a supernatural tale about a mysterious gothic mansion that tries to destroy those who live there. It proved to be a tumultuous production, with co-star Oliver Reed arriving on set still drunk,

Karen Black six months pregnant, and tragically, the director's daughter committing suicide.

On its release, *Variety* wrote that Davis "doesn't have much to do. Her role is that of a weak and pathetic old woman, hardly the kind of thing she does best. Unkind lighting and costuming make her resemble Baby Jane Hudson."

Television work proved to be more forthcoming, where she said she "spent most of my creative hours in this medium." She starred in *Madame Sin*, a 1972 ABC Movie of the Week in which she traveled to the Isle of Mull to play an elderly villainess who plans to steal a nuclear weapon and achieve world domination from her Scottish castle. She adored her co-star Robert Wagner, as well as the chance to once again wear costumes designed by Edith Head, which were shipped over to Scotland for her.

Another TV movie, *Scream, Pretty Peggy*, in 1973, was in the guise of *Baby Jane, Hush, Hush, Sweet Charlotte* and *Psycho* combined, with Bette playing an elderly recluse in white face powder and a girlish blonde wig. "The film had a Peggy in it, but no screams – except for my silent ones," she said.

In *The Disappearance of Aimee,* which aired on NBC in November 1976, she was teamed with Faye Dunaway in a drama about the notorious preacher Aimee Semple McPherson. When at Warner Brothers, Davis had pleaded with Jack Warners on many occasions to buy the rights to a book on the notorious Los Angeles evangelist, but she was considered an amoral figure by the Hays office, and they refused for her to be depicted on screen. When the film was finally made, she was deeply disappointed not to play Sister Aimee, rather her mother instead. The TV movie was advertised with the promise of an explosive pairing between Davis and Dunaway, and it spilled into real life. Bette was exasperated by Faye for holding up production because she'd been "riding around town all night in a chauffeur-driven limousine, sipping champagne in the backseat."

There was one particularly memorable sweltering hot day when two thousand extras were kept waiting inside a stifling church, as Dunaway was expected to be filmed delivering the sermons. "As a rule, these are the best of fans - unpaid, there for a box lunch and a glimpse of the stars," wrote Davis in *This n That*. "They ought not to be treated with discourtesy. To help pass the time, I went onstage and sang "I've Written a Letter to Daddy" from *Baby Jane.*"

She later added that "Compared to Miss Dunaway, Joan Crawford was a real pro."

Suffering from a shortage of cash, Davis went on tours of campuses where she played clips to an audience of appreciative students. In March 1975 she brought her "Evening with Bette Davis" to Australia and then Great Britain. After playing a series of famous scenes from her films, she would saunter on stage smoking a cigarette, look out over the crowds, and then utter the line, "What a dump." It always brought rapturous applause, and left the audience eating out of her hands.

As reported in the *Times* in October 1975, she performed to a Croyden audience who "gobbled up" her gossip on Joan Crawford and Olivia de Havilland, and they treated her like "an exhibition of Papal relics or miracle-working crutches." She said that her reward "is that when I do tours like this, many young people know about me."

The "Hag Horror" genre had shifted from cinemas, into drive-ins and then onto television, but by the mid-seventies it was no longer the lucrative space for older actresses to exploit. Gregory

Peck had brought gravitas to *The Omen* (1976), but horror movies were shifting in direction on the back of the monumental success of John Carpenter's *Halloween* in 1978, launching the craze for teen slasher movies that would mark the next decade.

Haskell, in *From Reverence to Rape*, explored the representation of women in cinema, and described how the testosterone-fueled New Hollywood movement left women, and particularly older women, severely under-represented. Men were now considered the main cinema audience, and so films such as *Easy Rider*, *Midnight Cowboy*, *Deliverance* and *The Sting* dealt with the male experience. As men explored their own sense of identity, violence was meted out against women in films like *A Clockwork Orange* and *Straw Dogs*. In the majority of output, women were relegated to being the love interest to support the "bromance" between the male characters, the eye candy, or as the crazy woman. Jane Fonda and Faye Dunaway may have taken on complex, challenging roles in films like *Klute*, *Coming Home* and *Network*, but for older women, the representation was practically non-existent.

In terms of New Hollywood, Robert Altman's *That Cold Day in the Park* (1969) offered an interesting depiction in its sympathy of a repressed middle-aged woman. Sandy Dennis plays Frances, a woman who lost out on life because she cared for her ill mother. She's surrounded by older relatives and her fellow members of the bowling club, so when she spots a young man being soaked by the rain on a park bench outside her apartment window, she invites him in. He tricks her into thinking he's mute, and her attraction drives her to care for him. She desires the youth culture he represents, but when he rejects her, she does what it takes to keep him in her life.

Despite the dearth of leading roles for women, there were other options for Hollywood's classic stars to remain visible. As well as the "audience with" format of shows that was proving popular, and which Davis had excelled at, talk show appearances treated them with the reverence they deserved. While they had once exuded a sense of mystery, these shows revealed their real personality and allowed them to entertain new audiences with their tales of the old studio system and gossip about their co-stars.

The disaster movie was also a prolific new genre for the seventies, although it was one that Davis wouldn't take part in. Sparked by the critical and commercial success of *The Poseidon Adventure* (1972) produced by the genre's maestro, Irwin Allen, these movies provided plenty of opportunities for older actors to be part of an ensemble cast. They were effectively Armageddon soap operas, with a slew of famous faces, old and young, being woven into the story. The anticipation and suspense was built around which ones would live or die.

The Poseidon Adventure starred Oscar-winners Gene Hackman, Ernest Borgnine, Red Buttons, and Shelley Winters. Despite putting on weight for the role, Winters got the chance to be an older action heroine on the stricken cruise ship, when her character uses her past swimming skills to rescue her fellow guests, and ultimately sacrifices herself. In *Earthquake* (1974) Ava Gardner and Charlton Heston, as an estranged couple, were given a grim fate in being washed down a sewer, and in *The Towering Inferno* that same year, Jennifer Jones topples to her death from the lift of the blazing skyscraper, while dapper con-man Fred Astaire, unaware of her fate, heartbreakingly searches for her.

The successful *Airport* series of films, beginning with *Airport* in 1970, which told of the plight of passengers during dramatic air disasters, featured big name stars like Burt Lancaster, Dean Martin, Jean Seberg, Maurice Stapleton, Charlton Heston, Gloria Swanson, Dana Andrews, Jack Lemmon, James Stewart and Olivia de Havilland.

Gloria Swanson wrote in her memoirs that after *Sunset Boulevard* "I vowed I would never play another aging movie queen. As recently as 1974 I made a feature picture in Hollywood and played in it an aging movie queen –myself, Gloria Swanson (In *Airport 1975*). So it's no use saying never."

She had initially been approached by Universal Studios to play the well-trodden cliché of an alcoholic aging actress, and immediately turned it down. However she was persuaded by producer William Frye, director Jack Smight and costume designer Edith Head, who promised they would make changes if she would agree to do it.

"After lengthy discussion, someone suggested I simply play myself, Gloria Swanson – not an alcoholic but a health-food freak, not a gin-soaked philosopher but a normal human being dictating her memories into a tape recorder. In my favorite scene in the picture, all the passengers have to prepare for a crash landing. Quick as a flash, I dump my jewels out of my portable, crashproof, fireproof safe and lock up the tapes of my memoirs instead."

By the time of her death in 1983, Swanson had an enormous legacy of work, as well as two daughters, six grandchildren and two great-grandchildren. In her obituary, *The New York Times* called her "the last great star."

In *Airport 77*, Olivia de Havilland played a passenger on a plane owned by James Stewart, which is hijacked and crashes into the Bermuda Triangle. She also returned to Warner Brothers for the Irwin Allen-produced *The Swarm*, about an invasion of Brazilian killer bees, which also featured her *Airport 77* co-star Lee Grant.

Olivia lived to the extraordinary age of 104, spending her retirement in Paris. She made one last appearance in 2009 as the narrator of the Alzheimer's documentary *I Remember Better When I Paint*. In 2017 she became the oldest person to be appointed Dame Commander of the Order of the British Empire.

Another opportunity offered to older actresses in the seventies was to work with Italian directors like Dario Argento in *giallo* horror films. *La Dolce Vita*'s Anita Ekberg played an immoral nun in 1978's *Killer Nun*, directed by Giulo Berruti, where she possesses a beautifully made-up face and displays her lingerie under her habit.

In her final film role, Joan Bennett was cast next to Alida Valli in one of Argento's finest films, *Suspiria* (1977), which explores a coven of old witches who rule the Tarn Academy of Dance in Germany, and like those in *Rosemary's Baby*, are hiding in plain sight. Suzie Banyon (Jessica Harper), an American student, investigates the brutal murder of a friend who was at the academy, until she must confront the grotesque and hideous Queen Witch, in order to destroy the coven. Bennett, as Madame Blanc, seeks to destroy the young women who get in the way of the coven's evil control. "We must get rid of that bitch of an American girl. Vanish! She must vanish! Make her disappear!"

Yvonne De Carlo, who had a role in Gloria Grahame's *The Girl on The Late, Late Show*, also embraced the opportunities for horror roles in the late 1970s. The Canadian actress, who was under contract with Universal in the 1940s, and was described by producer Walter Wanger in the 1940s as "the most beautiful girl in the world," found new popularity on television in the 1960s as Lily in the camp horror comedy *The Munsters*. By the 1970s, there were fewer roles available for the actress who was now in her fifties, and as she wrote in her autobiography, "There was a period of time when I was less selective than I might have been. If a job was offered, and if the price was right, I took it. I needed the money." Amongst the low-budget films she accepted, there was *The Intruder* (1975), co-starring Mickey Rooney, and which was never distributed, and slasher movie *The Silent Scream* (1979), where she plays the owner of a boarding house, whose daughter, played by horror regular Barbara Steele, is a homicidal maniac.

As the seventies progressed, Joan Crawford became further isolated in her New York apartment with only the company of her Tibetan lap dog Princess Lotus Blossom. Like Blanche Hudson, she positioned herself in a hospital bed, watching her own movies whenever they were shown on television.

"I hate being asked to discuss those dreadful horror pictures I made the mistake of starring in," she said, as she reflected back on her career. "They were all just so disappointing to me; I really had high expectations for some of them. I thought that William Castle and I did our best on *Strait-Jacket* but the script was ludicrous and unbelievable and that destroyed that picture. I even thought that *Berserk!* would be good but that was one of the worst of the lot. The other one William Castle and I did was the most wretched of them all and I just wasn't good at playing an over-the-hill nymphomaniac. Ha! Then came *Trog*. Now you can understand why I retired from making motion pictures."

In one of her last interviews, with Patricia Bosworth for *The New York Times* in September 1972, a reclusive picture was painted of the star, who seemed to be firmly stuck in the past, living in her apartment with plastic coverings on her furniture and sipping vodka as she answered questions. Bosworth described how Crawford "appears at the end of a long dark corridor as in so many of her horror movies; a little dog is yapping at her heels."

"I've decided to give an interview because people can't believe I'm still around," she told Bosworth. "But I'm still an actress! I want to act." She had just starred in an episode of the TV series *Sixth Sense*, on ABC, called *Dear Joan, We're Going to Scare You to Death*, about an older woman who is caught in a youthful black magic cult. "It's the kind of emotional, gutsy role I can sink my teeth into," she said. "My agent sends me scripts every week to consider but most of them are trash."

Despite a report in January 1977 that Crawford was planning to make a return to acting, with a part in a TV series called *The Silver Fox*, she was quietly suffering from stomach cancer and withdrew completely from public life, not telling anyone, even her children, that she was gravely ill. She died in New York on May 10, 1977 with the cause of death listed as a heart attack, as per her stipulations. In her obituary in *The New York Times*, she was described as "a quintessential superstar - an epitome of timeless glamour who personified for decades the dreams and disappointments of American women."

While she left money in her will to her two adopted twins Cindy and Cathy, she disinherited her two oldest children, Christina and Christopher. Christina would have her revenge with the publication of her memoirs, *Mommie Dearest*, which was translated onto the screen in the 1981 camp classic. Faye Dunaway had been convinced she would be nominated for an Oscar, but her over-the-top performance as Joan was one that her career couldn't properly recover from.

Despite never having uttering them, *Mommie Dearest*'s "Tina, bring me the axe!" and "No more wire hangers!" have become the most quotable lines of Crawford's, more recognizable than any from *What Ever Happened to Baby Jane?* or from the films she made at MGM and Warner Brothers. Faye Dunaway preferred never to discuss *Mommie Dearest*, but when taking part in *Inside the Actor's Studio* in 1995, James Lipton asked her some probing questions, and she called her performance "kabuki." She said: "It was by definition an exploitation novel, the first of its kind, and by definition, an exploitation movie. It was never modulated, directorially. I'm sorry to say, it became camp."

The film depicted Joan's obsession with cleaning, her tireless work ethic, and her vanity, where she plunged her face into a bowl of ice every morning. Yet it was a characterization that many of her friends, and Cathy and Cindy, felt was false and unfair. Out of all the horror movies that she did, it was Joan's real-life reputation, as a result of *Mommie Dearest,* that became the most monstrous depiction of all.

When asked her thoughts on her former co-star's death, Bette told Stanley Siegel, "I never knew Joan Crawford personally. We just worked together. We worked together of course once on *Jane*, and then she started on the film *Charlotte* and was taken ill, and oh no, I had never seen her after that. We were not personal friends at all." Despite their differences, she would always insist that Crawford was a professional through and through.

Joan Blondell died just two years after Crawford, on Christmas Day 1979, at seventy years old, from leukemia. She'd recently completed Franco Zeffirelli's *The Champ*, playing a wealthy racehorse owner, and had gained a new generation of followers with her small role as waitress Vi in *Grease* (1978). In her novel *Cen-*

ter Door Canteen, published in 1974, Blondell offered a thinly fictionalized version of her own rise to fame from vaudeville to chorus girl in Hollywood musicals, and Hollywood marriages, offering insight into a showbiz world of the past.

Blondell was nominated for a Golden Globe for Best Supporting Actress in *Opening Night* (1977), a psychological drama about the theater world, directed by John Cassavetes. Famous actress Myrtle Gordon, played by Gena Rowlands, struggles with her latest stage role as she's haunted by the obsessive teenage fan who she witnesses being knocked down by a car. The drama summed up all the themes of the horror films of the last decade. Myrtle, as a contemporary Margo Channing, turns to alcohol as she frets about her age. "I'm not going through menopause. I'm not ready to play grandmothers," she implores, as she worries that once she plays an older woman, she'll be trapped in those roles for the rest of her career.

It was a film that offered an alternative to *All About Eve*, if Eve, after waiting outside Margo Channing's dressing room in the rain, had been hit by a car and killed. Cassavetes had even initially wanted Bette Davis to play Blondell's role, that of Sarah Goode, the writer of the play within the film, called *The Second Woman*. He thought Davis would have been tougher in conveying her frustration as she tries to knock some sense into the destructive Myrtle. "Her time has passed, it's as simple as that," Sarah says to Myrtle, as she tries to explain the character she's playing. "How old are you Myrtle? You see, it's too late. You understand that, don't you? People change, physically. There's a hell of a lot of pressure one puts on oneself by demanding to stay competitive."

In March 1977, Bette Davis became the first female recipient of the prestigious Life Achievement Award from the American Film

Institute, and it triggered a slight career resurgence for her. She received promising offers of work, including traveling to London and Egypt to make *Death on the Nile* (1978). The Agatha Christie adaptation featured a multi-star cast, including David Niven, Angela Lansbury, Maggie Smith, Jane Birkin, Mia Farrow and Peter Ustinov as Poirot. Its predecessor, *Murder on the Orient Express* (1974) had also brought together weighty names including Ingrid Bergman, Lauren Bacall, Anthony Perkins and John Gielgud.

Bette was distraught by the death of her mother, followed by her sister Bobby, in 1979, and a few years later she would receive further devastation when her daughter BD wrote a tell-all book, sparked by Christina Crawford's success with *Mommie Dearest*. B.D painted her mother as an alcoholic with anger issues, and documented all the fights between Bette and ex-husband Merrill. "Her book left a deep scar and an emptiness in my life. At the time her book was published, I was told B.D. had become a very active member of a religious group which I had never heard of. She even went as far as to write me and tell me that God had told her to write the book," she wrote.

She continued to work, with roles in feature films and television movies, to fill the void she felt in her personal life. In 1983 she was diagnosed with breast cancer and underwent a mastectomy, which was followed by a debilitating stroke, which took all her strength to recover from, and which left her looking arrestingly thin and frail. The dramatic change in her appearance and physical condition made her almost unhirable, particularly with concerns around insuring her. "Acting had been my life. I wouldn't want to live if I could never act again," she said.

Producer Mike Kaplan came to her rescue by offering her one of the two leads in *The Whales of August* about two elderly widowed sisters who are opposites in personality. Davis was cast as the cantankerous and blind older sister Libby, with a long white wig which made her look every one of her years. Playing opposite her as the younger, kinder sister, Sarah, was Lillian Gish. Davis called *The Whales of August* "a very courageous film to make in this day. No sex. No violence. It was just a simple story of two aging sisters."

Directed by Lindsay Anderson, the film also cast veterans Vincent Price and Ann Sothern, and it was filmed in Maine, close to the house where Bette had lived with Gary Merrill. Bette was unabashed in announcing she would have preferred Katharine Hepburn as a co-star, taking every opportunity to slight Lillian Gish, as she was afraid of having attention directed away from her.

"She wasn't very nice to Lillian," said Ann Sothern. "I don't know why. I think she felt threatened because Lillian is a great lady."

While Bette and Lillian were thought likely to receive Oscar nominations, it was only Ann Sothern who was named in the Best Supporting Actress category. It had been Sothern's first film in seven years, having seriously injured her back in 1974 when scenery fell on her while performing in regional theater in Florida. Despite her debilitating injuries, she acted in a couple of exploitation movies after *The Killing Kind*, including *Crazy Mama* (1975) and the parasitical horror *The Manitou* (1978), also starring Tony Curtis and Susan Strasberg. Despite the acclaim, *The Whales of August* would be her last film role before her death in 2001.

As a follow-up to the success of *The Whales of August*, Davis held out hopes of being cast as another cantankerous old woman in *Driving Miss Daisy*, which she believed was the perfect part, but Jessica Tandy was cast instead. The only option that seemed tangible was to take a role in the low-budget black comedy *The Wicked Stepmother*, which began filming in April 1988, on her eightieth birthday. She had insisted her assistant and close friend Kathryn Sermak be made an associate producer, but still, she felt the director refused to listen to her suggestions.

After a week of filming, she was shocked by her appearance in the dailies and realized she didn't want to be involved. She became paranoid that she was being used as a prop, and aware of the poor production values and quality of the script, she feigned illness and abruptly quit. It was released direct to video in 1989, utilizing the fifteen minutes of footage they had of Davis, and changing the story so that her character transformed into a beautiful younger woman, played by Barbara Carrera. It would be her last screen role before her death in October 1989, at the age of eighty-one.

Her final appearance was as a special guest at The San Sebastian International Film Festival in 1989, where she had been invited to receive the Donostia award. As part of her visit, she answered questions from the audience. She said that Margo Channing "was a totally different kind of actress than I. Her frenzy about her age - I have never gone through this at all. I would have liked to stay young but even at a young age I played old parts. Queen Elizabeth, for example. I was thirty playing a character of sixty. No, Margo and I were totally different types of actresses."

Conclusion

The "Hag Horror" subgenre of movies may be one that is aligned with the sixties and seventies, but the themes of the movies, of tragic spinsters, damaging mothers and terrifying crones is one that has lived on in many different guises.

Friday the 13th (1980) may have been one of the new breed of horror movies unleashed in the eighties, but its villain, Pamela Voorhees, was aligned with the Crazy Old Ladies of horror that preceded her. Struggling to cope with the death of her son Jason, the mental torture and despair leads her to taking vengeance on the sex-obsessed teenagers at summer camp who she blames for Jason's death. Like Norman Bates taking on the persona of his mother in *Psycho*, and Danielle carrying out the violence of Dominique in *Sisters*, Pamela is spurred on to kill by Jason's voice, "Kill them Mommy!"

In her back story, Pamela gave birth to Jason at sixteen during a short-lived abusive marriage, and, like Norma Bates, is overly protective of her son. She possesses the sin of being a single mother, and becomes the omnipresent force that drives Jason to embark on further murder sprees in later films. As Jude Doyle writes in *Dead Blondes and Bad Mothers*, "At the heart of horror is a bad mother; the familiar and terrible vision of a woman corrupting the world, unleashing her own flaws upon it through her monstrous children."

In the 1980s, the desperate middle-aged spinster was transformed into a dangerous career woman, played to terrifying effect by Glenn Close in *Fatal Attraction* (1987). Alex Forrest appears successful and confident, but because she lacks marriage and children, she is driven to derangement. Like Shelley Winters' Helen Hill, jealousy and sexual frustration leads her to murderous intent, and to take out her rage on innocent pet rabbits.

As a film that built on the anxieties in Reagan's America that the family unit was in jeopardy, *Fatal Attraction* was the first of a series of "psycho" films where women are driven mad because of this sense of loss in not being a wife or mother. In 1992's *The Hand that Rocks the Cradle*, Rebecca de Morney plays Peyton Flanders, a nanny who plots to carry out revenge on the happy family unit following a miscarriage which left her unable to have children. As a review in *Entertainment Weekly* at the time noted, the film was "clearly designed to lure women into the theater. The paradox is that it trades on the most retrograde images of women imaginable — they're either '90s Doris Days or murderous destroyers." It was the same message that had been delivered forty years earlier.

In *Misery*, nurse Annie Wilkes (Kathy Bates) at first appears to be the savior of James Caan's bestselling author Paul Sheldon, after he suffers a serious car crash in the Maine wilderness. As a frumpy middle-aged woman, she is driven to psychotic behaviors as part of her unfulfilled role in life, and which also led her to having killed the babies that were in her care. She is an obsessive fan of Paul Sheldon's romance novels, and not only does she trap the incapacitated Paul until he rewrites the book the way she wants, but as she deteriorates further, she'll stop at nothing to keep him with her forever.

Old women in modern horror movies continue to follow similar tropes – they are witch-like in their possession of supernatural powers which threaten the younger protagonist. In *The*

Skeleton Key (2005) Gena Rowlands plays the mysterious owner of a creaking Louisiana plantation who lures Kate Hudson into danger. In *Insidious* (2010), Elise Rainier (Lin Shaye) is a paranormal investigator with psychic abilities. In Sam Raimi's *Drag Me to Hell* (2009), bank clerk Alison Lohman is cursed by an old woman, Sylvia, played by Lorna Raver, when she refuses to give her more time to pay back a loan. Sylvia is unrelenting in her revenge on the young woman, refusing to call off the curse, and the terrifying supernatural entities that are summoned.

In 1974, Molly Haskell named as a fundamental inequality the notion that women are "over the hill" at forty, when they are "with any luck, just coming into their own, sexually and intellectually, while men of that age are 'in their prime.'" She called it "symbolic of our prejudices as well as being one of the most profound injustices of our ego-maniacal society."

Times have changed and forty is no longer considered "old". Actresses in their mid-forties and into their fifties, sixties and beyond are becoming more visible, with opportunities that would have been unheard of decades before. Jennifer Lopez can still play a stripper at fifty, and Nicole Kidman continues to take on varied roles in film and television. We may live in a time when the superhero movie rules at the box office, but there are still options for women of all ages in independent movies. In 2021 Chloé Zhao won a Best Director Academy Award for directing sixty-three year old Frances McDormand in *Nomadland*.

"Middle-aged women have long been underestimated, disrespected and disregarded in the film and television community, and now that's changing," said Kate Winslet in reference to the plaudits she received for her role in TV's *Mare of Easttown*. "Look at the actresses who won at the Emmys. None of us were in our 20s by any means, and that's cool! I feel way cooler as a fortysomething actress than I ever imagined I would."

Helen Mirren, Meryl Streep and Frances McDormand are richly rewarded for the complex roles they take, but still, parts are often limited for other actresses. What continues is a repeat of the same stereotypes – the damaged single woman, the mother who is tormented by the loss of a child, the mysterious old crone, the grandmother.

As Piper Laurie said in 2021: "I had a good part about a year and a half ago, and Dame Judy Dench gets everything that comes along in that age range, she gets to do...I think it's too late for me, a lot of stage roles. Just a little late. I think I'm lucky to be able to do what I've done." But at the age of eighty-nine she still felt that she was ready and available to work.

Selected Bibliography

Books

Alain Silver and James Ursini, *Whatever Happened to Robert Aldrich? His Life and His Films* (Limelight Editions, 2004)

Bogdanovich, Peter, *Who the Devil Made It: Conversations with ...* (Ballantine Books, 2012)

Briggs, Colin, *Cordially Yours, Ann Sothern* (Bear Manor Media, 2017)

Byars, Jackie, *All That Hollywood Allows: Re-reading Gender in 1950s* Melodrama (The University of North Carolina Press, 2020)

Castle, William, *Step Right Up!...I'm Gonna Scare The Pants Off America* (William Castle, 2010)

Chandler, Charlotte, *Not the Girl Next Door: Joan Crawford, A Personal Biography* (Simon and Schuster 2012)

Considine, Shaun, *Bette and Joan: The Divine Feud* (Sphere, 2015)

Crawford, Joan, *A Portrait of Joan: An Autobiography of Joan Crawford* (Graymalkin Media, 2017)

Creed, Barbara, *The Monstrous-Feminine: Film, Feminism, Psychoanalysis* (Routledge, 2015)

Curcio, Vincent, *Suicide Blonde: The Life of Gloria Grahame* (Graymalkin Media, 2018)

Davis, Bette, *The Lonely Life: An Autobiography* (Hachette Books, 2017)

Davis, Bette, *This n' That* (Hachette Books, 2017)

Derry, Charles, *Dark Dreams: The Horror Film from Psycho to Jaws* (AS Barnes and Co, 1977)

Doyle, Sady, *Dead Blondes and Bad Mothers: Monstrosity, Patriarchy, and the Fear of Female Power* (Melville House Publishing, 2019)

Edwards, Anne, *Judy Garland: A Biography* (Taylor Trade Publishing, 2013)

Farrell, Henry, *What Ever Happened to Baby Jane?* (Mulholland Books, 2013)

Fontaine, Joan, *No Bed of Roses* (WH Allen, 1978)

Gordon, Ruth, *My Side: The Autobiography of Ruth Gordon* (Harper & Row, 1976)

Hafdahl, Meg, and Florence, Kelly, *The Science of Women in Horror: The Special Effects, Stunts, and True Stories Behind Your Favorite Fright Films* (Skyhorse, 2020)

Harrington, Curtis and Bartok, Dennis, *Nice Guys Don't Work in Hollywood* (Drag City Books, 2013)

Head, Edith and Calistro, Paddy, *Edith Head's Hollywood* (Angel City Press, 2008)

Hearn, Marcus, *The Hammer Vault: Treasures from the Archive of Hammer Films* (Titan Books, 2011)

Higham, Charles, *Olivia and Joan* (New English Library, 1984)

Kennedy, Matthew, *Joan Blondell: A Life between Takes* (University Press of Mississippi, 2009)

Laurie, Piper, *Learning to Live Out Loud: A Memoir* (Crown Archetype, 2011)

Levin, Ira, *Rosemary's Baby* (Corsair, 2011)

Lobenthal, Joel, *Tallulah! The Life and Times of a Leading Lady* (Harper Collins, 2009)

Newman, Kim, *Nightmare Movies: Horror on Screen Since the 1960s* (Bloomsbury, 2011)

Newton, Michael, *Rosemary's Baby* (BFI Film Classics, 2020)

Pastoureau, Michel, *Red: The History of a Color* (Princeton University Press, 2017)

Rebello, Stephen, *Dolls! Dolls! Dolls!: The Most Beloved Bad Book and Movie of All Time* (Penguin Books, 2020)

Shelley, Peter, *Grande Dame Guignol Cinema: A History of Hag Horror from Baby Jane to Mother* (McFarland & Company Inc. Publishers, 2009)

Signoret, Simone, *Nostalgia Isn't What it Used to Be* (Harper Collins, 1978)

Spada, James, *Bette Davis: More Than a Woman* (Author and Company, 2013)

Spoto, Donald, *Possessed: The Life of Joan Crawford* (Arrow, 2012)

Staggs, Sam, *Close-up on Sunset Boulevard: Billy Wilder and the Dark Hollywood Dream* (St. Martin's Press, 2003)

Susann, Jacqueline, *Valley of the Dolls: 50th Anniversary Edition* (Tiger LLC, 2016)

Swanson, Gloria, *Swanson on Swanson* (Random House, 1980)

Turner, Lana, *Lana: The Lady, The Legend, the Truth* (Pocket Books, 1982)

Turner, Peter, *Film Stars Don't Die in Liverpool: A True Story* (Pan, New Edition, 2017)

Wayne, Jane Ellen, *The Life and Loves of Barbara Stanwyck* (JR Books, 2009)

Weaver, Tom, *Science Fiction Stars and Horror Heroes: Interviews with Actors, Directors, Producers and Writers of the 1940s Through 1960s* (McFarland, Incorporated, 2006)

Welsch, Tricia, *Gloria Swanson: Ready for Her Close-Up* (University Press of Mississippi, 2013)

Wood, Robin, edited by Barry Keith Grant, *Robin Wood on the Horror Film: Collected Essays and Reviews* (Wayne State University Press, 2018)

Newspapers and magazines

Ann Sothern Has Had Four Careers, The Calgary Herald, Mar 12, 1963

A Well-Planned Crawford, Life, 21 February 1964

Adams, Val, *Gloria Swanson Weighs TV Role*, The New York Times, 12 October 1956

Adler, Renata, *Miss Davis's 78th*, The New York Times, 21 March 1968

Aldrich, Robert, *Director Now Reveals Background of Davis-Crawford Feature*, The New York Times, November 4, 1962

Aldrich: A Finger on Hollywood's Pulse, The Los Angeles Times, 02 July 1967

Archer, Eugene, *Dead Ringer review*, The New York Times, 20 February 1964

Archer, Eugene, *Fasten Your Seat Belts – Here's Bette Davis*, The New York Times, 7 March 1965

Archer, Eugene, The New York Times, *Bankhead Returns from the Wars*, 6 December 1964

Bankhead's Back, The New York Times, July 19, 1964

Bette Davis Dispute with Director Told, The Los Angeles Times, 12 May 1967

Brady, Thomas F, *Lead Role in Film to Gloria Swanson*, The New York Times, 21 February 1949

Brady, Thomas F, *Trio Considering Film on Industry*, The New York Times, 31 December 1948

Budding Star: Attractive Gloria Grahame has talent and Louis Mayer's backing, Life, 21 October 1946

Callahan Dan, *Fatal Instincts: The Dangerous Pout of Gloria Grahame*, Bright Lights Film, 29 November 2017

Canby, Vincent, *Screen: Chiller a la Mod: Games is Happening, Eerily, at the Sutton*, The New York Times, 18 September 1967

Canby, Vincent, *Screen: In 'Frogs,' the Animals Do In Ray Milland*, The New York Times, 6 July 1972

Cinema: Bette Meets Boy, Time, 29 October 1965

Collins, Amy Fine, *Once Was Never Enough*, Vanity Fair, 26 August 2013

Crowther, Bosley, *Socially Hurtful*, The New York Times, 21 June 1964

Divorced Film Stars Sign for Same Movie, The Los Angeles Times, 17 April 1964

Film on Violent Youth Agitates Readers, The New York Times, 28 June 1964,

Gardner, Paul, *Swanson's Way*, The New York Times, 7 March, 1965

Gleiberman, Owen, *The Hand that Rocks the Cradle*, Entertainment Weekly, 17 January 1992

Haber, Joyce, *The Los Angeles Times, Ruth Gordon Lands 'Best Part' Ever*, 16 January 1970

Hadleigh, Boze, *Last Kiss of the Spider Woman: Gale Sondergaard*, Scarlet Street Magazine, Summer 1993

Handsaker, Gene, *Seeing Stars*, The Day, 26 May 1967

Harford, Margaret, *Stanwyck and Taylor Star in 'Night Walker'*, The Los Angeles Times, 01 Jan 1965

Hopper, Hedda, *'Lady in Cage' Star*, The Los Angeles Times, 3 December 1962

Hopper, Hedda, *Dean Jones Named for 'Yum-Yum Tree'*, The Los Angeles Times, 15 February, 1963

Hopper, Hedda, *Under Hedda's Hat*, Photoplay, August 1963

Hopper, Hedda, *Under Hedda's Hat*, Photoplay, May 1963

Jenkins, Lin, *Actors pay tribute to Beryl Reid, 'one of the best'*, The Times, 14 October 1996

Joan Crawford, super star: a fearful joy, The Times, June 18, 1971

Joan Crawford talks of actors and directors, The Times, December 14, 1966

Joan Fontaine: The English rose who likes her briar patch, The Times, June 14, 1966

Kane, Christopher, *Movie Review*, Modern Screen, August 1950

Kim Novak Does Double Take as Film Queen in The Legend of Lylah Clare, The Los Angeles Times, 23 August 1968

Kinet, Beverly, *The Replacement…*, Photoplay, July 1952

Koury, Phil, *How Script for Sunset Boulevard was Born*, The New York Times, 2 July 1950

Lady in a Cage Filming is Unique; Paramount Finds Elevator Story is Confining in a Vertical Vein, The New York Times, 1 March 1963

Letters, Life Magazine, 26 June 1964

Lilley, Jessie, *The Woman in the Window: Ruth Roman*, Scarlet Street, Issue No. 12, Fall 1993

Los Angeles Times, *Joan Crawford Can Still Cry on Cue*, Philip Oakes, Sept 2, 1969

Marks, Sally K, *'Her Crawfordship' Conquers England*, The Los Angeles Times, 9 January 1967

Movie Call Sheet, The Los Angeles Times, 17 October 1969

O'Connor, John J, *TV Review*, The New York Times, Dec 11, 1973

Oulahan, Richard, *Movie Review: It's No Place for a Lady Like Olivia*, Life, 5 June 1964

Put the Blame on Nameless Evil, Folks, Cyclops, The New York Times, Feb 24, 1974

Ruth Gordon: Long Wait for a Very Good Year, The Los Angeles Times, 29 December 1969

Schickel, Richard, *Shock of Seeing a Hidden World*, Life, 1 Nov 1968

Shinnick, Kevin G, *Curtis Harrington*, Scarlet Street, Issue No. 12, Fall 1993

Skolsky, Sidney, *That's Hollywood For You*, Photoplay, February 1960

Still Weaving a Magic Spell, Screenland, December 1949

Swanson: Birthday Girl at 80, The Los Angeles Times, 02 April 1979

Thomas, Kevin, *Brass Ring for Ruth Gordon*, The Los Angeles Times, 27 April 1969

Thomas, Kevin, *Gloria Swanson: Between Glamor Puss, Old Shoe*, The Los Angeles Times, 24 February 1974

Thomas, Kevin, *Ruth Gordon Plays 'Aunt Alice' Role*, The Los Angeles Times, 20 August 1969

Thomas, Kevin, *The Anniversary Opens Multiple Run*, The Los Angeles Times, 08 March 1968

Thomas, Kevin, *Triumphant Madness Role*, The Los Angeles Times, 19 June 1965

Thompson, Howard, *Bette Davis as 'Nanny'*, The New York Times, 4 Nov 1965

Thompson, Howard, *Testament of a Roving 'Lady'*, The New York Times, June 7, 1964,

Thomson, Howard, *Circus Chiller*, The New York Times, 11 January 1968

Todd, Derek, *Bette Davis, Superstar*, Kinematograph Weekly, 27 May 1965

Valley, Richard, *The Killing Kind: An Appreciation*, Scarlet Street, Issue No. 12, Fall 1993

Wardle, Irving, *Bette Davis, Fairfield Halls*, The Times, October 7, 1975

Weiler, AH, *More Laughable than Shocking: Gloria Grahame Cast in 'Blood and Lace'*, The New York Times, 18 March 1971

Wilson, John M, *From Bees to Tarantulas: The Man Who Bugs the Movies*, The Los Angeles Times, 17 September 1977

Archives

The Margaret Herrick Library, Academy of Motion Pictures, Arts and Sciences.

Paramount Production records, F2633, *Lady in a Cage*, 3 January 1963, Bernard Donnenfeld to Mr. George Weltner, Paramount Pictures

Curtis Harrington, F33, Curtis Harrington to Ted McCord, 21 October 1966

Curtis Harrington, F33, Curtis Harrington to Charles Higham, Australian Press, The Bulletin, Sydney, 10 May 1967

Curtis Harrington, F33, Curtis Harrington to Bette Davis, 2 December 1969

Curtis Harrington, F33, Curtis Harrington to Quentin Tarantino, 28 January 1997

Curtis Harrington, F33, Letter, Curtis Harrington to Peter, 15 August 1966

Curtis Harrington, F33, Letter, Meade Roberts to George Edwards, 3 June 1966

Curtis Harrington, F33, Mr. Barnard L. Sackett, Adelphia Pictures Corporation, Philadelphia, to Curtis Harrington, 27 December 1967

Curtis Harrington, F33, Telegram from Curtis Harrington to Mlle. Simone Signoret, Royal Court Theatre, London, 19 October 1966

Hedda Hopper F998, Bette Davis & Joan Crawford, 16 July 1962

Hedda Hopper F998, Joan Crawford notes for interview, 8 September 1958

Paramount Production Letters, *Lady in a Cage*, Letter from Donnefeld to George Weltner, Paramount Pictures, 3 January 1963

Paul Henreid F18, Paul Henreid to Jack Warner, 23 December 1963

Paul Henreid, F371, Bette Davis to Paul Henreid, from My Bailiwick, 78 River Road, Weston, Connecticut

Paul Henreid, F371, September 17, 1963, Paul Henreid to Bette Davis

Robert Aldrich interviews, American Film Institute

Joan Crawford Papers, *T-Mss 2001-053, Billy Rose Theatre Division, The New York Public Library for the Performing Arts.

Hammer Horror Steve Chibnall Archive, De Montfort University, Leicester

The Anniversary, Pressbook, British

Fanatic, Pressbook

The Nanny, Final Screenplay

The Nanny, Pressbook

The Witches, Pressbook

Other

Author interview, Shar Daw, author of *Bombshell*
Author interview, Mark Lester
Author interview, Dennis Bartok
Author interview, Foster Hirsch
Interview with Piper Laurie, The Lamb's Club, 30 March, 2021
Interview with Stefanie Powers, The Lamb's Club, 11 March 2021
Marcus Hern, Jimmy Sangster, Renee Glynn, continuity editor,
    The Nanny DVD commentary, August 2006
Rosemary's Baby documentary, Inside the Criterion Collection

Printed in Great Britain
by Amazon

17074219R00224